FOR MY MOM,
WHO HAS ALWAYS BEEN.

CONTENTS

ix   *Preface*

xi   *Acknowledgments*

1   INTRODUCTION   Social Life to the Side

I DOMINATION

15   CHAPTER ONE   Old Man Tilley & the Land

23   CHAPTER TWO   Big Tim & Mrs. Taylor

31   CHAPTER THREE   The Chief & Bigfoot

41   CHAPTER FOUR   Jon & the Glittery Crow

50   CHAPTER FIVE   Carl & Waking Bakery

57   CHAPTER SIX   The Sheepdog Who Cried Wolf

70   CONVEYANCE I

II RESISTANCE

77   CHAPTER SEVEN   Ms. Reid & Her Boy

83   CHAPTER EIGHT   Ten & Two: How a Civil Rights Organization Fights Police Work

90   CHAPTER NINE   Mr. Cantale & the Community

101   CHAPTER TEN   Fred, Ken & Intensive Supervision

113   CHAPTER ELEVEN   Ruthie at Lunch

120   CHAPTER TWELVE   Seymour Green &
Political Party(ing)

129   CONVEYANCE II

   III   **TO-THE-SIDE**

135   CHAPTER THIRTEEN   Fred & the Declaration
of Independence

139   CHAPTER FOURTEEN   Herc & Prison on the Outside

152   CHAPTER FIFTEEN   The Lawyers & the Amish Market

160   CHAPTER SIXTEEN   The Spot Is an Alternative Space

173   CHAPTER SEVENTEEN   Henrietta & Annie: Forty-Five
Minutes from Life

180   CHAPTER EIGHTEEN   Shakes & the Pace of Connection

188   CONVEYANCE III

191   Epilogue

195   APPENDIX I   *Local History of Confinement
with Archival Pictures*

203   APPENDIX II   *Demographic Details of
People in Vignettes*

205   APPENDIX III   *Hand-Drawn Pictographs of
Arguments Sketched Prior
to Writing the Book*

211   *Notes*

221   *Bibliography*

223   *Index*

PREFACE

In 1986, reactor four at the Chernobyl Nuclear Power Plant melted and caught fire, burning like hell for nine straight days. Radioactive material released into the ground, water, and air was substantial. Pine trees surrounding the site rusted red. More than one hundred thousand people fled. A twenty-mile radius etched around the meltdown established a zone of restriction to human access and development. As I finished this manuscript, the details of this nuclear meltdown seeped into my mind.

This is because the zone did not remain a post-apocalyptic hellscape as people imagined it would. It became forest overgrowing abandoned buildings; bears frolicking in unlit streets; packs of wild horses, boars, and gray wolves roaming; flora and fauna swarming home gardens and sidewalks and fields. Humans returned—scientists, workers, even so-called squatters reclaiming life beside a smoldering nuclear core. And while toxicity levels remain high in the soil, in the animals, in the plants and insects, life floods the zone, unexpectedly filling what human endeavors all but snuffed silent.

Prison facilities are a bit like nuclear power plants. Except, even when operating as planned, they produce sprawling zones of restriction in places the wider society prefers to avoid. The southeastern border of New Jersey that is centered in this book has five facilities, trapping more than 6,400 people each and every day. Like nuclear spillage, confinement radiates through the region's ground, water, and air. It attaches to animals, plants, and humans, saturating the landscape in rusty hues. Toxicity levels are high. And they could very well stay high into the next century. But the relentless pulse of social life nevertheless beats on. This is the inevitability I hope to convey in the pages that follow. Prisons will get their due. The fallout zone of confinement is going nowhere soon. But to believe in the totality of its greedy grip, to see only the reach of prisons, is something akin to the effects of radiation poisoning. When we get close enough, way, way down beside it, we can feel the force of common life, surrounding confinement's false image, everywhere on the move.

ACKNOWLEDGMENTS

I could not have undertaken research for this book, much less written it, without a sprawling network of supporters, friends, family, comrades, and mentors. I offer this project in honor of that collective. Especially to my friends and collaborators in South Jersey, who took me in and cared for me as if I were your own, may this small work somehow reflect the beauty of life that your labors continually bring about, and may it honor your resiliency to build the worlds you believe in amid the world you have inherited, with hope that it gives courage to all who struggle for social life beneath the grinding mechanics of racial capital and market democracy.

Unending thanks to Bridget Purcell, whose love, encouragement, support, and razor-sharp critiques since the first day of research kept me and this project going. To my little boo, Wilder Marxley, who takes me into new worlds each and every day with wonder, joy, and love. Deep and everlasting gratitude to Sharalyn Hyman, my mom, and Mark Hyman, my pops, who love me without account and who always direct my feet when I cannot find the path. Thank you to Brittney Pearson and Drew Pearson, who prop me up and carry me along with love, fellowship, and humor. Thank you to "Bluegill" Bill Pearson, my grandpa, who modeled regimented consistency even when I wasn't paying attention. And in memory of my grandparents, Ray and Wilma Markley, and Gloria Pearson, who loved me unconditionally.

This project was cultivated, nourished, pruned, and expanded by a community of scholars and comrades who always kept me close and kept it real: Imani Perry, Carol Greenhouse, Laurence Ralph, Fred Moten, Eddie Glaude, Ruha Benjamin, Mark Lewis Taylor, Melissa Burch, Kevin Miller, Del Doughty, Abdellah Hammoudi, Geddes "Pop" Hanson, Derecka Purnell, Dylan Rodriguez, Wendy Belcher, Arjun Shankar, Neil Gong, Brandon Hunter-Pazzara, João Biehl, Andrew Edwards, Orisanmi Burton, Avery Gordon, Quincy Amoah, Benjamin Fogarty-Valenzuela, Kessie Alexandre, and Marcus Johnson. And especially to my closest, who have moved with me these many years, from plucky graduate students to radical scholars: Nyle Fort, Matthew Harris, and Tyler Davis. T. D., words are insufficient to express my indebtedness to your steady hand and my gratitude for your expansive insight on this project across these many years. I hope you feel proud of what it has become.

Thank you to the people at Duke University Press, especially Ken Wissoker, Ryan Kendall, my anonymous reviewers (whose careful insights, suggestions, and critiques catapulted this book into another stratosphere), and those who worked on editing and design. Thank you to my colleagues in the Anthropology Department and the Justice and Peace Studies Program at Georgetown University, and to my former colleagues in the Society of Fellows at the University of Michigan.

Thank you to those with whom I have shared meals, listened to music, made magic, walked the streets, and discussed every manner of thing under the golden sun—my friends, artists, intellectuals, unpaid comedians, and loved ones who have surrounded me with unwavering love and support: Amaury Acosta, Michael "Shaka" Allen, Chad Biddle, Ross Bitzel, Brett Blum, Gabi Blumberg, Matt "Winkie" Brown, Amos Caley, Sarah Trovato Caley, David B. Campbell, Christine Chalifoux, Matt Conner, Jessica Cooper, Emma Shaw Crane, Chloé Samala Faux, Joseph Feldblum, Amelia Feldblum, Jonathan Fox, Wallace Gaffney, Cait Gault, Tyler Gault, Thalia Gigerenzer, Nathan "Freedom" Gray, Onur Gunay, Ma Hanson, Sarah Harris, Eric Helvie, Julia Hori, Arthur Horn, Jonathan Jackson, Kyle "KJax" Jackson, Rebecca Jackson, JoEllyn Jones, Matt Kendig, Amy Krauss, Emmanuela Kucik, Al Kurtz, Bryan Lamb, C. J. Majerski, Sean "Bloodbath" McGrath, Shinjung Nam, Mitchell Newberry, Jordan Phillips, Amanda Plett, Matt Plett, Tim Power, Natalie Purcell, Jeremiah Schlotman, Xian aTunde Adjuah, Janet Shinn, Veronica Sousa, C. C. Thompson, Alex Turpin, Rob Weinstein, Jeremiah Wilson, and Mel Wilson.

My research received material support from the Program in American Studies (Princeton), the Center for Health and Wellbeing (Princeton), the Center for Culture, Society, and Religion (Princeton), the Wenner-Gren Foundation, the Fellowship of Woodrow Wilson Scholars (Princeton), the Charlotte W. Newcombe Foundation, the Charlotte Elizabeth Procter Fellowship (Princeton), the Anthropology Department (Princeton), the African American Studies Department (Princeton), the Society of Fellows (University of Michigan), the Program on Justice and Peace (Georgetown), and the Department of Anthropology (Georgetown).

SOCIAL LIFE TO THE SIDE

> The Premises from which we begin are not arbitrary
> ones, not dogmas, but real premises from which
> abstraction can only be made in the imagination.
> **KARL MARX** | *The German Ideology* (1978)

> Every day, I live prison on the outside.
> **HERC NELSON**

Shakes was sick, so I was on my own for lunch. I jammed the phone into my pocket and drove a few short blocks from the Spot to the Mill, across the street from the county courthouse. The dining room was stuffed with chattering professionals, but the oblong bar had a few empty stools, so I plopped down.

"Are you in a hurry?" the bartender asked, wiping the bar's surface with a grimy-gray rag.

"Nope," I replied.

"Good."

She made her way around the oval bar, snatching up empties, pouring coffee, delivering fresh bottles of beer and plates of food and joking with the white-haired lunch crowd. Ten minutes later, she was back in front of me.

"You're new in town, huh?"

"Yes," I replied. "I have been here for about nine months and will be here for another year or two."

"Why would you move *here*?" Setting the coffeepot on the bar, a hand on her hip.

I laughed. "Because I am doing research."

"Ohhhh, I know who *you* are! I've heard of you. You're here to study the prisons or something, aren't you?"

"Umm, yeah, I am here to study how the prisons have impacted the area. How did you know that?" I laughed. "Who told you?"

"I-I-I can't remember," she stumbled sheepishly, perhaps not expecting the question. "Do you want to hear what I think about how all the prisons have impacted this town?"

"I would love to hear your perspective." I slid a small, gray notebook from my pocket. "That's why I'm here."

"*Nada!*" Raising a hand in my face in the shape of a zero. "I'm sure that's not what you wanted to hear, but they haven't had any impact on this town whatsoever. And I would know—my daughter and two of my sons-in-law *work* as corrections officers!"

The bartender speaks from the side, where regular old workdays, personal opinions, and multigenerational family interests gather in the accumulation of lived experiences that happen in a place called home. Like most residents I met, the bartender never once heard the phrase "mass incarceration" or spent any time scrolling through editorials about the failures of the criminal justice system. Her thoughts on the county's five facilities were rooted in family relationships, in what they provided for her children and grandchildren, in how they sustained the region, even as the factories and farms fled. For the bartender, prisons were part of the place, like anything else.

Life beside Bars showcases social life in a region with five correctional facilities. The stories take place in Cumberland County, located way down along the southeastern border of New Jersey, where three state prisons—two of which share a working dairy farm—one federal prison, and a regional jail have been squeezed into a twenty-mile radius.[1] On any given day, 6,400 people are confined across the five facilities, plus many thousands more on probation or parole. Another 147,000 people live in the area surrounding the facilities.[2] The county has the second-highest concentration of correctional jobs in the country.[3] And this does not include the thousands of people who are employed in the court system, legal offices, social services, prison-adjacent nonprofits, and police and sheriff departments, and the friends and family of those who are confined. As Carl, a local pastry baker in part 1, said to me: "There is a lot of corrections going on."

This book is about slowing down to spend time with many different kinds of people who have carved out meaningful and sometimes radical social life adjacent to large-scale human confinement. It is easy to think of correctional facilities as institutions that are set apart, tucked away, impermeable, and functioning far outside the activities and concerns of daily life. And for many people across the United States, this may be true—prisons exist somewhere else. But for the millions upon millions upon millions of people who live in close proximity to prisons, who rely on them for employment, who regularly visit, write to, think about, and care for people trapped in them, prisons are a regular feature of social life. My aim in this book is to emphasize close contact with folks who have spent the better part of their lives navigating the spaces that surround Cumberland County's five facilities. And my hope is that in meeting all kinds of people who occupy the same to-the-side spaces as the bartender, readers will learn something about prisons and their function within one locale, catching a glimmer of the alternative rhythms, a spark of the resilience and resistance, an appreciation for the beauty of social life happening in a place that was developed through the mechanism of confinement.

I began fieldwork on the wave of national protesting that marked the early and mid-2010s, supercharged to challenge the owner class and to continue organizing with others toward the abolition of the system of prisons and policing. I also became entangled with prisons and policing on a personal level and learned quickly how confusing, overwhelming, exhausting, and impossible it was to try to support a loved one who was confined or in process. Fighting in the courts, like fighting in the streets, exhausts one to the bones. And my family was ill prepared to face off with the so-called criminal justice system. We were working class with no money, zero extra time, and scant political connections, stretched between multiple low-wage jobs. It was enough simply trying to keep up with the normal demands and expenses of everyday life. Never mind piling on the weight and cost of a loved one's (potential) imprisonment. So, I wanted to use ethnographic research to connect with others who also had firsthand experiences—people who, from my perspective, had been largely ignored in the wider conversation happening despite their lifelong efforts in developing skills and forging relationships in a land-scape dominated by militarized policing and multiple prisons.

I thus set out to write a prison "history from below."[4] Or, more correctly, to write a prison history from the spaces beside a whole bunch of prisons. I was committed to following the tradition of radical historians, theorists, and anthropologists who took seriously the ideas, the actions, the relationships, and the politics of people who were finding ways to build robust social life within the nooks and crannies of capitalist systems of domination—people who were daily targets of police, who had spent time confined in a prison, or who, perhaps, had friends and family in prison. But, at the very same time, I also wanted to speak with people who benefited—directly or indirectly, intentionally or unintentionally—from the sprawling social, political, and economic possibilities produced by prisons. Because, as with the bartender, if a person was a resident of Cumberland County, then they most certainly had some kind of tangled relationship to the prisons and the policing that helped fill them.

The range of relationships to the prisons encountered in the vignettes that follow, then, are something like the diversity of experiences high-lighted by Tania Murray Li among the highlanders of Sulawesi, who, in the 1990s, were introduced to the savage process of capitalism ordering the privatization of their ancestral lands.[5] Many highlanders quickly lost family parcels and thus their present and future livelihoods. Like a plague of locusts, the gobble of privatization chewed across the land, hungry and teeming, laying boundaries over what had been eternally shared and fraying social relationships beyond repair. And, exactly as most people experienced devastating loss and debilitating debt, a few highlanders, some lucky and some shrewd, turned around to find themselves at the top of the hierarchy—more land, better crops, bigger savings accounts, and even able to profit from extending credit to people they once lived and worked with in common.

The same is true of the prisons and the militarized police depart-ments that patrol the streets. The early days of drug war policing hit many by surprise, squarely in the mouth. Officers raided homes, blew up corners, seized vehicles, patrolled school hallways, and targeted young people—especially black, brown, and poor people—with a supreme viciousness that left so many dead, broken, incarcerated, and sometimes, with the aid of lengthy sentences handed down by the courts, permanently confined and separated from friends and family. As the war clawed along, the prison population grew and grew. But those who were lucky enough to stay out found all kinds of ways to prosper and even build social and political power. Corrections officers in this part of New Jersey, for example, make considerably more in annual salaries than teachers, and they exercise vice-clamped control over certain public spheres, like one of the school boards, where they have held nearly all the elected seats (including president) for almost two decades. Other corrections officers have amassed statewide political power, bending the ears of governors and congresspeople and media personalities alike. Police officers, who also make far more in annual salaries than teachers, have gained local power, as well as fast cars, access to weapons of death, and, perhaps most importantly, a kind of personal and familial immunity from the attention and surveilling of drug policing itself. Still others, like retired high school teacher Mickey Kite, saw opportunities in snatching up the increasingly available foreclosed or devalued housing while paroled people with few alternatives were suddenly in need of qualified housing.[6] Even the prison-adjacent nonprofits have created wealth and social power for a handful of (mostly white) people. Prisons, like private property, have created cascading economic and political opportunities for a few as they dominate life for the many.

For those who are trapped on the underside of the prisons' domination, though, it is never the only dimension to their existence. Far from it. Robin D. G. Kelley makes this point in *Race Rebels*. Beginning in the late-1970s kitchen of a Pasadena McDonald's, employees who were ridden by the constant surveillance of swing managers and treated as stupid and lower class by the customers developed "inventive ways to compensate" for their exploitative working conditions, like liberating boxes of cookies, making too many burgers and fries near closing time, or offering to clean the parking lot so they could linger outside with friends.[7] Kelley defines these acts as both rebellious and political, and he centers them as endeavors to retain personal dignity while transforming the routinized work of fast food into pleasurable play.[8] Kelley builds on the insights of James Scott and Lila Abu-Lughod, bringing them into a California fast-food kitchen, to argue that these everyday acts of rebellion are, on the one hand, illuminative of how structures of domination reproduce across time and place and, on the other, are instructive in expanding our imagination of what another world might look, feel, and sound like.[9]

This, too, is similar to what I found scattered across Cumberland County. Tucked into the everyday grind of the region's relentlessly hostile landscape were sparks of resistance and bursts of joy, spaces that were momentarily broken open for sharing, supporting, laughing, and communing and collective acts that at times conjured momentary alternative worlds swaying to rhythms all their own. Like old-school thirty-five-millimeter slides, these tiny moments were difficult to glimpse on their own, from a detached distance with untrained perception, but up close, when sitting in the company of others who knew how to see, hear, touch, and feel them, light passed through to cast into relief a radically different social world not in some grainy, yellow-tinted future but in the very present, nestled right beside systems or moments of domination: a public defense attorney who reconciled with the recently paroled person who murdered her brother, a group of formerly incarcerated men sharing a small business storefront, a young girl riding her bicycle in squealing joy as the family picks up the fractured pieces of life after a devastating police raid. The carceral system of domination in the region remains powerful and merciless but is also incapable of silencing social life, of crushing people into acquiescence, of confining them out of existence.

Instead, folks who were targeted and subjugated in the region, especially those who belonged to families that had lived locally for multiple generations, inherited an understanding of how (their local) domination worked, as well as a cluster of practices for resisting it that had accumulated through decades if not centuries of collective life. Cedric Robinson refers to this accumulation of knowledge, imagination, and practice across privatized space and capitalist time as "the socialist impulse," which names the persistence of the human spirit to carry on and reinvigorate "visions of an alternative order" irrespective to the political or economic systems working to dominate life and land.[10] For many people I met, their families had been targeted, policed, corralled, confined, and exploited as controllable, exploitable labor across hundreds of years. They had learned tactics of resistance and calculated cunning of the ways the present system of confinement functions, of how police officers actually behave in the streets, of who could be trusted and who could not, from their parents and grandparents, friends and siblings, and of course through their own experiences. Keeping someone free of confinement was a gargantuan collective effort, a local fact as relevant to the present as it had been to the past. This is why I frame the study through the ongoing reproduction of confinement rather than the specific entrance of the prison facilities.

Barbaric systems for human confinement have been central to the region's political economy for nearly four hundred years. The genocide of the Lenni Lenape people and the theft and enslavement of African descended people for agricultural work established a rigid order over land as it entrenched a hierarchy of labor. Brutal conditions for farm workers remained long after the collapse of slavery. In the ramp-up to the United States' entrance into World War II, the largest farm in the region (and in New Jersey) built on-site labor camps to house thousands of recently "interned" Japanese Americans brought by train from the West Coast. They expanded the labor camps by transplanting prisoners of war and other displaced people from Europe. Then they filled the camps after World War II by recruiting people from Jamaica and elsewhere. The farm folded in the late 1950s, and within a decade there was a gleaming new state prison that was shortly thereafter surrounded by an operational dairy farm where imprisoned people were put to work. The three additional prison facilities were added over the next three decades (1970s–2000s). Cumberland County is not a region that lost industry and then randomly fixed it with prisons. It is a region that has used systems for human confinement to establish and reproduce its political economy across four hundred years. Confinement and (then) capital. Today's prisons are only the current system.

And even still, in each era of confinement, people were wily and unpredictable, resisting and refusing the overseers of confinement every step of the way. Enslaved people in these parts constantly broke tools, sloughed work responsibilities, held illicit meetings, and escaped regularly. Folks did the same during the era of Seabrook Farm's labor camps. And almost before the paint dried on the new state prison (Leesburg), people escaped. Most famously, George Wright, who liberated the warden's car, hopped on and then redirected a commercial flight, and eventually made his way to Portugal, where today he lives with his family in a little white house near the shore. No matter the system or style of confinement, targeted and trapped people have always found ways to avoid or undermine capitalist working conditions, escape confinement when the moment presents itself, and build robust social life along the way.[11]

It is the consistency of unpredictability, of the impulse for social life, of the refusal to be defined or determined by systems of domination that led me to the vignette form this ethnography takes up.[12] The primary aim of each vignette is to make space for people to speak and act on their own terms from the flow of their own contexts. The moments that make up the book are intended to encapsulate particular relationships to, experiences in, or perspectives of the prisons and policing while also illuminating the unexpected breaks where the pulse of social life manifests.[13] The vignettes do not revolve around one heroic person and their relentless will. And they are not driving toward a singular finale like a detective novel. There are no conclusions or solutions to be found anywhere in this book. Instead, the vignettes revolve around collectives, groups of people, families, and friends, and they highlight the significance of strong, supportive relationships as the grounding of social life to the side of capitalist domination.

The vignettes are organized into three parts—part 1, "Domination"; part 2, "Resistance"; part 3, "To-the-Side." There are no composite characters or fabricated scenes. And a list of each person's age, race, class, and occupation can be found in appendix 2. The conversations that unfold in each vignette are based on the time I spent with people across three years of in-person research. All but a handful were recorded on my phone. I have cut them into vignettes to crystallize differing experiences, histories, opinions, dreams, and clusters of relationships or political orientations as they relate to the organizing category. For example, in part 1, I introduce people who are targeted by policing and prisons, people who do the targeting, who desire to do the targeting, or who benefit from others being targeted, and also people who sit back safely, protected from the domination of being targeted, and muse on all of it. Each and every resident, though, necessarily contends with the context of capitalist domination that has been created by four hundred years of human confinement. The simple point is that each experiences it in radically different ways. This is the core of tending to everyday life to the side of domination. Most of the time, there is no tidy resolution or simple solution;[14] there is only life in the flow, on its way, messy, mired, and to the side, complex and contradictory, ambitious and accidental, refusing and resisting, reaching for connection with others. What makes the people and events in these vignettes unique is the extreme context of multiple prisons and militarized policing around which all of this stuff happens.

Part 1 centers prisons as the current system of confinement used to maintain social control through the hierarchization and exploitation of humans for labor. It elucidates the idea that confinement is the engine driving the region's social, political, and economic systems while teasing apart how prisons have in fact advanced capital production by eliminating the need for commodities, and thus also the requirement to set labor to work making commodities.[15] "Domination" names how systems of capitalist reproduction function in and across time and place. My specific use gestures to Stuart Hall's "Race, Articulation, and Societies Structured in Dominance" but most specifically builds on Clyde Woods's critical-historical approach in *Development Arrested*, where he traces the *longue durée* of plantation power relations in the Mississippi Delta. Woods meticulously reveals how the owner class (those he calls "planters") plotted and manipulated to perpetually reshape the political economy in order to maintain "plantation-centered development" and hegemonic control over the land and labor.[16] He shows how the legal edifice for slavery was disassembled and put back together in bits and pieces, preserving the social, political, and economic logics and practices of the plantation system. The same is true of confinement in Cumberland County. It has been disassembled and remade across hundreds of years, always in ways that preserve the labor hierarchy and modes of social control similar to those established during the era of plantation slavery. This is not to suggest today's prisons are "the same" mode of domination as slavery, Lenape reservations, or World War II labor camps, but the prisons (with the militarized police forces) target black, brown, and poor people for elimination or containment; order the landscape; structure the labor hierarchy; and function within and for the political economy in ways similar to past systems.

Part 2 features a diverse landscape of people who are explicitly working against, organizing, and fighting the domination of prisons and policing. It revolves around the distinct ways that people become entangled in collective efforts of resistance, how the system itself manages to incorporate its own opposition in order to stifle dissent, and it highlights the many ways organizers struggle with others to fight back. It fractures and challenges the idea of a uniform philosophy, politics, or practice of resistance. Everything is messy, compromised, and in the flow of life. As Avery Gordon reminds us, "It is a fact of great analytic importance that life is complicated," and we must hold tightly to this if we are to "see deep into the heart and soul of American life and culture, to track events, stories . . . and history-making actions . . . to the point where we might catch a glimpse of . . . society and imagine otherwise."[17] Following people whose efforts are sliced through and bound up by competing and oppositional commitments, as most all of our efforts are, provides a glimpse of the culture of this region of southern New Jersey, perhaps even of wider US society. There is no monolithic approach or political orientation that unites people who resist the prisons' domination across the region. It instead appears in many different forms, spearheaded by people with different and sometimes opposed aims, orientations, and visions for the future. The common thread of resistance is neither politics nor practice but how the mode of domination perpetually works to define its own resistance. And how it works to bring into itself those who stand against it. Part 2 offers a glimpse of the deep-seated punitive or carceral logic, and it reveals complexity at the core of people who must, on the one hand, find ways to build sustainable life in a region that specializes in correctional jobs but who, on the other hand, feel compelled to work collectively to fight the prisons and police in the hopes that they can bring about long-lasting change. "Resistance" limns what society is, what it might be, and how people are working to make it happen, and it illuminates the many difficulties in disentangling one's beliefs and activities from the dialectic of domination—resistance.

Part 3 moves through conversations with people whose efforts and activities unfold in places that are blurred to the side, outside the gaze of politicians or police, and away from noisy fights in the streets.[18] If the region's political economy is an outcome of different systems of confinement across hundreds of years, then "To-the-Side" names the unruly (spaces) that do not conform to the values, temporalities, or logics of the system—not because they are accepting it or resisting it but because they are moving in other ways, at other speeds, quietly beside it. I first took note of life to the side when reading an archived letter from World War II. A local mayor—writing to C. F. Seabrook about the arrival of interned Japanese Americans—states that "securing . . . American-Japanese citizens for labor [is preferable to] the undesirable southern Negro labor, [who are] unruly and are continually causing the local police considerable difficulty by fighting and continually behaving in a disorderly manner" (see appendix 1 for the full letter). This reminded me of Fred Moten highlighting Immanuel Kant's inadvertent acknowledgment of "the prior resistance (unruly sociality, anarchic syntax, extrasensical poetics) to that politics that calls it into being."[19] That is to say, Moten turns attention to what he calls the "unruly sociality" that exceeds (in all directions) political and economic domination. It manifests and disperses before the before, after the after, in the break, or, in my language, off to the side of domination and resistance. I first learned to recognize it at the Spot—a small men's clothing store in one of the old downtowns that is owned and managed by two lifelong residents who were entangled with prisons and targeted by drug war policing in their twenties and thirties.

One afternoon, a large group was standing outside the Spot, debating the intersections of federal politics, state prisons, and the social health of the town in light of what needed to change. This vignette appears in part 3. The primary need was the creation of places where "interdependent" community with others could be possible. Interdependent community comprises horizontal relationships that foster mutual care and resource sharing[20]—what might be thought of as something like small-scale, mostly disorganized socialism[21] that is also committed to sharing in the process of personal healing. The people who spent time at the Spot were deeply committed to building and maintaining this space, however momentary or fleeting, where joy, possibility, healing, care of all forms, and even freedom might be possible. Soon, I looked to the side everywhere.

I conclude with vignettes organized to the side because outright resistance is only one mode of living amid and collectively undermining capitalist systems of domination. Or, as Saba Mahmood writes in the 2012 preface to *The Politics of Piety*, "acts of resistance to relations of domination constitute one modality of action, [but] they certainly do not exhaust the field of human action."[22] That is to say, meaningful social life is constituted by far more than negotiating, plotting, and fighting racial capitalism. These spaces and brief moments challenge the totality of domination by tending to the parts of life often neglected and suppressed amid the dizzying work of fighting back (or theorizing about fighting back). Cedric Robinson contends on the first page of *An Anthropology of Marxism* that "the ultimate Marxian objective [is not the outcome of resistance but] the recovery of human life from the spoilage of degradation."[23] The vignettes in part 3 illuminate how people recover, tend to, and care for their own humanity and that of their family and friends. This is an important point to hold onto, because following people whose efforts are in excess of the dialectic suggests that social life, and practices that facilitate something like small-scale socialism, are not only the outcome of overthrowing capitalism but are, also, prior to, in the middle of, to the side, and far beyond it. "To-the-Side" casts light on these spaces, moments, conversations, bursts of laughter, acts, and relationships in unapologetic hope that they are not only appreciated for their own sake but that they are inspirational for all who carry on and, at times, fight like hell beneath the blistering weight of capital.

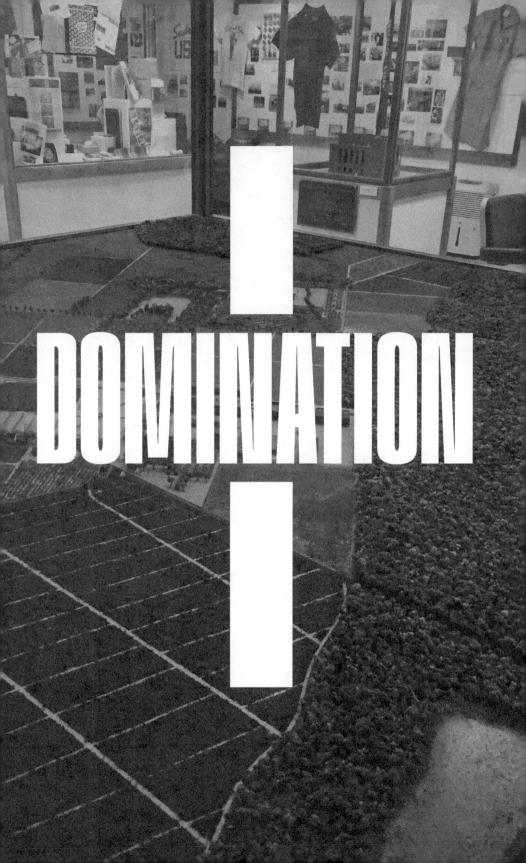

DOMINATION

CHAPTER ONE
OLD MAN TILLEY & THE LAND

As successive terminal moraines result from successive
glaciations, so each frontier leaves its traces behind
it, and when it becomes a settled area the region
still partakes of the frontier characteristics.
FREDERICK JACKSON TURNER | "The Significance
of the Frontier in American History" (1893)

The power of capital always involves and
relies on domination.
SØREN MAU | *Mute Compulsion* (2023)

I always parked in the back. Old Man Tilley's Lexus was usually parked next to Doris Tilley's Lexus. This restaurant (the Mill) was like a scene from *The Sopranos*: deep drapes and heavy furniture and carpeted floors that felt accustomed to pinky rings and cigar-smoking whisperers with gravelly voices. The tables were crammed with professionals, especially aging and retired professionals, and the oblong, wooden bar was generally noisy with chatter. The Tilleys sat in the middle of the dining room.

"Hello, hello." I sat down. "Have you been waiting long?"

"Well, hello, Heath," Old Man Tilley said smiling, blue eyes twinkling. "No, Doris just arrived—and I arrived a few minutes before her."

I knew a club sandwich was already on the way for Old Man Tilley. And I knew he would box up half to take home. Doris was less predictable. I ordered soup and salad. We were recording the lunch meeting—our fourth in two months, not counting phone conversations—and, so, I tuned in momentarily to the chatter at other tables, mostly because I was feeling twitchy. It had been two months since police officers interrogated me in a windowless room and told me to stop asking people questions about the recent police shooting.

"I'm very concerned about this business with the police department," Old Man Tilley said. "Do you think it would be best if I made a call down there? I can talk to the chief and tell him this kind of behavior is unacceptable. Maybe we can get to the bottom of this?"

I noticed a retirement-aged white man at the next table craning to listen to our conversation, which may or may not have had anything to do with me. Since the Tilley family had a kind of local fame, other residents regularly stole glances in their presence or paid respects with a hello and handshake. The Tilley brothers were the last of their family in town.

"Thank you very much," I said as I side-eyed the eavesdropper, "but I think it might bring me more trouble than relief. Maybe we just let it go for now."

"I'm very concerned." Old Man Tilley frowned. "But you will let me know?"

"Yes, I will let you know, I promise. For now, I am more interested in hearing about your experiences with the internment camps confining Japanese Americans that you mentioned yesterday on the phone," I redirected. "I had never heard of that."

"Those were concentration camps." He threw a corrective finger in the air. "I'm very insistent on correcting people who say 'in-tern-ment.'" He slowed for each syllable. "The US government stole their possessions, took their homes, lands, and family businesses, and then put them into concentration camps and held them at gunpoint." Doris shook her head. "I remember as a boy watching them unload for the first time at the farm."

"Wait, you mean you were actually standing there—in person as they marched by?!" I had missed this detail.

"Well, OK." He lit up. "So my family moved to that land, which we still have [in Cumberland County], in 1748. My great-grandfather and one other man got the railroad stop here in 1869, which enabled local farmers to send their produce to Brooklyn in five hours. So, the more assertive people in town started to make a tremendous amount of money. My great-grandfather was a great visionary."

Old Man Tilley liked to collapse personal memory with historic events. A question to him was more a provocation for time travel, which could ground you just about anywhere in time as long as it was this place in space. From our discussion of Japanese American concentration camps, he leaped back to the mid-1700s, then up to the mid-1800s, and up again to World War II. For him, knowledge of what happened in a particular time connected to his family's land ownership and business ventures. By highlighting shifts in how the land was ordered for capitalist production, he filtered national history through the lens of family ownership. In this conversation, it was his great-grandfather, a few years after the end of slavery, who brought a railroad stop into the downtown, which altered the landscape and how workers related to the rhythms of that new order—selling fruits and vegetables (by train) in Brooklyn produced different job demands and new rhythms of time than selling produce at local grocers. In an earlier conversation, it was the public school system built in the late-1990s, outside of the city limits, which today brandishes his family name, and which, he felt, resegregated local education and deepened the growing economic divide.

"OK, I called the library to make sure that they were open," Old Man Tilley continued. "They are open, and they have a volunteer that comes in at lunch. So, I'll be very concerned about protocol. This thing is very internal to me, and my mother used to do the guided tours, when she was living, around the family property, showing people exactly where, on our land, the artifacts were found."

"Oh, wow." I imagined his mother trekking across the lands in a muddied dress, *Little House on the Prairie* style.

"They recorded where all these artifacts were found," he relayed excitedly. "And the journals go back. They are all lined journals, and there are thousands of entries, because the collection is somewhere between twenty-two thousand and twenty-three thousand pieces," he stressed. "When Father died, I took the entire collection to the tribal leaders and offered to give it back. It never belonged to us. But they did not want the collection, so that's how it ended up in the basement of the library. I'm in the process of establishing a more permanent home."

During his youth, Old Man Tilley's father regularly journeyed throughout the family land, which had been earlier occupied by Lenape people, to dig up broken pots and jugs, arrowheads, and even human remains in skeletal form—"Shhh, we still have some of those skeletons in the family house," he whispered. Doris shivered, and he laughed, before recounting a story that happened some sixty-odd years earlier, when she still slept in the family's guest bedroom, before they were married, and, one late night, woke up with a fright, certain the skeletons lining her room had creaked back to life. Old Man Tilley laughed and then reconstructed in vivid, thrilling detail finally getting to travel with his brother and the archaeologist (hired by his father) to a corner of the farming estate to dig up the Lenape bones and pots.

"My older brother and I were going to help dig up some already-found pots not yet fully removed," he went on.

It was six months before I encountered a resident of Lenape descent. It happened one day as I walked the two short blocks from the Spot to the public defender's offices to visit Henrietta. The door *dinged* as I entered the tiny storefront. It was stuffed, floor to ceiling, with trinkets, woven rugs, and thick blankets, all crafted in Mexico, according to the labels. A person behind the desk, chatting on the phone, acknowledged me with a nod before returning to the tasks at hand. I thumbed my way through various items, thinking I might buy something.

The person hung up the phone. "What can I help you with today?"

"Hi." My voice was eager. "I'm an anthropologist doing research here and thought I would stop in. I didn't know you all were here!" (I am embarrassed to include this line.)

The person looked back to the phone and said, "*Harrumph*. Let me know if I can help you with anything," and dialed a call a few seconds later.

They were uninterested in chitchat. I fiddled with a few more blankets and bolted out the front door.

"We still have that land." Old Man Tilley chewed his club sandwich.

Father Tilley and the archaeologist took the brothers to that distant edge of farmland they had never been, gave them digging tools, and instructed them on how to carefully remove the old Lenape bowls from the earth. Light digging here, tap-tap-tapping there, using their tiny hands and simple tools to extract fragments of a buried existence that would

1.1 Photo of taxidermied birds and reassembled Lenape pots and arrowheads, taken in the basement of a public library in Cumberland County.

1.2 Photo of reassembled Lenape pots and arrowheads, taken in the basement of a public library in Cumberland County.

eventually be reconstructed into a perfectly shaped water jug for decontextualized display in a fluorescent-lit basement.

In excitement (he remained excited telling the story), the brothers dug and dug, removing earth, exposing pottery fragments, and, in one swift moment, Young Man Tilley brought his pick firmly down with the childlike force of timelessness, cracking through a prized piece, fragmenting a fragment. Father Tilley was none too happy. The brothers were taken to the car and left to await their fates. Never again were they allowed to dig.

"After we visit the museum, would you like to ride around with us and see the family property?" Old Man Tilley asked. "Do you have time for that?"

"I would love to ride around with you," I replied.

Leaving the museum, I folded into the front seat of his plushy Lexus—Doris insisted on sitting in the back—and we drove up, down, and across Cumberland County, especially Bridgeton and its adjacent farmlands, as he pointed out what happened here in 1958, and what happened there in 1883, before even his own father was born, and which tree their children once played around, all with a kind of enchanted excitement born of a lifelong capacity to move freely upon the land.

"Would you like to see where our family's grocery store was located, which served the Japanese Americans who lived at Seabrook Farms during World War II?" he asked.

"Of course!" I said.

"Most people around here were not too happy about their arrival," he said.

"They were such hard workers!" Doris exclaimed from the back seat.

"Yes!" Old Man Tilley agreed. "C. F. had purchased the technology to freeze fruits and vegetables from Birds Eye—well, more like stole the technology—and he needed them to . . ." Old Man Tilley was perhaps repeating what he heard his father say long ago. He enjoyed rewriting the myths of Seabrook in the same way he delighted in correcting the fantasies of the United States—by reframing through the lens of his family's experiences.

"Dear," Doris interjected from the back seat, "you shouldn't say that!"

"Well, it's true. My family knew about it." Old Man Tilley shrugged and chuckled. "Father started an on-site general store for the Japanese Americans, since they were not allowed to shop in town, even though he did not approve of exploiting their labor. Mother was pretty anti-Japanese at the time, and she was upset that they were being brought into the area," he chuckled again. "But we soon set her straight on that one."

"They were so talented at sports, and they never complained," Doris added.

"Nope! The whole group kind of undertook a biblical turn-the-other-cheek approach, and they were not bitter at all."[1] Old Man Tilley nodded.

We turned onto a long, seemingly dead-end, dilapidated road that cut through a large expanse of field, where abandoned farm machines rusted brown like metal dinosaurs. He pointed excitedly to an area where eighty years prior, the family's general store stood.

"My father worked with C. F. on many things." Again he threw a finger into the air. "But he did not share C. F.'s willingness to undertake shady deals," he assured me—and himself?

Old Man Tilley shows us that since capitalist owners control the means of production, they will always benefit from the systems of confinement. He sees his own ancestors as "great visionaries" and hard workers who strategically navigated the dramatic changes that happened across the centuries. Within one decade of the system of slavery's collapse, his great-grandfather strategized with one other person to establish a railroad stop that opened Brooklyn food markets to local produce. When the "government stole" the homes, possessions, businesses, and livelihoods of Japanese Americans at gunpoint before marching them to "concentration camps," and eventually to labor camps at Seabrook Farms, his father strategized with C. F. to open a grocery store that exclusively served them. Today, the primary family business is coal and oil, but they continue to farm large portions of the land by employing people who migrated in from Mexico and Central and South America. Irrespective to the era of confinement, the Tilley family has figured out how to generate great profits for the family businesses.

He views the different systems of confinement as moral failures and extreme overreaches undertaken by the US government. His commitment to setting the record straight, whether it is correcting his mother or returning unearthed artifacts or reframing the brutalities of internment and concentration camps, is rooted in a detached capacity to analyze and critique the situation. He never seems to make the connections between the necessity of confinement to the functioning of the political economy. Or at least he never admits this to me. The mayor's letter to

Seabrook, however, which can be found in full in appendix 1, does not suffer from the same lack of clarity. In the letter, the mayor speaks openly about the strict and necessary order of racialized confinement for capitalist production. He acknowledges that residents and politicians alike are not in support of Japanese Americans being moved locally to work the farm, but he insists, nevertheless, that residents must be willing to accept whatever is necessary to aid the production efforts of Seabrook Farms (and, ultimately, the war efforts of the US government). And since the farm requires workers who can be fully controlled (there are multiple references in the letter to the "unruliness" of black laborers), using interned Japanese Americans makes good economic sense, which, in turn, creates robust political support. The mayor's letter, in contrast with Old Man Tilley's history, then, does not frame the labor camps as a gross misstep or moral failure but as a matter-of-fact necessity for large-scale production under capitalism. He understands that systems of confinement are essential to economic viability, whether residents support their use or disagree with it, and, so, he must throw his own political weight behind them.

CHAPTER TWO

BIG TIM & MRS. TAYLOR

If only because ethnography is opening always
outward in time and space, the discourse of
solutions [is] always seeking containment.

CAROL GREENHOUSE | *The Paradox of Relevance* (2011)

Following a morning spent sifting through archived newspapers in the library, I drove elsewhere for a quiet lunch. Retreating to noisy restaurants was my occasional respite. I received a text message just as my food was delivered. An organizer in Philadelphia wrote to me in all caps: PROSECUTORS ISSUE NONINDICTMENT FOR OFFICERS WHO MURDERED JERAME REID!!! CALL ME ASAP. I slammed the food and raced downtown. The few blocks of streets were rolling-tumbleweed quiet. My heart raced, and I was sweating from the humidity. I ran into the Spot to the *ding* of the door. Shakes was unloading boxes of T-shirts and jeans in the back storage room.

"My man!" He walked to the front. "What's good?" He grabbed a folding chair. "Let's step outside."

"Did you hear the news?" I skipped the greeting.

"What news?" He tapped a Newport short and flicked a lighter.

"The nonindictment. I just got a text . . ."

"The nonindictment of who?" He looked over.

"Of the police officers who shot and killed Jerame." I lit my own cigarette.

"Ahh, man, no." He shook his head. "No indictment, huh? That ain't right."

"Do you know anything about protests happening because of it?" I asked.

"No, man. I don't know anything about any of that."

"OK." I exhaled. "I'm just kind of wondering what to do?"

"Let's go over to Timmy's [Shakes's son] and see if he knows anything." He snuffed the cigarette.

We walked across the street to Big Tim's barbershop. He was lining someone up. The clippers buzzed slow and steady, his nose millimeters from the customer's head.

"Have you heard the news?" Shakes's voice boomed as he plopped down backward on a folding chair he placed in the middle of the room, in front of the large television and still in view of the Spot's front door.

"What news?" Big Tim cut off the clippers.

"Tell'im." Shakes waved his hand.

Big Tim had not heard but offered multiple places to check for people protesting in the streets. I left in a flash.

The courthouse: empty.

The city police station: empty.

The prosecutor's offices: empty.

The numerous country roads I got lost on: empty.

The street memorial on the side of the road where Jerame was shot six times and killed: empty.

I knelt at the side of the road, bringing myself eye-level with the memorial, to read the poem next to the picture.[1]

After a few minutes on my haunches, a voice spoke over me, as if answering a question I had not yet asked: "You know Officer Days and Jerame were sleeping with the same woman, right?" Mrs. Taylor shook her head. "My kids can't unsee *that*." Her voice thinned. She was pacing and smoking. "He was shot *right there*," she said, pointing across the street.

"Umm, hi!" I blurted. "No, I did not know that. Do you mean that Officer Days was sleeping with Jerame's wife?"

"No. I mean Officer Days and Jerame were sleeping with the same woman, and she wasn't married to either of them. And *she* is the one that called Officer Days on his cell phone, not 9-1-1, his *cell* phone, telling him

2.1 Photo of the Jerame Reid memorial, taken in front of Mrs. Taylor's house, across the street from the site of the police killing.

that Jerame had a gun up in the glove box. There was no gun. I watched every single minute of the police cleanup from right here." She dragged deeply from the cigarette.

"Well, it's very nice to meet you." I stamped out my own cigarette, stood, and extended my hand. "My name is Heath . . ."

"I shouldn't say *cleanup*," she corrected, shaking my hand. "I had to go the next morning and cover a bullet hole and clean blood from the grass, sidewalk, and street so my babies wouldn't have to walk to school in it. During the cleanup, the cops were laughing and having a good ol' time eating donuts and drinking coffee. They didn't even bother to remove the bloody investigator's gloves and scissors from the ground before they all drove off."

"Are you serious?" I asked.

"And look—" She fixed her eyes on mine. "I don't hate the police. My daddy was a cop in this town for twenty-five years. He just retired. He lives down the road from here." She pointed over my shoulder.

"And what does he think of all this?" I managed to squeeze in. Mrs. Taylor speaks fast.

"And another thing—" A young boy appeared at her hip, clinging at her waist, and she wrapped an arm around his narrow shoulders. I did not know whether she was comforting him or he was comforting her. "Mrs. Reid [Jerame's widow] came down here the other day, thanking me for keeping up this memorial in my yard, and she handed me fifty dollars! I asked her, 'Where did you get that?!' and she said, 'The police came by my house and paid me, and they told me if I stopped protesting after the nonindictment was released, then they would pay me again in October.' So, she is getting paid off by the cops, who already knew the nonindictment was coming, to keep quiet and to quit protesting. And *trust* me, it *must* be true. She got that money from *some*where because that woman never has two nickels to rub together."

I imagined the young boy at Mrs. Taylor's waist, perhaps eleven or twelve, watching the shooting, maybe shielding his eyes, maybe sneaking a peek through his fingers, a faint silhouette at the second-floor window, his mother's arm still wrapped tight, sidestepping bullet holes the next morning while his tiny backpack bounced around his shoulders. Notice that Mrs. Taylor cleaned up the remaining blood from the ground, left there by the officers, but she did not mention shielding her children from witnessing the shooting. If her children are to survive until adulthood, they must know how to stay safe around police officers. That is to say, they must understand who police officers are and how police officers behave.

"Did she tell you how much the cash payment was for?" I asked.

"Ten. Thousand. Dollars. Twice." She stressed each word.

We finished the conversation. I hopped into my car and raced back to the Spot. My head was spinning with the new information. Stories of police officers using cash bribes or planting drugs or guns are common. They represent a shared understanding of standard police work by people who must know how police work. But I had never been this close to what I imagined was a scandal. My heart was racing again. This time I busted through the Spot's front door like a bat out of hell, eager to break the news. Shakes hustled from the back before realizing it was only me again.

"What did you find?" he asked, mostly with disinterest.

"Not much," I replied. "But I spoke with Mrs. Taylor, who lives across the street from where the shooting happened. She witnessed the entire event."

"What did Mrs. Taylor have to say?"

I relayed the collected information, one crumb at a time, action-movie style, assuming that the crumbs would lead us out into the streets to get rowdy!

"Hmm, yeah." He scratched his chin. "I knew all that, except I hadn't heard about the cash bribes."

"Wait—you already heard everything else?" I asked, dumbfounded. "The shared girlfriend? The lack of a gun in the glove box? The false 9-1-1 dispatch? You *knew* all this?!"

Information that was revelatory to me was routine to Shakes. He was not shocked by news that police officers were bribing Jerame's widow to stay quiet. Once upon a time, he, too, was a young black boy who had to learn who police officers were and how they behave.

"Yeah, man. Let's go over to Timmy's and see what he thinks."

The barbershop was quiet. Big Tim sat in his barber's chair, smoking a Swisher Sweet, squinting at the television. Shakes plopped down as he had earlier. Rodney, the second barber, sat on the opposite couch, half-watching NBA highlights and half-twisting the ends on his James Harden-esque beard as he scrolled Twitter. On this day, he waxed poetic about majority-black towns with poisoned water systems (i.e., do not drink the tap water). Less than three months after this conversation, Flint, Michigan, made national news for poisoned water (that remains poisoned).

"Have you heard anything?" I sat on the couch across from Big Tim.

"Nah, man," he answered. "You broke the news to us this morning. What did you find out?"

I relayed every piece of information to him.

"It wouldn't surprise me in the least. They're fucking cops." He exhaled thick, sweet smoke. "They can do anything they want to do."

"So, you believe they bribed Jerame's wife with $20K?" I asked.

"*Of course* I believe it," he emphasized. "I have no idea if it's true, but I believe it."

"So, what are we going to do about it?" I asked.

"About what?" Big Tim cocked his head.

"A . . . about the nonindictment . . ." I hesitated.

"There is no *anything*." Big Tim dragged deeply from his Swisher. "*This* is what it means to be black. *This* is who it is. There's nothing *we can* do. Those are cops." Smoky puffs puffed around each word.

Big Tim and Mrs. Taylor show us different experiences of domination. With Old Man Tilley, the centrality of prisons, like the necessity of labor camps, was more about musing on the similarities of what he saw as egregious missteps within a family history of ownership and successful production. His understanding of racist policing, confinement, and punitive labor conditions was detached from real-world stakes. He may have stood beside horrific spectacles of confinement like the parade of Japanese Americans being moved onto Seabrook's farm, but he could not make the explicit connection to the region's prisons. He has kept himself shielded from bearing witness to the similar ways that police officers round up residents at gunpoint to march them into spaces of confinement (and sometimes put them to work). Because of this, he does not view the prisons as grossly unjust moral failures the way he does the labor camps, and he does not recognize that police officers are like soldiers maintaining a system of domination for the ruling class. He thus holds to the belief that police officers can be expected to behave in specific ways, as evidenced, first, in his shock at my mistreatment and, second, by his insistence that calling the police chief would resolve the situation. Like the old Lenape artifacts on the dank basement shelves, the fragments of fragmented life that have been shattered by police work are cleanly sealed off in glass for his detached observation. He does not know who police officers are or how they behave because he does not need to know.

Residents who are poor or racialized minorities do not have this ruling class, white privilege. They grow up learning what they need to know. This means that very little of what I found out about police work was new knowledge to Big Tim or Shakes or so many others. Officers will "do whatever they want to do," and eight months later, prosecutors will refuse to issue indictments, as they almost always have in the thousands upon thousands of officer shootings and aggressions over the previous decades. Big Tim's answer to my question about what we are going to do ("About what?") thus peels open and exposes my eagerness for street protests by asking me what I believed the object of change should or could be. I stuttered to answer. He did not believe much in the possibility of change, and he wanted me to understand that standing up to police is not only useless, like punching at the wind, but incredibly dangerous, since the smallness of the town means that protestors are easily identifiable and thus swiftly punished for their civil disobedience—something I, too, learned after being questioned in custody for doing research in the area. People in part 2 will have firsthand experiences with these kinds of punishments. Big Tim understands that policing is central to the region's order. And, like privatizing land and resources into the hands of a few white men, policing is a technology for maintaining domination.

Mrs. Taylor offers a similar view of the local order, but she does not accept domination or hierarchy as the only or last words on the matter. Instead, she pushes our sight past the pessimism of unchangeability by tending to a memorial that is off to the side, repairing it when people trashed it or knocked it down in the middle of the night, making sure there was evidence of care and love and remembering in a place beside the place where life was stolen. It took me years and years to grasp the significance of her efforts. When Mrs. Taylor's children were exposed to the ways that policing maintains order through the butcherly force of department-issued revolvers, she began working to make sure they were exposed to the other forces of the neighborhood as well. She could not stop police officers from firing their pistols, or bullying and bribing residents, or occupying the streets and sidewalks of her neighborhood. But she could make sure their forces were not the only ones in the neighborhood. Mrs. Taylor cleared and cleaned the ground, covering up the blood on the sidewalk and in the street, hewing a path through the destruction where her children and others might play and chatter and hop and skip and freeze tag and walk together to schools or parks or corner stores once again. Month after month after month, Mrs. Taylor's children witnessed this work, her persistence, her commitment to making and keeping something beautiful out of something very ugly. Leaving Jerame's blood pooling on the sidewalk, like leaving Michael Brown's body lying cold in the hot Ferguson streets, is a technique police officers use to perform dominance on city blocks and in neighborhoods—an effective reminder for demonstrating their state-sanctioned power over life and death. But Jerame's memorial is a testament to other kinds of powers. It is testament to the life that preceded police officers' savage acts of domination, to the collective life that remembers, that lives on, that continues to work the ground. And, perhaps just as significant, it is a sign of the incompleteness of those officers' acts of domination. Mrs. Taylor was teaching her children, and the neighborhood, and me that even in death, she and others will do whatever is in their capacity to care for one another, to keep alive the memories of life, to open space for communing on earth that has been silenced by the pop of bullets, by way of memorializing and honoring and building and planting and beautifying—insisting, in this neighborhood, on these sidewalks, death speaks neither the first nor the final word.

CHAPTER THREE

THE CHIEF & BIGFOOT

I nervously fiddled at a small brown desk in a small taupe office with no windows that was reserved for part-time prosecutors. Millsy was the day's part-time prosecutor. I looked obsessively over my shoulder at every sound. It had been only a few weeks since police officers held me in another windowless room just down the hall from this one. I would not choose to be inside this police department alone, but Millsy arranged the meeting, and I trusted her to keep me safe.

"So, these two guys are retired cops?" I asked. "And they agreed to talk with me? Are you staying in the room?"

"Yeah, they were both eager to speak with you," she laughed.

Residents who were eager to speak with me made me nervous—especially when those residents were police officers. Millsy was a lawyer for a private firm who worked part-time as a county prosecutor. I suspected she had political ambitions. She had developed friendly ties with Chief Jones and Detective "Bigfoot" Blanke, who worked regularly as courtroom cops in their retirement. I met Millsy through Henrietta, who served as a public defender (I will introduce her later). She never told me outright, but I suspected Millsy went to the police chief of this department and threatened him with stories of Princeton-money lawsuits coming if his officers continued harassing me. The door swung open, and two hulking men lumbered into the office.

"Heyyy, Chief! Detective Blanke!" Millsy enthused. "Thanks so much for coming. This is Heath, the one I told you about. He is doing research on the impact prisons have had on Cumberland County."

Both men greeted me, right arms outstretched, with hands strong enough to crush cans before stuffing their oversized frames into chairs on either side of me—a position, I must confess, that made me sweat almost immediately.[1] We exchanged pleasantries and began.

"Chief and I both came on about a year apart, back in '68 to '69," Detective "Bigfoot" Blanke started. "At the time, [police] academy was six weeks. It's now six months. You came on and basically you walked downtown. You were given a beat downtown. You got to know the stores, the people, everybody walking around. Anytime anybody needed a police officer, they knew if they came downtown, they could grab one right away."

"Notable difference," Chief Jones cut in, throwing a finger in the air. "We had no radios. So, when you walked the beat, you walked the beat. It was on *you*. You were the law on that beat. So, whatever came up, you handled it. So, it was pretty much a different world than it is now."

This is a moment when knowledge from opposing sides about the function of policing intersects in agreement. Local residents regularly refer to officers as "the law." This is what Big Tim meant, for example, when he said that officers can "do anything they want to do." The actions of officers in the streets, on the ground, is "the law" irrespective of state or federal legislation. His understanding is rooted in tradition passed along by elders and through his own experiences with police officers. On the other side, knowledge of "the law" from a professional position means knowing legislative details and perhaps histories. Chief Jones references this kind of knowledge later in the conversation. But, at this moment, like so many other residents, the chief also believes "the law" is the point of contact where officers "handle" residents in the streets.

"This was about the time the Panthers, the Black Panther Movement, was executing police officers, you know?" Bigfoot said. "We both grew up here, but I was shocked when I started walking the beat . . . what the back alleys looked like."

This was also the time (between 1968 and 1971) when police officers and other domestic soldiers across the United States were assassinating members of the Black Panther Party for Self-Defense. I recorded numerous stories from retired high school history teacher Donald Tice, including one where he and a few friends, both white and black, were pulled over by local police, yanked out of their van, and thrown to the concrete. An officer placed the barrel of a shotgun against his throat before finally tossing everyone in jail overnight. His voice still tensed as he recalled the officer unlocking the shotgun's safety and pressing the steel barrel against his larynx.

"As a normal person living in the city, you see the storefronts of the stores. Now you start dealing with alleys and all that stuff," the chief added.

"So, what kinds of things were you experiencing on the beat?" I asked.

"We used to deal with burglaries a lot," Bigfoot answered, "because, you gotta remember, back in the '60s, the late '60s, they didn't have burglar alarms. So, you actually had to be there and listen for glass breaking, listening for strange noises."

"What were you telling me," Millsy jumped in, "how over all your years on the force, how many police shootings was it? And how many there are now?"

"I don't think—" Bigfoot looked upward, scratched his chin. "I don't think from '69 up to probably, oh, what, '75? When Flip shot someone?"

The chief nodded in silent agreement.

"That was the first shooting I can remember." Bigfoot nodded.

"Flip shot a guy in the—"

"In the leg!" Bigfoot cut the chief off. "But that was 'You run, I'll shoot.' He ran, and he shot. It's not like today."

"But why is it not like today?" Millsy pushed.

"Times have changed," Bigfoot sighed, folding his hands.

"What changed?" Millsy pushed again.

"Everybody is carrying a gun," the chief said.

Reliable gun statistics are elusive. There are more guns in the United States now than fifty years ago, but the percentage of households with guns has remained largely steady, even revealing a slight decline over the decades, which likely means both that more households have multiple guns and more households have no guns. The chief, like most police officers, believes that a far greater number of people now carry concealed pistols than they did in the late 1960s.

"Oh." Millsy rested her line of questioning. "OK."

"Back then, nobody carried a gun," Bigfoot continued.

"I had a guy shoot at me." The chief leaned his face directly in front of mine, eyes wide open. "Point-blank range, and I mean, closer than me to you. And he missed. After he missed, I took off running to chase him and grabbed him jumping over a wall."

"Why didn't you shoot him?!" Millsy laughed.

"Umm, well, he turned around and started running before I could grab my gun," Chief laughed.

"It was really frowned upon to shoot people in the back in those times," Bigfoot explained, as they continued laughing.

"Well, that's one thing that has changed around here," I stated flatly.

"Yeah." Bigfoot scratched his chin.

"The gun was in his back pocket." The chief insisted on finishing his story. "And I pulled him down off the wall and came up with him and his gun and found extra rounds in his pocket, and it actually went to trial. And the judge only sentenced him to six months for attempted homicide!" Chief leaned forward, scanning face-to-face-to-face. "I look at the judge, like, *What?!* And he said to me, 'Well, he missed, didn't he?!'" Everyone laughed.

"Stop." Millsy leaned back. "Are you serious?"

"We are getting a little off track here, so maybe we can bring it back," I redirected. "You both retired within a few years of the new prisons coming in, so, from your perspective, how has that changed things?"

"Today, we have more gradations of crimes," the chief picked up. "You know, when we started, I think things were much more harsh. What we have done now is fill cells with people doing short stints. And also, in the early '70s, we changed our mental health laws across the nation.[2] A lot of times, I would ask the prosecutor to send people to jail because it was going to be a cold weekend and I don't want them outside freezing."

The chief and Bigfoot seem to suffer from a heavy dose of nostalgia-induced delusion about their past policing. They claim that the problems with policing "these days" has to do with the fact that everyone is carrying pistols and running away from police officers while they simultaneously yuck up story after story from the 1960s and 1970s about residents pointing pistols at them and running away from arrest. But the chief manages to identify the lessons for survival exactly right: even grandmothers participate in teaching the children who police officers are and how they behave.

"So, you're saying a person's relationship to crime has changed?" I asked.

"The prisons brought in a much worse criminal intellect," Bigfoot replied.

"Once in a while—" the chief started.

"So, how do you see policing as having changed across the country, then?" I cut him off.

"The war on drugs is really where it started," the chief answered.

"I don't think the police officers of today know anything about the people they police." Bigfoot pivoted away from the chief's point. "They go from point A to point B, and as soon as they're finished with point B, they're gonna go to point C. They're not in the downtown area with all the bullshit, talking to people and everything. When Chief and I came on, we had five cars—"

"Plus, the ambulance," the chief clarified.

"Plus, the ambulance," Bigfoot acknowledged, waving his hand. "And the police handled all the ambulance calls on top of the policing calls."

"But more than the resources police departments have or don't have," Chief cut in, "is recidivism and the way we handle juveniles in our criminal justice system. We have several generations of criminals that we have produced in our flawed criminal justice system."

The chief sometimes surprised me.

"So, then," I said, trying to steer the conversation, "back to the war on drugs: What do you think that war has done to policing and police-community relations?"

"I don't honestly think we've made a dent in drug use," Bigfoot replied matter-of-factly.

"I don't either," the chief momentarily agreed. "I think of all we've done—ummm—there is a lot of people doing a lot of time in prison. But the broader question is: Do I think it's necessary for them to be a criminal? And yeah, I do."

"So then—"

"You got me started on something here," the chief cut me off. "You can see the difference in police officers. That's a major shift. When we took the service test, it was a general knowledge test, similar to an IQ test. You reached a certain standard or you couldn't go to the department. And they lowered it and lowered it and lowered it. We had a chance back in the '70s when we wanted officers to be more educated. They offered officers free education to go back to college. I took them up on it. Now, they've lowered the standards so much that you can get in with a GED. They have kids coming out of academy that can't write a report because they can't put a paragraph together, and we find it difficult to prosecute the cases. Officers are now in this environment where everybody has a camera, everybody is taping everything, and there is a lot of anti-police sentiment out there." The chief paused for affirmation.

Here the chief unpacks a more traditional understanding of "the law" and a police officer's relationship to enforcing it amid the local population.

If the job description were spelled out in a newspaper advertisement, he insists, then the expectations would include a thorough understanding of the intricacies of criminal law and a lightning-fast wit to apply it in all contexts. He believes the perpetual lowering of standards undertaken by the higher-ups produced a generation of officers with low levels of intelligence.

Bigfoot started: "Well, the investigations have gotten so deep now, an officer shoots somebody—which it should be, because you need to decide: Did he do it right or are we going to indict the officer? Like, when we investigated Jimmy shooting into Rosy's house. We get the call, the neighbors called, and we go to the door and yell in, 'Hey Roosevelt—Rosy, what's going on?' And instead of answering, he fires a shot at the officer. Jimmy leans in and fires off two rounds—he's protecting himself; he's returning fire."

"Well, it's so quick," the chief raised his voice. "When are you going to deploy your weapon? When are you gonna pull your gun?! At what point? When somebody pulls one on you?! It's too late. These days, we may be years answering for what happened right here, right now, just in a matter of seconds. I once had a guy pull a gun and stick it to my forehead." He pointed his own finger into his forehead, looking up at his finger. "And I didn't shoot him."

This is the third story about residents pulling guns on officers during the era when people supposedly did not carry guns.

"I can remember one case: Big Wanda," Bigfoot began. "I shouldn't be naming these names, but Big Wanda was a Philadelphia gang member that moved in. We got the call when we were downtown that she and her boyfriend were arguing in the front yard of their house. By the time we get there, she is walking out with a gun and neither of us have a vest on. I have a shotgun next to me and we pull up while she's walking across the street. I throw the car in park and crack the door open, and she turns and *BAM! BAM! BAM!* she fires three rounds through the car door." He punched his fist into his palm with each "*BAM!*" "Just like that! I threw the gun up, cocked it, it was a shotgun, and I'm yelling, 'Wanda, drop the weapon!' And I've got the shotgun pointed at her because the entire time she's turning, I'm squeezing the trigger. . . . That shotgun should have gone off . . . because I was gonna dust her."

"So, I'm interested in hearing your take on police practices, and in how you understand what's going on with the increase in incarceration from the drug war and, more specifically, police relations with residents," I said, in an attempt to redirect.

"I wonder sometimes about the friction within the community, especially the black community, and a lot of times I don't understand it," the chief replied. "I do with some of the officers. A few officers are making a very negative impact. When I walked the beat though, it was all black people, and I never had a problem in the world. I had people on that beat that would back me up in a heartbeat."

"Yep," Bigfoot nodded. "You made friends with them. . . . But not only did you make friends with them, you treated them like you wanted to be treated."

The implications here seem to be that white people and black people were different and were thus policed differently, in a region where friendships did not cross race lines.

"But what do you do when there is a corrupt police department in a poor town like this? What do you do?" Millsy pushed back on my behalf.

"Sometimes you have to dismantle it," the chief pulled back. "Sometimes you go in with the AG's [attorney general's] office and clean house. One of the things that bothers me a great deal though is, 'Oh, we're going to demilitarize the police.' What?! Who are you going to call—" He leaned forward and looked from face-to-face-to-face. "Worst-case scenario, who are you gonna call when ISIS decides to reach out and strike ten kindergarten classes to bring the nation to its knees? Gonna call the military? No. They're not available. Who you gonna call? There's only one place, one agency, that can be called to combat terrorism, and that is our local and state police. We need to have police in a mode that is ready to secure their communities against terrorist threats. But dealing with corruption in police departments . . ." He stared at his hands for a long pause before looking up. "I wonder how many police departments are actually corrupt. I mean, I can't go around to every single one—look, crooked cop, bad cop, I'm going to excise them like a cancer."

"Yep," Bigfoot nodded.

"I have moved to prosecute many officers as a chief. I mean, not a little bit—"

"Back in the day," Bigfoot cut in, "if we had somebody doing something, now I'm going back to the '70s [and] '80s, we had someone who was doing something *not quite kosher*, we take them in the back parking lot and have a little heart-to-heart [read: a few officers beat the out-of-line officer within an inch of his life], because 99 percent of the guys wanted to keep the department straight, and every once in a while, you might get a bad apple."

"So, then, umm, regarding the drug war, you think . . ."

"I think it may have curbed—" The chief paused. "I think, well, I think that it has kept drugs out of some hands—at least, to some degree, out of the mainstream culture as being acceptable. Um . . ."

The chief claimed that the drug war was not only about policing so-called drugs but about shaping what people believe and understand about them. From his perspective, drug policing is propaganda with a message as much as it is brute enforcement maintaining order.

"I think," Bigfoot cut in, "if anything has worked as far as drugs, it would be the DARE program, where they go into the schools for fourth, fifth, sixth graders with a police officer, in uniform, preaching to them about the dangers—"

"I remember that as a kid in Indiana," I laughed.

"You have to realize the intellect of the person you are dealing with when you are dealing with me," the chief said. "When you say, 'The war on drugs,' because all throughout my career I was dedicated to that. I thought they were destroying kids, destroying communities, and if I could do anything possible to remove them from the community, it was not only my duty, it was my joy and my great pleasure to get them out of here. So, to sit back and examine and say all these years it's done no good . . . I can't abandon the idea that it has helped." The chief sat back.

The chief contradicted his earlier statement when he agreed with Bigfoot that the drug war did nothing to stop the negative impact of so-called drugs on the community.

"Think of Terrell!" Bigfoot said excitedly. "He was using his nephew to hold for him. So, we kicked down his door, raided his house, went through everything, and we weren't gonna find anything. So, we tapped his phone and got him on conspiracy charges—possession with intent."

"And we ended up confiscating his white BMW!" the chief gushed.

"And *every*body in the community knew whose car it was," Bigfoot laughed.

"So, I had it, I put police decals on it and overhead lights and we used it in the parades. We got word one day that 'Oh, Terrell is gonna burn the car,' and so I had the car parked at the fire station, right by the main road, and sent word back that I *daaare* him to try and burn it," the chief laughed, rubbing his hands excitedly.

"You realize—" Bigfoot circled back, "the main reason we're never gonna win that war? Too much money. These cartels are making billions and—"

"Yeah," Chief agreed.

"And, you know, all the people who are making money on it in a, umm, a legal manner," I added. "Police officers, prosecutors, corrections, the private corporations that operate in prisons, politicians. It's a massive cash cow for more than just so-called drug dealers."

"Oh yeah. And all the rehab centers popping up everywhere," Bigfoot added, "they're *all* making money. It's like a revolving door. They're coming in today and they're rehabbing them and six months later they're coming back again. It's like cancer research. Never gonna cure it."

———

Chief and Bigfoot are retired police officers who saw their work as maintaining order, for example, between a resident like Old Man Tilley and a resident like Big Tim. They were first responsible for standing and walking around the downtown streets "with all the bullshit," and then they were tasked with driving vehicles "from point A to point B," as policing came to rely not on an officer's presence in a place or personal relationships with residents, but on dispatch responding to 9-1-1 calls. Both spoke in nostalgic terms for the era when policing was more assimilated into the community (from their perspective), and both hold a clear difference in how they view alleged lawbreakers prior to the drug war and after. Both also lamented the perceived cultural shift in attitudes toward their profession, with the chief, specifically, pondering that he does not understand the "negativity." But they seem to know and provide possible reasons for that "negativity," even if they are unable to admit it to me or themselves.

The so-called drug war removed officers from the streets and put them into vehicles with radios, which alienated officers from the people and places they were allegedly tasked with policing. At the same time, conceal and carry laws across the country laxed, and the number of people carrying handguns on a daily basis increased.[3] The standards for acceptance into work as a police officer were lowered, and the rigor of basic training was reduced. This is not anecdotal. Even a pro-police organization like Police1 has been thoroughly critical of the lowered standards for becoming a police officer in the United States.[4] This is the context in which officers like the chief developed an obsession with the object of the local drug user/seller as enemy number one. It is not merely that officers "don't know the people they police," as Bigfoot interprets—it is that officers have learned to hate the people they police. Like Captain Ahab, they are filled with an obsessive desire to track and surveil, to capture, to lock up residents who are deemed enemies simply because of an alleged relationship to illicit substances. There is no evidence at the national scale that drug policing lowered sales or use or addictions. It is very likely the opposite. And at the local scale, both officers admit: "We're never gonna win that war." And yet the chief cannot "sit back and examine and say all these years it's done no good . . . I can't abandon the idea that it has helped." He has been dragged into the murky depths of unending combat by a rope connected to an alleged drug dealer. It is thus not surprising that he enthusiastically speaks of the next phase of policing as fighting so-called terrorism on the domestic frontier. Policing is not about protecting. It is about standing in between those who own much and those who own little and implementing the tactics of surveilling, targeting, and ultimately eliminating (be it through incarceration or death) in order to maintain the growing gulf between the owner class and everyone else. Order does not eliminate chaos. It channels it against people who are already targeted.

Despite the chief's alleged confusion over policing's "friction within the [black] community," then, it is not difficult to understand why even grandmothers must take up the task of helping to train the next generation on how to live in a region produced by confinement. The context that poor people and racialized minorities must navigate is one marked by police officers who find "joy" and "great pleasure" in surveilling neighborhoods, in kicking "down . . . door[s]" and "raid[ing] . . . houses," and by prosecutors who refuse to investigate or indict, and from an owner class that sits back and occasionally muses on all of it. Residents had better learn to run and hide and lie and rely on others and erect memorials and build safe spaces within the fissures of this order. Because something far worse than the drug war sits just past the horizon. And the chief seems to anticipate it.

CHAPTER FOUR

JON & THE GLITTERY CROW

A couple miles north of downtown is the Glittery Crow—a diner serving a standard range of Southern home-cooked-style meals. It was common to know people at other tables. I ate there so regularly that even the owner and host often greeted me by name.

"Hello, my friend. So good to see you," the owner greeted Jon. "And hello. Back for dinner, eh?" He turned to me. I laughed in slight embarrassment. I told you I ate here a lot. "Where would you all like to sit today?" We took a table by the window, passing Pastor Bert, who later surprised us by paying for our meals.

"So, what did you think about last night's [*Game of Thrones*] episode?" I began.

"Oh, it was great." Jon had read all the books but disagreed with his brother. "I still think it opens up a different perspective than Martin's novels." He prided himself on not being one of those "purists" who complains about the television writers getting it all wrong.

"I didn't care for it," I replied.

Jon grew up here and began working with the county's housing authority after graduating from college. The housing authority building is clean and flat gray. Employees generally greeted me with smiles, though the many people milling about outside, smoking and joking, usually stared at me in what seemed to be a mixture of amusement, bewilderment, and anxiety whenever I passed. The housing authority primarily serves people with financial needs and often serves people with physical and mental disabilities. Employees must be capable of working with residents whose alternative would likely be (or already has been) prison.[1] Employees often appeared overworked and stressed, despite their smiles, as they navigated the demands of their jobs and managed the material needs of others.

When Jon moved back after college, he got a downtown apartment near the housing offices, above what is now a nonprofit, because he had long wanted to live in the area. It was the late 1980s, and the entire region was undergoing a major reordering of the land (aligning with the shift in policing discussed by the chief and Bigfoot). Seabrook Farms had long since closed. Smith-Illinois glass, pronounced "Illi-Noise" by many locals, the area's second largest employer after World War II, had finally closed after a steady decade of layoffs. And all other factories had closed or severely cut their workforce. People from Mexico and Central American countries began moving in to work seasonal agricultural jobs.

"By the time I moved out of my apartment in 2009 [twenty years later], I was one of only two people still living downtown. Everyone else had moved out, and most of the businesses were closed," Jon said.

In the late 1990s, after the state and federal prisons opened, the board of chosen freeholders voted to rezone downtown buildings as exclusively commercial. The mid-nineteenth-century buildings with second- and third-floor apartment units could only be domiciles if the occupant owned the building. For decades and decades, businesses had supplemented their mortgages and business costs by renting the apartments, which meant the downtown was always full of people and full of stores. It also meant that finding an affordable apartment was easy (many could be rented for fifty to seventy-five dollars per week). Jon now spends his days trying to find adequate housing for people while dozens upon dozens upon dozens of apartment units sit empty all around him.

The downtown where the housing authority operates, for example, has only a few remodeled buildings—most businesses simply operate within the bones of the dilapidated storefronts that preceded them. For example, a check-cashing business used the old jewelry racks of the previous occupants to advertise paycheck advances and check-cashing options. Since Jon was grandfathered into his apartment lease, he was able to continue living and working downtown while he watched businesses and residents trickle away. As the factories on the outskirts of town and the small businesses in the downtown disowned their buildings and their land, government offices also shuttered, consolidated, and moved services elsewhere. This means, for one example, that residents without vehicles must travel by bus more than an hour (one way) if they need to access the offices of social services. And after the hour-long ride, passengers are dropped off on the side of a heavily trafficked state road where they must walk more than a half mile with no sidewalk to arrive at the social services offices. The day I took the trip, I walked with two women, Maria and Rose, who had to push strollers while also leading toddlers along the side of the highway without the advantage of a sidewalk. Both were making the arduous journey just so they could book appointments with a physician for their children because, at the time, the offices were refusing to take appointments by phone. Maria anticipated that by the time it was all said and done, they would each spend about six hours simply booking the visits with doctors and then another six hours the following week to take their children to the actual appointments.

"It's sad. As a kid, I remember walking downtown on Saturdays with my family. The downtown should be amenable to people supporting small, local businesses," Jon lamented, shaking his head and squirting more ketchup on his fried potatoes. "I walked and played around downtown all the time as a kid, but now I wouldn't walk around alone during the day *or* the night. People blame me if they or someone they know didn't get housing. The dip in work ethic around here may not be a direct result of the prisons," he pondered, "but when your environment is one of handouts, then kids learn to live that way."

"So, is anything new happening at work these days?" I asked, between bites of scrambled eggs and biscuits. "I was sitting outside the Spot last week with Shakes, and we watched a bunch of officers in SWAT gear raid the housing authority's apartment units. Any idea what happened?"

"No, I must have been away," he replied, gulping water.

"OK. Well, if you hear anything, let me know. A bunch of black cars pulled up to the tower and then officers in plain clothes and officers in SWAT gear entered the building, guns already drawn, with some positioning themselves around the back and side entrances and some charging through the front door," I relayed with dramatic pauses. He was unfazed.

"You know, when I first started working for housing, we had two officers that walked the beat, which included the housing tower, and they

4.1 Police officers who raided the Cumberland County housing authority. They are eating lunch in Chick-fil-A and still wearing bulletproof vests.

were so great. They knew peoples' names; they played with kids and talked to residents as if they were real people, as if they were neighbors who needed assistance. Now, police officers have no relationship with anyone. They talk to everyone as if they are enemies. They bust in and just make the situation worse."

This contradicts a point made many months earlier, during our first dinner together, when he said officers carried out their jobs mostly well given the "PC culture" they must navigate. Jon was a person inclined to give state-sanctioned authority figures like police officers the benefit of the doubt regarding their intentions and behavior. This is not surprising, since his work position is also made possible through the authority of a state-funded institution. But when he shared personal stories rooted in experiences and the events he had witnessed over his decades of work, he inadvertently critiqued policing as only capable of making situations worse. His reasons for why this might be the case—officers have no relationships with residents whom they view as enemies—align with the chief and Bigfoot.

"Do you want to grab a beer after this?" Jon asked.

He loved microbrews. Each time we met, he showed me an app that tracked his diverse microbrew consumption. He and three friends took pictures and uploaded each new microbrew onto the group message board, making the consumption of small-batch brews into a kind of treasure hunt. I still send him pictures sometimes if I drink a random local microbrew. He generally responds by telling me the name of the beer that I should have tried. We left the diner and drove to a sports bar twenty minutes away, because, he believes, "no bar is safe enough" to share a drink in this particular downtown after 6:00 p.m.

We arrived at a kind of local TGI Fridays, entering a dimmed room with a large wooden oval bar in the middle. We grabbed stools. Bright television screens littered the walls. Jon ordered two beers. He told me about living in his house alone, and it occurred to me how little I knew of his personal life. He is very private. Perhaps because he has spent so much time listening to other people's struggles and then figuring out creative ways to get them housing, he has developed skills for keeping his own personal life hidden. He is single, I know, and has never mentioned an ex-partner or children. But I do not pry my way into his (or anyone's) intimate life unless they insist, because I am not here to force confessions or read private journals. I am an anthropologist and not a therapist. So, our conversation jumps around as we kick back a few beers. He tells me about a trip he is taking in the summer with his microbrew-drinking buddies. And he continues to speak candidly about the region's struggles and ways to help bring about change.

"A few years back, I wanted to start a comic book festival in one of the downtowns." He leaned back and looked to the ceiling, sipping his beer. "Since there was a 1970s issue of the Batman comic that placed Gotham City smack dab in the middle of our county, I thought it would be a great way to rebrand our image and perhaps reorient our economy around something other than prisons.[2] It's like, the only ideas anyone ever has in this town are ideas about how to lock people up. I thought a comic book festival would get people traveling into town, staying overnight, and maybe create a little buzz. But nobody was interested. No one wants to think outside of the box. Now the local downtowns are nothing more than ghost towns."

"Why think outside the box? It's far more profitable to lock people into boxes," I replied, joining in his anger. "Hell, if the original settlers had known how profitable incarceration is, they probably would have skipped the genocide altogether and built prisons for Lenape people." The beer was loosening my tongue. "Do you still want to go with me to check out the hotel?"

"Yeah, let's go," he said, chuckling and slugging down his remaining beer.

We drove twenty minutes back—which means Jon would have to drive twenty minutes back to his home. The downtown hotel where I

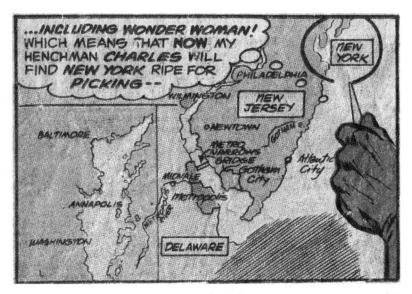

4.2 Image of a newspaper comic strip, *World's Greatest Heroes*, released in 1978, where Gotham City is located in Cumberland County. Image courtesy of "Gotham City Is Actually in South Jersey and This Map Proves It," from NJ.com, October 6, 2019.

was staying, four blocks up from the Spot, had red lights blinking ROOMS AVAILABLE next to a red and gold entryway. The front bell *ding-donged* as we walked in, and a man in his mid-fifties stepped out from a back room, peering at us from behind bulletproof glass. We looked an odd pair, judging by his sideways glances, and I believe it to be true. Jon is a large, middle-aged person who dresses like a computer programmer, and I am an undersized thirty-something person who, according to Shakes, dresses (and acts like) the nerdy guy from *Criminal Minds*.

"I'd like to rent a single room for the evening." I placed my mouth near the circular cluster of holes in the middle of the bulletproof glass.

"For just you and for the entire night?" he asked, tilting his body sideways and looking past me at Jon, who was smiling widely and squinting through glassy eyes.

"Yeah, just me." I turned and chuckled. We both had bellies full of beers. "This is my friend. He's only here to make sure I get settled in OK. He's not staying the night."

Jon continued smiling and half-waving at the man behind the bulletproof glass. "I'm just here for support," he added in hushed laughter.

The hotel owner gave a disinterested "hrmphh" and disappeared to retrieve a few papers for me to sign. He seemed skeptical of the story perhaps, but primarily disinterested, and I was too tired to give a damn about which it was—I had been working for almost fifteen straight hours. I signed the papers, took the key, and we headed upstairs, joking and jeering.

It felt like the hotel was decorated after the owners robbed a casino. But instead of taking money, they stole the carpet, the fake paintings, and the gold-plated everything. It smelled like ashtrays and disinfectants. I could hear sheets shifting across the hall. They probably were not staying long. We entered my room, and Jon raced to the mattress.

"Normally I wouldn't let a friend stay here, but since it's under new ownership, I wanted to see what it's like." He got down on one knee—if only the hotel clerk could see us now—and swished the orangey-yellowy comforter away from the corner, lifted the mattress high up into the air, and began examining, like an old jeweler seeking the diamond's imperfections beneath a bright light.

"Are you checking for semen?" I asked, laughing.

He dropped the mattress corner to belly laugh. "No, nooo. I'll leave the semen up to you. I'm just checking for bed bugs."

"Oh, shit. I'd prefer the semen. Do you see any?"

"No. Surprisingly, it passes the eye test. It looks clean."

Lifting, examining, and releasing the mattress corner again, he told me goodbye.

"Well, this place looks pretty clean, pretty safe. I wouldn't spend much time hanging around outside, but I think you're fine to stay here for a night. Just make sure you stay in your room until tomorrow morning."

Over the next six months, each of my friends would rebuke me in wide-eyed amazement when they found out I was spending evenings in this hotel. Drug raids, sex work raids, robbery hideout raids, gang hits, you name it—the hotel was a local landmark of activity. I put on sweatpants and snuck downstairs, into the back parking lot overlooking the slow-rolling river, and burned a skinny marijuana joint I had rolled at home. After settling back in my room, I clicked on a Cleveland Cavaliers game and lazily remembered the day as police sirens intensified and faded on the streets below.

Jon is a person whose job positions him between the brute force of police raids and the vulnerabilities of residents who have economic and social needs. He regularly works alongside officers since the residents he connects to public services often have legal entanglements. Like the chief and Bigfoot, he, too, articulates a deep sense of nostalgia for the old days of policing when, he recalls, officers knew residents by name and brought calm into tense situations. Some version of this memory of policing was a common refrain. Most residents were not interested in abolishing any of the police departments as I was, even though a great number of them told me they knew there were numerous corrupt officers. Instead, residents like Jon wanted police officers to serve the community and perform their jobs with integrity, as all other public service workers are expected to do. This kind of policing, from Jon's perspective, would not only change his job for the better but would dramatically impact daily life for folks who are already socially and economically vulnerable.

Jon also highlights changes to the downtown as significant. He lived through the final moments of vibrancy, and he recalls watching residents pack up and move elsewhere for the better part of a decade. It is similar to Old Man Tilley's memories as a child, when he watched confined Japanese Americans being herded into labor camps on Seabrook Farms. Both are lamenting the savage procession of empire-forced movement that chugged along beyond their control. But Jon pushes past Old Man Tilley's analysis by centering elected leadership as culpable. He had an idea to tap into an international community of Batman comic book fans who would be excited to visit the "original Gotham," but his visions were stifled by an elected leadership that has turned all the downtowns into "ghost towns" because they are only interested in "ideas about how to lock people up"—in more ways than one, perhaps.

I will explore the ghostly afterlives of one of the region's downtown areas in part 2. But Jon's primary point is worth pondering a bit longer. Elected leadership seems incapable of thinking outside the box of racialized confinement. When they imagine how to strengthen the local economy, they are only able to reproduce the imaginations of their inheritance: criminalizing nonwhite people for confined labor. And in one form of confinement or another, it has always managed to maintain a certain kind of segregated order that provides the local economy with a particularly vulnerable labor force that is easily contained and exploited. Jon attempted to inspire another kind of vision for how the downtown might take shape—a vision that conjured his childhood, where kids and parents alike filled the space with excitement and wonder. His ideas are straightforward and revolve around a simple belief: a dynamic community is capable of healing the fractured and evacuated downtown.[3] And I experienced his vision of a downtown marked by care and joy, when he drove forty extra miles (round trip) just to inspect a hotel mattress before I slept there alone. He did not want me to experience the isolation and potential dangers of the downtown hotel at night. In this act of care we see that order can change, and it can be experienced differently—yes, by an owner class with profit-driven aims but also by residents who are willing to extend themselves, to prioritize their relationships, to create moments of care and support for others in time and place.

CHAPTER FIVE

CARL & WAKING BAKERY

I gazed at glazed donuts with drippy sides, next to double stacks of twist buns, next to triple stacks of crème-filled submarines, next to piles of poked-out donut holes, next to rows of cookies, next to triangle-shaped strudels oozing gooey jellies, resting in a glass display case as old as World War II at least, with a cash register that *dings* and *clings* and *rings* as it did, no doubt, when Carl's dad dressed the cakes forty years prior. Waking Bakery, located in the county, is *the* stop for baked goods in South Jersey.

"What can I get for you today?" a high school–aged person behind the counter asked.

"Hmm, well—" I leaned over the case with dreams of smashing a glazed donut. "For now, I think I'll hold off, since I'm here to interview Carl. Is he around?"

"Ohhhhkay." The register worker hesitated. "And what is your name?"

"My name is Heath . . . uh . . ."

"OK, Keith, let me—"

"H-Heath. With an *H*. Like the candy bar . . . or the dead actor," I chuckled.

"Ohhkay?" the worker responded in confusion.

"Hi, Heath." Carl, the owner of Waking Bakery, suddenly stood large behind the person behind the register. "I see you've already been introduced to our twist buns," he chuckled. "Do you want to come back here so we can talk? I need to ice this cake first, and then I will show you around the kitchen."

"Sounds good." I followed. "Do you mind if I record this on my phone? I won't—"

"Umm, sure, but I don't really understand why you want to talk with me . . ." Carl replied while laying out meticulously, as one imagines a brain surgeon might do, onto the gleaming stainless-steel workstation, one at a time, three squeeze tubes for icing, a small spatula-like tool, another shiny stainless-steel doohickey, and, of course, the anniversary cake with gleaming white frosting over three stories of white, circular cakes. "I don't know much about the prisons. So, is there a specific reason you are coming here to talk to me? Did somebody suggest it to you or was it your idea?"

"That's OK." I fiddled with the phone. "It was my idea. I really want to talk to everyone here. Long-term business owners have an especially unique experience and perspective, since I am interested in how the prisons have shaped the economy and in how businesses that have survived the shift have changed their approach, et cetera, things like that . . ."

"Well, so, how does this fit in with Elizabeth [a nonprofit director and CEO who introduced us]?" he asked.

"Actually, I met Elizabeth last week, just a few days before I met you, when I was attending a meeting of pastors [including Pastor Bert] and nonprofit workers who are trying to build actionable plans for fighting homelessness and reducing recidivism," I replied.

"OK, well, what we do is we help a number of people become employees and not end up in prison," he laughed. "If they have a useful life and support themselves and do it in such a way as to not be a negative influence. People who are not responsible people are not going to be able to hang around because we try to give them responsibility on the job. When they used to have the glass house, and people were going to work to pick up bottles, stuff like that, working the line. As long as you showed up and didn't drop the bottles on the floor, there was not a whole lot involved—not a whole lot of self-management. But here, people have to manage themselves quite a lot." Carl leaned forward, squeezing a thin green border line along the top of the cake.

"Right." I pushed the phone closer to Carl's downward-focused face; the hum of the kitchen was as loud as a highway. "So, compared to working at the glass factory—"

"And people who can't self-manage or deal with the consequences are the types of people who, of course, end up in the prison system. They don't think of the consequences when they are bashing somebody's face in or knocking over stores. So, that might seem like an awful lot of pontificating, but it's the answer to your question. As a person who is a Christian, I think people were designed to have a sense of self-satisfaction and accomplishment in work."

"Hi, umm, sorry to interrupt, but did you get the change?" a college-aged person asked Carl.

"Yes, I did. I dropped it off myself this afternoon," he replied, still squeezing green frosting. "I think that's part of what it means to be human." Carl set down the green and picked up the yellow. "I think if people don't have a sense of satisfaction, they're going to find it wherever they can get it, whether it's legally or illicitly."

"So, how did you come to own a bakery here?"

"Well, my dad had the bakery for twenty years. My parents were divorced when I was ten and he, at the time, ran a bakery in Philadelphia that belonged to my grandparents. The business went under, his marriage was broken up, and he basically had nothing. He moved down here because a bakery came up for sale, and the owner just held the building mortgage and allowed him to make monthly payments over time to purchase the business. That was in 1961. So, I worked in the summers and weekends with my dad because I still lived in Philly with my mom, and, eventually, me and Ethel moved down here. At the time, this was an interesting area with a tremendous amount of business. More small-town America. Now it's a hollowed-out downtown. Ethel's degree is in education, certified K through 8, and my degree is in photography. Obviously," he laughed, "we are not doing precisely what we went to college for."

"So, you purchased the business from your father in 1981? I seem to remember you telling Elizabeth that the other day."

"No. My dad had a heart attack and we moved down here in 1981. We planned to help him through the recovery and then move back to Philadelphia, but he did not recover. We were already familiar with the day-to-day operations, and we already had a staff and a large following in this region, so I decided it would be ridiculous to walk away from that, when I was an entrepreneurial person anyway. So, we've been here ever since, and it's worked out for us." Carl again picked up the green frosting to write letters in cursive.

"Would you like me to clean the large oven?" another teen-aged employee asked.

"Yes," Carl replied. "We did not know the business-management end when we took over, so we had to learn that part."

"So, you learned how to bake because you were around it as a kid?"

"I had the familiarity, yes, and then as I got older, my dad taught me how to bake cakes, which was handy, because, eventually, by the time I got into my high school years, I would come down here every weekend and all summer, so he didn't have to decorate cakes."

"You learned how to bake the rest of the items, then, from your dad's recipes? Or—?"

"My dad had his recipes the way all bakers used to keep their recipes: if you looked at them, you couldn't make any sense out of them. They were deliberately written that way so somebody couldn't look over your shoulder to steal recipes. When my grandfather died, no one else had the recipes and everyone had to learn new recipes from scratch while trying to keep the bakery going. Fortunately, we didn't have to do that, because a year after he dictated the recipes to us, he was in a coma, never to recover."

"By 1981, then, you and Ethel have a pretty good handle of how to make the baked goods but not how to run the business?" I asked. "So, what was your experience at that point, when you were trying to learn how to run a small business in a small town?"

Carl set down all the frosting tools, the scrawling tools, the brightly colored icing tubes, and finagled the cake into a large refrigerator.

"At that time, the big glass house had started to phase down. At its height, there were, like, seven furnaces. It was, like, the biggest glass factory in the world." Carl stopped. "OK, why don't I take you around the back here so you can see how everything is made? There was a lot of opportunities for people who didn't have a college degree, didn't have a lot of education, so they could support their family and help their kids go to college someday. Now, what has taken up the slack? The prison system. Now, you can't be an uneducated person working in the prison system. So, you know the bar has been raised. Where, as long as you could read and write and show up at the right time, you could get a job at the glass house . . . I suppose. But the up-and-coming occupation became corrections, because there is a federal prison about fifteen minutes from here; there's the county courthouse, which has the county jail; there's Bayview on the other side of town, that's a state prison; and there's, I think, two others around here. So, there is a lot of corrections going on. The thing is, you don't have to be local to do that, whereas the glass house tends to be local people because not a lot of people drove in to work at the glass house. But people will drive from a distance to work at a prison."

Carl effortlessly weaves his large frame through freakishly oversized mixers, straightening large baking sheets in tall stacks, pointing to large ovens that bake cakes, medium-sized ovens that bake this, smaller ovens that bake that, squeezing through passageways formed by the leftover spaces between all these ovens and racks and mixers, grabbed a few screwdrivers and set into working on fixing the hinges and deadbolt on the bakery's back door.

"Right. And the pay is very good for being a corrections officer," I added.

"Everybody's got a car now, and it makes it worth it to put the gas in the car."

"What was your staff like in 1981?" I asked.

"In '81, we had a professional full-time baker. We had Bob the production manager, who was also the store manager, and he had been doing that since he was a teenager. So, again, he was a lifetime career person. And we had George, who was an older guy who had been a baker his whole life. He was probably about eighty years old. Then we had an older lady who was working for my dad in the store. She wasn't the store manager, but she was the other full-time store person. And we would have one or two other girls that worked in the store in the afternoon, and one guy in the back who cleaned up. And then the baker had an assistant baker. Basically, all adult people who are doing this as a career for their life. You didn't have college students and high school students rolling in and out the door. So, one change has been that we are geared more toward a model like a restaurant, because a restaurant doesn't have one chef who's been there for forty years. You got a lot of younger people who have not been trained in food service; they're just waitering on the side. You can't just pull bakers out of a hat—especially around here. And another change is that we would just go downtown and get supplies and stuff, but there's not a lot of downtown stores anymore."

Carl fixed the door hinges and then ushered me to the front.

"Please grab a few complimentary pastries before you go."

"Oh, thank you so much!" I said.

And Carl was gone. I squatted down and scanned the pastries once again.

"I'm gonna need one of those twist buns, please. And a glazed donut . . ." I wondered: How many free pastries can I get away with?

Carl articulates a belief that people in prison are people who avoided working so-called formal or licit jobs because they did not understand that there would be consequences to their actions. As a Christian, he believes people were intentionally designed to find satisfaction in working hourly wage jobs. For Carl, being a hard and responsible worker is the essence of being a good human. This is similar to the typology articulated by the chief and Bigfoot: normal people (who are workers), police officers, and criminals. For Carl, Waking Bakery helps to develop people into responsible workers, which means, simultaneously, that it keeps people from spending life in prison. The suggestion here might be that Carl holds an oppositional view between people who work and people who are incarcerated.

Within this oppositional vision of worker versus convicted criminal, if the economy is to continue humming, workers must be responsible and forward-thinking while criminals must be isolated and removed. Carl's understanding, however, relies on the mistaken idea that the region's so-called formal economy is sustained by its so-called normal workers. And it is not. Like the line between workers and criminals, he also draws what he believes to be an obvious line between the formal and informal economies. But with five correctional facilities, numerous police and sheriff departments, and 6,400 people confined behind bars on any given day, that alleged line is more akin to a perforated edge. The so-called formal economy relies almost entirely on the so-called informal economy. But even better, one might stop thinking of the local economy as broken into two distinct units and instead recognize a kind of singularity—a complex in/formal economy that stretches up, down, and across the region. Even though Carl believes that being an "entrepreneurial person," like himself, is in opposition to being a criminal person who is incarcerated, it has long been the case that the "normal" person and the criminalized person are *both* workers within a unified labor structure.

When a person is criminalized, a multifaceted response of corporate and government agencies, institutions, and professions kick into gear (all of which rely on dealing with so-called criminality for their existence). Carl believes that an incarcerated person is a burden on the local economic and political system. But what if he recognized the ways that workers and so-called criminals belong to the same economic and political system? He might first acknowledge, for example, that the collective incarceration of 6,400 people annually draws about 500 million state and federal dollars to the region.[1] Like the government contracts during World War II that were fulfilled through confined Japanese American labor, incarcerated people today are responsible for generating nearly half a billion dollars of state and federal money streams into an otherwise economically defunct region. Carl might then consider how many professional jobs in the region are produced by and dependent on this system of confinement (to list only a few: oversized state and county police departments; private attorneys, public defenders, and county prosecutors; administrative officials and corrections officers within the prison facilities; a range of jobs in the court system; a range of jobs in the division of probation and parole). Or he might simply take the time to speak with and learn from any one of the thousands and thousands of his neighbors who have been confined in the prisons. But the system of confinement is highly effective at keeping people separated, at breaking the possibility of meaningful relationships. Perhaps this would keep him from "an awful lot of pontificating" about people and situations he seems to know very little about. Around here, workers and criminals have never been opposite one another. They have always been located at different degrees on a single labor continuum. Order does not mean removing criminals from workers. Order means criminalizing and confining some workers in order to change their status for greater control and exploitation.

CHAPTER SIX

THE SHEEPDOG WHO CRIED WOLF

I parked in the lot behind the community college auditorium. Police vehicles and other cars were parked any which way but within the yellow lines. It was chilly and dark. I was paranoid as hell. Inside the atrium, a ticket taker at a folding table signed people into the event—"Awakening the Sheep"—as they flashed their hard-to-come-by tickets. Hundreds of middle-aged white men waited outside the auditorium's many double doors. The high ceilings did not keep the room from becoming loud and stuffy. The ticket taker glared suspiciously before requesting my license. Curious, since she did not make this request to the people in line ahead of me. She then nodded and pointed and greeted the person after me with enthusiasm. The doors flung open and the men squeezed through and then expanded into the auditorium. Police officers stood in a choppy blue line at the back, opposite the stage, chattering and guffawing. I took a seat near the last row, pulled my ball cap down low, and turned on my phone recorder. One of the police officers who questioned me in that windowless room tapped me on the shoulder to say hello before taking a seat only four rows ahead.

Sheepdog Seminars is a Christian organization based in Hurst, Texas, that, according to its "About Us" page, has sent retired police officers to thousands of church congregations across the United States in order to "awaken the protective instincts that reside in the hearts of all men (and many women). It is our firm conviction that violence will have its way unless certain people (we call them 'Sheepdogs') intervene . . .

[because] they are driven by the most powerful force in the [*sic*] all of the universe: LOVE." And the home page for Sheepdog Seminars contains this message: "EVERY AMERICAN IS ENTITLED TO PROTECTION FROM VIOLENCE. NOT JUST POLITICIANS, CELEBRITIES, AND THE WEALTHY. However, the average American does not have access to the necessary funds for such elite service. Thus, our motto: *I am my family's secret service*." Sheepdog Seminars was founded by Jimmy Meeks, a white man who is a retired police officer and ordained Christian minister. Jimmy is tonight's keynote speaker. He was introduced by a county prosecutor and Steve Brown, a white man who was his former partner, now serving as his on-stage hype man.

The prosecutor tap-tap-tapped the microphone: "Welcome to everyone here this evening. Good to see so many people in the audience. We had about two hundred people register for this event and we set up 244 seats." She scanned the audience and pointed to the many clusters of men seated on the floor. "Which means we have a packed crowd!"

Everyone clapped.

"I'd like to thank our police chiefs," she continued. "I'd like to acknowledge the chaplains in the audience—please stand to be recognized." The crowd clapped again. "At most events I go to, our county is at the top of all the wrong lists, and we're working on that daily. But we are at the top of the right lists with our chaplain program. This is a program that's homegrown, and I can tell you that it's grown from the county to spread throughout our state and really spreading throughout the nation. I got a call from Chaplain Smith asking me about the 'right to carry' laws and how that interacted with churches in the community. As prosecutors, we are not allowed to give legal advice. But after that, I reached out to some people about what we could do. Some of you may know, if you read the paper, that we've had some disturbing incidents that we need to guard ourselves from. We have to be mindful of the realities that there are people in the community that for whatever reason—it might be mental illness, it might be a domestic disturbance, it could be *ter-ror-ism*—that are out to harm our congregations, and we just want to make sure that you're armed with the tools to address that and that's what this program is about tonight."

Applause intensified throughout the auditorium.

The prosecutor identified New Jersey's strict no-carry gun laws as a shared problem for church communities, prosecutors, and police officers alike. Then the prosecutor relayed to the crowd that their office is not allowed to give out legal advice. In response to this constraint, the county prosecutor's offices organized a public forum to give out legal advice. The prosecutor then creates a common enemy, criminalizing mental illness and equating it with "domestic violence" and "terrorism," stoking fear in the audience that the county is widely under attack. Finally, the prosecutor claims the event is designed to "arm [them] . . . with the tools" to pastor a church in a no-carry state like New Jersey, which sounded like a dog whistle for *get guns in your hands.*

"Now, let me introduce you to Lieutenant Steve Brown!"

The prosecutor full-body-hugged him and exited the stage.

"Hello. I have to tell you, I'm very, very nervous." Steve adjusted his shirt collar. "I retired from the New Jersey State Police last August, and I travel all over the country giving seminars in hostage negotiation. I was just in Baltimore, spoke for six hundred cops, and I was not even a little bit nervous."

Steve opened by humble-bragging about his itinerant speaking events. In a room full of pastors, boasting about delivering a lecture to six hundred Baltimore cops increases his credibility as a skilled orator who can also handle his own in front of tough men.

"Can I ask a favor of you guys? Can you give me a little leeway? I have a cop's sense of humor. I am introducing this guy, Jimmy Meeks, and at one point he tased me when we were going through training, and I was on the ground screaming like a little girl," he laughed, as did the crowd. "And Jimmy was sitting there laughing at me. So, if you get the chance, ask me about that!" The crowd laughed loudly. "I don't know if anybody's curious about why we call this seminar 'Waking the Sheep'?" Steve turned the moment of laughter into a serious question. "Lieutenant Grossman has a philosophy, and I think it's believed by *most* people in law enforcement, firemen, and clergy alike: There are three types of people." He scanned the crowd and paused to build anticipation. "The majority of people are—what do you guys think?"

"SHEEP!" the crowd shouted in unison.

"Yes! And then, there's a small portion of people that are what?" he asked.

"WOLVES!" The crowd was nearly bursting.

"Correct! But there's an even smaller group of people who are what?" Steve hushed the crowd's roar.

"SHEEP . . . DOGS!" they screamed.

"Yes! You guys are the leaders! Police, military, firemen, clergy, chaplains, and the like are the leaders. Most people want to be led. Most people want to be told what to think, how to drink, and what to drink. So, we have a responsibility to your flock, to your sheep, to protect them. You don't go to church thinking you could be a victim of a violent attack, but it happens more often than you think. Jimmy Meeks, Sheepdog Seminars' founder, is a police officer *and* an ordained minister who travels the country showing churches how to keep their congregations safe. Please, join me—" Everyone was already clapping. "—in welcoming Jimmy!!"

For the first time, the crowd stood, shouting and clapping.

The prosecutor opened the event by merging the interests of police and pastors within a context that is under attack ("We have to be mindful . . . that people are out to harm our congregations"). Steve built on that construction by offering a typology of humanity that "most people" believe: Sheep, Wolves, and Sheepdogs. What made my skin crawl in this moment was not the typology itself, which is rather common in white supremacist visions, but in how the crowd was able to shout the typology in accord before Steve said it, thus strengthening his claim about its universality. It is a flash of the same typology articulated by the chief and Bigfoot and even Carl: good Christian people at home (Sheep), minding their business, while evil/criminal people surround them (Wolves), with heroic white men maintaining the divide between the two (Sheepdogs). Finally, the interests of pastors, prosecutors, and police officers unify on stage in one person: retired police officer and ordained minister, Jimmy Meeks.

"It's an honor to be here, sir, thank you." Jimmy shook hands with Steve and turned to the crowd. "Now *you say* there are three kinds of people in the world: Sheep, Wolves, and Sheepdogs. The Sheep is the Sheep, you know; they just love peace and that's fine. They just want things nice and quiet. We all do! But, unfortunately, there is a Wolf that will attack the Sheep, but even more fortunately, there is a Sheepdog that will defend the Sheep and take on the Wolf. We need to have Sheepdogs *every*where. We know that *no place is safe* anymore, but we certainly need them in church and there are reasons for that."

Jimmy tossed the typology of humanity back to the crowd, giving them credit for it: "Now *you say* there are three kinds of people." This inception-like rhetorical move further naturalized the idea that the typology is a universal truth, and it built on the ongoing emphasis that Christian churches in Cumberland County are under threat. Jimmy then expanded the problem of safety from Christian churches into the wider community: *"No place is safe!"*

"Why is that?" Steve teed him up.

"The statistics are staggering." Jimmy took a swing. "Most people don't know, but we're up to at least 473 confirmed violent deaths on church and faith-based properties since 1999. Already this year we've had ministers beaten to death, we've had people shot coming out of church, four kids were shot at a church playground in North Carolina a few weeks ago. There's a lot of violence going on, on church and faith-based properties, and that doesn't even take into account the fact that we have somewhere between fifty and one hundred reports a week of sex crimes that are occurring on church and faith-based property."

The crowd shushed.

The phrase *violent deaths* is used without any context. The total number of deaths cannot be verified, but in the figure he cites, at least 166 of these 473 deaths, scattered across 348,000 US churches, have been determined by police investigators to be suicide.[1] Removing the category of suicide drops the number of "violent deaths" allegedly perpetrated by Wolves on church properties to 307. To put that number into perspective, police officers on average have killed almost three people a day for (at least) the last ten years.[2] Extrapolating this rate across the same stretch of time (1999–2016) provides us with a helpful comparison: since 1999, Wolves have allegedly killed 307 people on church and faith-based properties, and police officers have killed 18,768 people everywhere else.

"Listen—" Jimmy held his right hand up, as if testifying under oath. "We don't want to assemble an army; that's not what we're trying to do. We are trying to keep the people of our congregations as safe as possible without letting someone take advantage of our softness. And we are soft, and we often have a mindset that, you know, we're God's people and God will protect us, and he will, and he does . . . he does in a lot of ways. But you know, I don't know if you know, but we're in a very *different kind of a world* right now, very different. Those of us who were around during the sixties, it might have some similarities with one glaring difference: in the sixties they respected God, or at least many did, and houses of worship. Those things don't exist as much today. It's very different."

Every person in the auditorium stood to their feet, clapping and yelling.

Jimmy referred to the 1960s as the era when people "respected God." He did not reference any of the shootings or bombings perpetrated by white supremacists against black churches between the 1950s and 1970s. And he blatantly omitted Dylann Roof's shooting spree, the deadliest church attack in US history, which happened only seven months prior to this event. More generally, according to the Center for Strategic and International Studies, a Cold War–era think tank, right-wing attacks have accounted for the majority (58 percent) of all terrorist attacks in the United States since 1994, and that number jumps to almost 70 percent of all attacks since 2019.[3] Jimmy's elisions and misrepresentations are not accidental. Stating that white men are the primary perpetrators of terrorist violence in the United States would disrupt the ideological conceits that Christian white men are under attack. And it would erode their capacity to be awakened as Sheepdogs.

"You need to promote observation within the church. Everybody just walks through kind of like this." Jimmy looked to the ground and walked in circles. "And they don't look at other people. You need to look. If someone looks or behaves suspiciously, report it. If it looks like a duck and it sounds like a duck and it acts like a duck, it's a what?"

"A DUCK!" the crowd screamed.

"So," Jimmy continued, gaining momentum, ratcheting up the intensity, "if someone comes in with an overcoat and they're walking like this, and they have a limp—" He looked around like a guilty person and walked with an overacted limp. "They may have a weapon on them. You know, they might not. But, you know, you have to keep an eye. You should promote, you should try to get the father—nothing against the women—but try to get the husbands and the fathers to sit on the outside of the pews. Why? Because if something happens, you want the scariest, hairiest guys going to the scene, OK?" The crowd laughed. "Fathers and husbands should be prepared to fight. There are plenty of potential weapons in the church. I don't want to offend people, but can you think of any weapons that are in the church?" he asked, working the crowd.

Jimmy added people with physical disabilities to the growing list of Wolves potentially lurking about church properties. He also denigrated women, which was the easiest way to provoke laughter from the crowd. Jimmy then essentialized "the scariest, hairiest" white men and their inherent Sheepdog capacities, arguing that using violence to protect women and churches are the "things a man just has to do."

"Chairs!" someone yelled.

"Chairs." Jimmy pointed. "Your Bible, your keys. If someone's in your church and they're shooting, if you get close, stab them in the face with a pen. Worry about the legal ramifications later. There is an active terrorism investigation going on in every single state in this country, no doubt,

100 percent. Steve and I arrested a guy a couple years ago who beheaded two people, cut their hands off, and he was a terrorist."

Jimmy emphasized that Sheepdogs should not consider legality when acting. This claim is made with legal authority, since he is a retired police officer and the prosecutors who planned the event are seated behind him, smiling. He then moved from his pleas to ignore the law to a story about arresting a "terrorist" on the side of the highway. There was no explicit correlation with Wolves killing people on church- or faith-based properties, but his mention of terrorism tapped into a familiar storyline for Christian white men by evoking the shadowy world of the US military's "by any means necessary" torture and interventionist tactics that marked the so-called war on terror. The story also continued to pull the original thread that enemy Wolves are encroaching, driving down their highways, lurking around any and every corner, seeking out Christians to behead or behand.

"It is important to practice lockdown scenarios in your church," Jimmy continued. "Evacuation scenarios. Learn what's going on in other people's churches. All scenarios should be as realistic as possible without harming someone. Contrary to belief, you will not rise to the occasion. You need equipment—ballistic armor if you can afford it. Talk to your police departments, because a lot of times they'll get rid of their old armor. It says it's expired, but I know, Steve and I did some testing with them, old armor will stop a round. It'll stop a rifle round. It'll stop a shotgun, a pistol. Radios and earpieces. They look cool! And they're very practical. Restraints. Surveillance cameras. We don't expect you to go out tomorrow and come back with a big duffel bag full of handcuffs and battering rams and all that stuff . . . but if you did, it would be cool!"

The crowd stood again, cheering and yelling with intensified clapping.

Here we witness a moment where the motivations behind the seminar manifest. All men (and a few women) already have the Sheepdog within themselves: "Protective instincts that reside in . . . hearts." But an "awakened" person's instincts are not enough ("You will not rise to the occasion")—even the best Sheepdogs must be trained and disciplined by police officers and tactical experts. But again, training and discipline are not sufficient. Sheepdogs also need duffel bags full of retired military gear and weapons. This is because, first, Sheepdogs must be recognizable in clothing and weapons amid their forays into vigilante violence. And second, they must have access to guns and other weapons of death, which is more difficult in a no-carry state like New Jersey. This is where the 1033 program for surplus military gear becomes essential. Since 1996, when Congress remade Section 1208 into the 1033 program, 70,000 firearms, more than 5,000 military vehicles (including tanks), and 358 aircraft have made their way to urban and rural police departments, with a total value north of $1.7 billion.[4] But police departments, like the military, do not have unlimited space to stockpile the weapons and wares of war. Christian church congregations controlled by Sheepdogs are the ideal sites to be converted to military weapons storage facilities, which have the added bonus of little to no government oversight.

Jimmy settled the crowd back down.

"It's not the function of anybody on the safety team to minister to someone, but if you come into the church and you're creating a disturbance, my job is to get you out of the sanctuary and make sure everybody is safe. There should be a zero-tolerance policy for drug or alcohol intoxication. If they're drunk, like I said, they're not hearing anything anyway."

The crowd erupted in laughter. Jimmy added people who have consumed drugs or alcohol to the list of potential Wolf characters. He then broke apart what the event previously merged: pastors and police. Though we all have the same mission, *we* are the Sheepdogs and *you all* are the Shepherds. The implication of this break is that Sheepdogs (police and police-trained church security) can reach their full potential only through training and discipline. Being a white Christian man, even a pastor, does not make one a fully realized Sheepdog.

"The Shepherd must tend to his flock," he slowed. "You guys and gals are the Shepherds and I'll fight off the Wolves. The Wolves are there and they're multiplying! And they're going to be here! They may not be in the county yet, but they're coming."

Repeating the event's opening message: no place is safe anymore!

"Now, I know this sounds unlikely—" Jimmy doubled down. "Hard to believe, but I'm going to show you a video of some stories you may not have heard about, stories of violence happening on church properties."

Jimmy turned to a large screen on the wall as the lights dimmed. A soundless montage of grainy surveillance footage played, primarily featuring elderly white people getting purses snatched in church entryways. The most aggressive act was by a nonwhite person: hoodie up, grabbing a tithe plate, shoving an elderly lady to the ground, and taking her purse before running out the doors.

The crowd was hear-a-pin-drop silent as the lights snapped back on.

"Now—" Jimmy broke the silence. "Let's have a show of hands: How many of you pastors have personally dealt with a church attack in your church ... ?"

For the first time this evening, well over an hour into the event, the crowd sat in extended, chair-shifting silence. Many people stole glances over their shoulders, scanning the auditorium for a single raised hand. Any hand. Jimmy flashed a look to Steve. In this muted moment, a raw laugh slipped out, which I swallowed almost immediately. Everyone in my vicinity turned to glare.

After what seemed an eternity, an older white man near the front row, on the other side of the room, raised his hand, took the microphone from the person roaming the aisles, and asked: "If someone shows up and threatens my congregation ... and I pull a gun, which, let's say I keep in my pulpit," he snickered while looking around the crowd, "and I fire at him, will I go to prison for—for protecting my flock?"

The crowd erupted in cheers and clapping.

The silence generated by the collective recognition that nobody in attendance, including Steve and Jimmy, had experienced an attack on church property was overcome when the pastor tapped back into the familiar narrative that Christians must protect themselves because they are under attack. He even managed to suture the role of Shepherds back to Sheepdogs. It is unclear if his story was an admission to concealing guns in his pulpit or if it was simply a juicy fantasy playing into the wider affective landscape. Either way, the crowd received it enthusiastically. I personally imagine that the pastor imagined himself re-hiding the gun in the pulpit, straightening his tie, and finishing the sermon.

"I will let the prosecutors answer that later on in the seminar." Jimmy looked back to the prosecutors' table and nodded. "But make no mistake, terrorists are coming, gun violence is coming, the threat of Wolves is serious, and we need to be prepared!"

The crowd stood in thunderous applause, cheering with all their voices.

Jimmy used the pastor's fantasy, similar to giving them credit for the Sheepdog typology when he began, to reaffirm that church communities are in danger. And by tapping back into the narrative, the collective lack of experiences with anything remotely resembling violent attacks on church properties was fully resolved, and the prosecutor's opening claim thus still rang true: enemy Wolves are surrounding us!

Jimmy then began screaming: "I am a Sheepdog under the authority of God!" His face flushed a deep purple-red, and his neck veins bulged. "A child of the one true God! I am endowed by my creator with unalienable rights, empowered by my Constitution to bear arms, inspired by my forefathers to fight for this land I love." He was screaming at the top of his lungs: "I AM A SHEEPDOG UNDER THE AUTHORITY OF THE GREAT SHEPHERD, AND THIS IS AS FAR AS THE MINIONS OF HELL ARE GOING!"

The crowd remained standing, roaring in applause, clapping, cheering, yelling.

"Now, let's turn it over to our prosecutors to answer your questions." He quietly exited the stage.

The Sheepdog Seminar demands a different kind of interpretive reading than the ethnographic moments that precede and follow this section. Since Jimmy and Steve travel the country giving the same written speech and using the same canned video footage, I intend to challenge their arguments, ideas, and visions with a suspicious reading. That is to say, unlike the interpersonal conversations that make up the bulk of this book, where I explicitly work to understand a person within their own context and on their own terms, I will not take the performance or the message in good faith. Instead, I highlight the event's own incongruences and inconsistencies, and I critically analyze the messages to make a claim about Sheepdog Seminars' underlying motivations.

First and foremost, Sheepdog Seminars is committed to expanding the daily exercise of the right to kill beyond police officers and other domestic soldiers. This stands in direct opposition to the views articulated by the chief and Bigfoot, who lamented the perpetual lowering of standards for police training. Sheepdog Seminars instead encourages weekend training sessions with tactical experts, and they offer coupon codes on their website for organizations that conduct these events. They are working to construct the conditions for a kind of patchwork militia of white Christian men that can access countless local church buildings across the country as home bases stockpiled with military gear.[5]

This patchwork militia is outfitted through an extension of the distribution line of retired military gear that has filled local police departments over the last century, since about the time that C. F. Seabrook was employing off-duty officers to brutalize labor organizers. By creating a path for off-loading retired gear, state and local police departments were stockpiled as domestic military forts, and police officers were outfitted as domestic soldiers, which enabled them to carry out a domestic war against black, brown, and poor people beneath the facade of a war against drugs.[6] But police departments also need to keep the weapons moving, since they, too, have limited space to accumulate. Christian church buildings provide numerous unregulated, fort-like safehouses where military gear can amass.

In a strict no-carry state like New Jersey, however, expert training and stockpiled military gear are not enough, since the penalties for carrying guns are severe, with mandatory minimum sentencing guidelines. There is thus also a second point of emphasis: the need for ideological discipline. The event tackles this in two primary ways. First, the county prosecutor claims that "disturbing incidents" are on the rise in the area. And Steve and Jimmy reemphasize this point—"No place is safe!"— throughout the almost two-hour presentation. It did not seem like the men in attendance needed much to convince them that this claim was true, even as everyone shared the same moment when more than three hundred police officers and pastors were unable to recall a single time they had experienced an act of violence on a church property.

So, how might an organization encourage hundreds of men—who both live in a strict no-carry state and also have no experience with violence—to unleash their weapons against potential Wolves? Teach them what to do with their fears. Jimmy stresses that in these situations, people are likely to become gripped with fear and thus "will not rise to the occasion" when they are surrounded by Wolves. This means they need disciplined training to harness their fears. On the other hand, if a Sheepdog does happen to kill a Wolf during an alleged church attack, they will need to know what to do with their fear if they are charged by their county prosecutor. In Cumberland County, prosecutors had a crisp track record of refusing to indict police-officer Sheepdogs for killing unarmed (black) people, and their presence at this event sent strong assurances that they would not be pursuing charges against other Sheepdogs who shot and killed unarmed people. But, in the event that a Sheepdog is charged, they must understand the legal and political benefits of articulating their feelings of fear as a defense for their actions. It has become a widely used trope for police officers to provide testimony that they acted from a position of fear.[7] And this fear trope has been picked up and put to use by non–police officer white men as well, like Kyle Rittenhouse, whose tear-stained testimony convinced the courts that carrying an assault rifle across state lines in order to shoot three unarmed people who were participating in street protests proved nothing more than self-protection amid his feelings of fear. This position of fear is a near-guaranteed tactic for avoiding indictment or conviction. This is one reason the event does not lower fear through education and training but ratchets up feelings of fear everywhere the Sheepdog might find himself (especially at church), assuring him that his fear is justification for the right to shoot and kill.

This brings us to the third point of emphasis. There is an attempt to minimize political significance and the use-of-force authority at the national-federal-state realm in order to expand it across the local landscape and, in fact, to situate that authority within the Sheepdog himself. Sheepdog Seminars play on the widespread feelings of fear around national politics and a "very different world" that is being overrun with Wolves to build adaptable power structures through much smaller units of authority. Since the prosecutor vocalizes support of the event's message, the evening becomes a kind of green light for getting Sheepdogs excited to (illegally) shoot guns and kill Wolves. In short, Sheepdog Seminars is working to raise an unlicensed domestic militia, with access to stockpiles of retired military gear, who are accountable to no one but themselves.

Now, how does all of this relate to the rest of part 1? Jimmy expresses a vision of a world that is entirely consumed by hatred for an enemy object. If the chief and Bigfoot represented a moment where there was a general shift in an officer's perspective of criminal/ity, as one aspect of the so-called drug war, then Jimmy stands in for a policing that has not only embraced that shift but is actively working to intensify and expand it. Criminality is no longer relegated to the downtown alleys "with all the bullshit" or among people who are allegedly connected to so-called drug economies. Criminality is everywhere! "No place is safe!" This is the foundation of Jimmy and Steve's "very different world." It is a vision that can only be produced by minimizing the significance of residents' lived experiences. Discussing the area's many prisons with Old Man Tilley, for example, meant journeying through a critical remembering of past systems of confinement intended to more accurately frame the current order. His response to that rehistoricization, even as we criticize its obvious reproduction of class and race hierarchies, was to memorialize the found objects of the Lenape people who were most directly impacted by those past violences. That is to say, he intervened in the present order with a curated reminder of the violences that happened in their past.

Jimmy and Steve take a different approach. They articulate nostalgia for a past that never existed, "when people still respected God," and they sound alarms of current dangers that no one has ever experienced in order to conjure a fear-based future that is reliant on Sheepdog white men with guns hunting Wolves. This is evidence of imaginations that are fully constrained by the order of domination, and it offers a window into a future world that Sheepdogs and so many other white men are working to make real. Order is not merely cover for owner-class domination. It is a false vision of the contemporary that reduces the significance of personal experiences by manufacturing feelings of nostalgia for an imaginary lost past to make the predictions of a violent future all the more terrifying, which produces a clear need for more white-man police officers and militias.

CONVEYANCE I

In this area of New Jersey, confinement has perpetually structured the system of capitalism, shaped the decision-making of elected officials, and dictated social relationships as well as individual movement. Confinement is and has been central to all that is reproduced. To show the economic, political, and social significance, for example, of Seabrook Farms to the rest of the region, C. F. began to pay his workers in silver dollars that he stamped. The curator of the Seabrook Educational and Cultural Center told me that within a few days, every store in the county, and many beyond, had registers loaded with silver dollars—a not-so-subtle flex of his farm's power and influence over the region's social, economic, and political viability. It was the confinement of racialized labor that kept everyone else's businesses afloat. The four prisons represent an equally overwhelming amount of power and influence. But it is no longer the confinement of racialized people that makes the production of commodities for profits possible. Confinement is now the product. Each year, almost $500 million stream into the region based solely on the number of people who are being confined. No goods need to be produced and unleashed on the market for this money to flow. In this sense, prisons as the mode of confinement are the most recent and most efficient form of capitalism to order the region.

Prisons are not like chattel slavery or labor camps in other ways as well. These past systems of confinement were designed to contain and control labor by dominating the movement, activities, and work of specific racialized populations, always in forms that would serve capitalist production. And they required workers to labor out in the fields alongside other people who were doing the same. On

Seabrook Farms, for example, this created the possibility for people to skip work, cheat the weigh-in system, or just simply slack off in the shade. The demands of production created small spaces for confined people to stretch out and, sometimes, even if only for a moment, break free. Prisons do not extend this same logic of labor and production. Instead, prisons helped advance the historical function of confinement by detaching it from the process of production. Prisons do not produce products because they do not need to produce products. This has had profound effects on the rest of the labor hierarchy. The current system of confinement is not about enabling the wider economy to be more productive. Other businesses do not attach themselves to the expansion and support of the production and transport of specific commodities, as they did during the days of Seabrook Farms. Instead, they model themselves to be in service of prisons, to cater to the wide range of people employed in or adjacent to prisons, or to take advantage of the increasingly large population of formerly incarcerated people who can be legally discriminated against and easily denied the same rights as other workers. This is why one of the county's mayors was working to get a second federal prison sited: they needed and wanted to expand their product.

The prisons do continue some of the longstanding traditions of warping, alienating, and breaking apart meaningful relationships. Confinement's capacity to determine relationships is easy to recognize in past contexts. For example, Old Man Tilley's failed return of the unearthed objects could be understood as his attempt to reach for and establish a meaningful relationship with Lenape people. Perhaps his remorse over this refusal to take back the objects was fueled by his own inability to recognize the ongoing relational detachment. But what might have happened if he instead started with a smaller, humbler step, like going to lunch or conversing on the phone as part of his commitment to building relationships with willing Lenape residents? It may not have produced the same public spectacle as returning twenty-two thousand objects, but it could have created an opening for a more sustainable, balanced, and meaningful relationship moving forward. Confinement, however, is premised on hierarchically controlling all forms of relationship.

This dynamic of confinement as necessary for reproducing ruling-class hierarchies reminded me of many of the nonprofit organizations that claimed to be working on or implementing solutions for the area's "prison problems," even as they employed zero people with personal experiences working for, being confined within, or tending to family held in the prisons. These examples are more than just a detached naivete seeking to remedy problems. They depict how the span of social relationships quickly becomes overdetermined by and fully structured through the logics of the prisons. For the most obvious example, corrections officers are paid to keep people confined in cages—their employment is premised on their willingness to maintain brokenness in relationships. And this does not stop after they are no longer formally confined. The system extends far beyond the walls, explicitly determining where formerly incarcerated people can live, whom they can spend time with, and where they are allowed to secure employment. The system divides the entire local population according to a resident's specific or assumed proximity to illegality and criminality.

The system of confinement structurally determining relationality across time and through space is precisely what we bear witness to in the Sheepdog Seminar: hundreds of white men with no interest in relationships, with no concern for evidence, with a rabid disregard for due process, holding no knowledge gained through experiences or even tactical training, who seek only to surveil, hunt, and kill, who imagine themselves to be defending and capturing not so-called enemies in a foreign land but their very own neighbors. In this way, Sheepdogs are not examples of anachronistic white men clinging to a fading past. Sheepdogs are clanging bells alerting us to the terrors of our shared future. For those who reject the warmongering culture epitomized in the Sheepdog Seminar, who seek to fight rather than further build the system of confinement, both present and future, there are scant alternatives: fleeing town, standing up to and fighting the system, or finding another beat.

Mrs. Taylor shows us a glimmer of what it looks like to find another beat. She did not assume the mantle of organizing or protesting. She did not join the middle-class white people who fled to the surrounding boroughs and neighborhoods. She neither shrunk nor scattered beneath the weight of domination. Mrs. Taylor instead tapped into a tradition of remembering, of reaching back to the life that preceded stolen life, of stretching outward to the life that carries on. She tilled the earth for a voice that was silenced, creating an opening where residents might also learn how to care and find ways to listen to and convene with Jerame and others. Similarly, Jon's actions suggest that not all relationships are fully structured by the system of confinement, even when a resident is afraid of the context it has produced. Even Old Man Tilley can be understood as trying to resist the structured determinations of past and present systems of confinement, revealing something other than dominance. Dominance is everywhere. Dominance is incomplete.

RESISTANCE

CHAPTER SEVEN

MS. REID & HER BOY

I drove three hours north to Newark to have lunch with Ms. Reid, mother of Jerame Reid. I was nervous about the meeting. We had been connected through a chain of friends in the wider movement who vouched for me and the research. And I did not want to let anyone down. I parked and hopped out of the car and two men chattering on a porch yelled out: "The bed and breakfast place is right there." They pointed. "Just right up there," they repeated.

"Oh, no. I'm here to have lunch with Ms. Reid. Do you know which house is hers?" I hollered back. All this neighborly back-and-forth reminded me of my Indiana home, sitting on the porch with friends and family, chattering the days and nights away.

"Ohhh, OK," they responded in unison. "There she is." Both pointed.

"Hello, dear," she called out to me while waving to the two men across the street. "How are you? Did you hit any traffic on the way up?"

"No, I didn't." She grabbed my arm to stabilize, and we made our way down the steps.

Ms. Reid walked gingerly, slightly favoring one leg, which, she told me, she had injured earlier.

"Would you still like to eat lunch at Applebee's?" I asked, closing the passenger-side door after she settled into the seat.

"Oh, yeah!"

Since Jerame, her son, had been shot dead by two police officers ten months prior, she had been a tireless force around New Jersey and New

York, protesting in front of the Department of Justice in Newark for twenty-two straight Mondays, organizing with locals in Cumberland County, working full-time for the People's Organization for Progress, and sharing her family's story everywhere, from cramped living rooms to university auditoriums. We sat down in a booth and ordered.

"I would like to record our conversation," I said to her. "Are you OK with that?"

"Of course. Anything that helps you get what you need."

"So, I think it would be best if you tell me what you want to tell me. I will ask questions along the way, but you don't need to answer anything you don't want to, and you can stop the conversation at any time. I would like to leave this space under your direction," I emphasized.

"My name is Sheila Reid. I'm Jerame Reid's mother—the mother of a son that got killed on December 31st, 2014, at 11:43 p.m. He was shot by two officers, a white officer, Officer Roger Worley, and a black officer, Officer Braheme Days. Officer Days was stalking my son. He literally shot my son seven times. The seventh shot was in the head. He shot him dead. It's on YouTube, because they had a dash cam and you can hear Officer Days saying from the time he got out of the car 'I got this' until the time he shot my son. They shut the dash cam off after the captain came. He told them to shut the cam off." She paused, closed and then opened her eyes, and continued. "My son is laying cold in the ground. I think that . . . no, I don't think, I *know* that Officer Days is guilty and so is Officer Worley. Both officers need to go to jail, but I would like to see something happen to Officer Days. My son was in jail behind an earlier arrest made by Officer Days, and that time he got beat up in jail by a group of corrections officers. He got his eye socket beat out and his ribs, and they threw cold water on him and tased him." The city of Bridgeton paid Jerame more than $300,000 following a civil suit for this encounter.[1]

"They did not give him any medical assistance for two hours. I am heartbroken, I am torn up inside, and I want justice. I want peace for my son, and I want justice for me," Ms. Reid repeated.

"I am so sorry you lost your son," I repeated. I was at a loss for words. Ms. Reid folded and refolded her exhausted hands. She began swiping through pictures on her phone.

Ms. Reid had spent the last nine months organizing full-time, using her body and her voice to stand against police and prosecutorial power. The long-term exposure seemed to be taking a physical toll on her.[2] My grandma would say that Ms. Reid was tired to her bones. But her commitment to fighting for justice was unwavering. On the three-hour drive home, I reflected on how she had been robbed of seeing her oldest son grow old, of seeing him bring his own children to her home for Sunday dinners and holidays. A six-second act perpetrated by Officer Days stole decades of collective life from Ms. Reid and her family. While it would be easier to remain quiet and slide into retirement, she was spending her days lighting New Jersey on fire with relentless energy and charge.

"This is what I wear when I show up in the streets." She handed me her phone. "Swipe to your left." Each image showed her wearing brightly colored wigs. In streets, in crowds, on courthouse steps, you name it, there she was—wig popping from the screen.

"See, I wear different wigs and sunglasses when I'm out in the streets, so these cops can't identify who I am or what I look like. We can't be too careful when we are demanding justice. My other son taught me this. He's a police officer in DC."

"Your other son is a police officer?" I was shocked. "Wow. So, then, what does justice mean for you and the family in this situation?"

"For me, justice means putting these officers away for life. We want you to join us before it happens to you. Well, not *you*, per se." She pointed at my white face. "But before it happens to anyone else. We are here, not just for Jerame, not just for my son, we are here for everyone. Every-one. *Ev-ery-one*. We need to convict the police officers that are out here murdering civilians," she emphasized. "Excuse me: murdering *unarmed* civilians," she corrected. "Not getting too off track, but let me give you a good example: Radazz Hearns. He was a fourteen-year-old boy that got shot seven times in the back. He survived. He got a wound in his butt, he got one, I think, in his hip, and one in his stomach. And the officer that shot him, Officer . . . umm, well, I can't remember his name [New Jersey State Trooper Douglas Muraglia shot fourteen-year-old Radazz Hearns in the back], but he got an award, I guess for shooting that child. He's not locked up. They didn't charge him. But he got an award from the state police. These officers are getting away with murder. Not just getting away—getting promoted, getting awarded. They are sitting at home on administrative duty, getting paid, and justice, for me, is getting them all locked up."

This sentiment stood in conflict with the wider demand, at the time, for abolishing prisons and police departments alike. But for many organizers at the local scale, at the personal, familial scale, until the entire social, economic, political, and legal systems are made anew, fighting the terrors of policing most likely necessitates strategic use of the judicial system that is currently in place since there are few alternatives to holding officers accountable for their on-duty behavior.

"So, what is your relationship with other folks in the family? Doesn't Jerame's immediate family still live locally?" I asked.

"Yeah. Well, I have a niece there, and we're close. As far as my son's wife, no. We are not close." She stopped answering the question abruptly. It felt like a moment when we both chose to ignore an uncomfortable topic. If I had already heard the rumors about the $20,000 bribe allegedly intended to keep Jerame's widow quiet and out of the streets, then she almost certainly had heard them as well.

"What is it that motivates you to keep pursuing justice in this way?" I asked.

"I think Jerame is in spirit, and he's with me in spirit, and he's telling me, 'Keep pushing, Mom. I know you're sick, I know you're tired, but don't dwell on it.' He's with me, and he's patting me on the back. I'm hurting on the inside, but I won't let anyone see it on the outside. I miss my son, I miss talking to my son, I miss calling that boy. I want justice. I don't want this to happen to anyone else. And I want to stop it before my grandson, Jerame Jr., gets old enough to walk around. I don't want him standing on the corner in a few years. I don't want him with a gun in his hand. I don't want him locked up. And I don't want him six feet underground."

As a mother who lost her son to a police killing, Ms. Reid has lived an utterly horrific and yet not uncommon experience. Jerame's murder drew her into organizing and protesting work, and she intends to remain defiant, to keep fighting for justice, for at least two reasons. One reason is that she still hears the voice of her deceased son, who speaks words of encouragement and hope to her and who motivates her to keep pushing. The second reason is that she does not want to see her grandson, Jerame Jr., standing on street corners or getting buried six feet underground.

Ms. Reid embodies the relentless energy and steely nerves that are required for fighting police work. She wants the US judicial system to hold police officers accountable when their actions break the law. She does not hate police officers, and she has no interest in abolishing the institution of policing. She simply wants them to be held to the same legal standards as everyone else. I am skeptical about fighting policing with more punishment, but I am also sympathetic to her demand for this version of justice being served as a response to policing. Some justice, any justice, is preferable to the injustices she has been fighting to the edges of total exhaustion. Ms. Reid places her body in the street, day after day after day, lining it up across from police officers dressed in military gear who are armed to the teeth, and it is a brutal grind. The stresses pile and pile, wearing down even the youngest and most energetic. For the great majority of people who are willing to do even this, it often ends a few hours later—at most a few days. Ms. Reid was entering her tenth consecutive month of street protesting. She was facing one of the great strengths of US policing: its unendingness. It can outlast, outspend, outbody, and outshoot even the most defiant demands for accountability. Policing can simply exhaust you until, one way or another, nothing is left.

Ms. Reid's relentless energy to push through the exhaustion, her courage to stand unarmed against armed soldiers, is fueled by her continuing relationship, her regular communing, with Jerame. She still hears his voice as a restless spirit who has been denied peace, whose living family members have been denied justice. She is committed to listening to the voice of her murdered son, to hearing what he needs, what he has to say, and to receiving care and support from him. Organizing work is not simply about shouting in the streets or drumming up more support or speaking truth to power. It is also about being quiet long enough to hear the voices of the prematurely dead and to follow their lead. Ms. Reid's work is an outcome of the ongoing love and care reciprocated between herself and Jerame. Like Mrs. Taylor keeping Jerame's memorial alive, Ms. Reid was working to keep Jerame's voice speaking, however quiet his whisper may have been. I could not give this answer or speak to this relational love when Big Tim asked what my goal was for getting noisy in the streets. But following Ms. Reid's lead might mean shouting less so that the voices of the prematurely dead filling our streets can be heard more.

Listening and learning from voices in the streets who still speak might then center the primary goal of fighting police work, which is not policy reform for better policing. Much to the contrary. The goal is the creation of sidewalks and corners that are spaces for celebration and life. Although Ms. Reid believes that officers should be held accountable when they break laws, her end goal is not passing more legislation. Her end goal is to reorder the streets so that her grandson and others can live freely. Standing in the streets to demand justice is simultaneously a mode of resistance and an act of living freely, both of which cast into relief police departments as violent military units wielding unnecessary force against unarmed people. Ms. Reid envisions a collective future that can grow from these dual acts, where streets are places for celebrating, where children play and are carefree, and where police officers are not permitted to gun people down whenever they damn well please. As Sheepdogs proliferate like rabbits, they work to build a future world where children—especially black, brown, and poor children—will never be able to play and bounce and celebrate on street corners and sidewalks. But that does not stop Ms. Reid, because she listens to a voice that police work tried to silence, and so she knows that while their dominance may be thunderous, destructive, world-shattering, it is resoundingly incomplete. And she remains committed to exposing, exploiting, listening to, and ushering life into the spaces of that incompleteness.

CHAPTER EIGHT

TEN & TWO
HOW A CIVIL RIGHTS ORGANIZATION FIGHTS POLICE WORK

I met up with David Johnson and Pastor Bert for dinner at the Green Tomato, located in the outskirts where small suburban neighborhoods are clustered. Mr. Johnson had worked as a corrections officer in one of the state prisons for twenty-two years and, upon retirement, was continuing to work and consult within the system. He was also campaigning for a reelection bid to serve another term as president of a powerful civil rights organization in New Jersey. Pastor Bert was angling to become president of Cumberland County's community college, so he was hoping to secure a recommendation letter from Mr. Johnson, whose name held weight around town. This dinner was not about me asking questions. Mr. Johnson did not know Pastor Bert was bringing me. But when an opportunity presented itself in the form of an appetizers-being-delivered-to-the-table-induced-conversation lull, I seized the chance.

"Is it OK if I ask a few questions?"

Mr. Johnson seemed taken off guard momentarily, but with a smooth and confident wave of his left hand, he replied, "Of course."

"So, from an outsider's perspective, it may seem like someone who is a retired corrections officer would have a conflict of interest in leading his fellow residents in the fight for civil rights. Obviously, you don't see it as a conflict, so can you talk about how you negotiate that dynamic with the people you work with?"

Mr. Johnson stopped with a forkful of salad halfway to his mouth and shot Pastor Bert a *WTF?!* glare but quickly recovered.

"Yeah, well, I think when you're talking about incarcerated individuals, and we know this has disproportionately impacted black men, you are talking about a lot of men with great talents who are being incarcerated for marijuana possession or whatever—it's nonviolent—and these men may get caught when they are very young, and then the rest of their lives are essentially determined before they even get a shot. But people work in the prison, they learn a skill, and I'm telling you, some of them are highly skilled workers. But, of course, they are making $1.50 a day, and when they get out, they can't get hired. Because they have a record now, none of these employers who are taking advantage of their labor, for virtually no cost while they're in prison, would ever dream of hiring them on the outside." He finished his bite of salad.

"Right, OK, I see that. And so how does your lifelong occupation in corrections help you to meet these challenges?" I asked the question again.

"Well, as a corrections officer, I understand the men in prison. When they get out, they have no opportunities. So, then, what are people supposed to do? They have the option of being homeless and broke and all these things, or they can go back to their former occupation, which many were pretty good at. What are *you* gonna do?" He pointed his fork in the direction of my face. "You have to eat. And these guys feel they have paid their debt to society, and they should be allowed to move on, to become contributing members of society without something they did as kids, in some cases, hanging over their heads for the rest of their lives. So, what I have been working on aggressively with some others around New Jersey is the legalization of marijuana."

"So, you're working for medical use or full legalization?" I did not repeat the question again.

"We are working for full legalization, but you have to realize that Governor [Chris] Christie is adamantly opposed to legalization and in fact has said that if he is elected president, he will work to overturn laws in the states that have legalized it. So, we are fighting a no-win battle in this state as long as Christie is governor. But if we can get everything in place for when the next governor takes over, who will almost surely be a Democrat, then we can get this through. And furthermore, we can attach the legislation that will immediately enable so many to be released from prison."

"But don't you think it's a problem to assume we can do anything like get people out of prison and keep them protected when police officers are working to put them right back in? And places like this county, where these prison facilities are located, are supposed to do what, exactly, with their workforces and their local economies that have been entirely produced by maintaining a confined population? It's not clear to me that legalizing cannabis is a plan that will actually keep people out of prison." I was winding myself up.

"Well, we have to be more imaginative when it comes to keeping our local economies strong and going, instead of relying on something like a few prisons to prop up what was lost when all the manufacturing left town. But that's not easy. And I'm not sure what can be done about that at this point, but . . ." He trailed off as the entrees were delivered to the table.

Mr. Johnson is not exactly correct that the prisons are propping up the economy. They are driving it. His own upward mobility and growing political power across the state of New Jersey is evidence of this phenomenon. But he is onto something important in stressing that people need new imaginations. The conversation stopped and moved elsewhere while we each dug into our food. As the meal concluded, a resident approached the table and greeted Mr. Johnson and Pastor Bert. The topic of Jerame Reid came up. When the person said goodbye and left the table, I asked Mr. Johnson, even though I already knew the answer, if the civil rights group he led had joined or helped to organize the street protests and education classes.

"No, we did not," he responded curtly.

"So, then, did you . . ." I started.

"Here's the thing . . . of course there are good cops and there are bad cops, and there are plenty of bad cops out there." He raised his voice. "But it's like I told someone just the other day, the idea that cops are out to get black men is crazy! And the media turns them into these people who are all crooked and all bloodthirsty and all only interested in policing and killing black men. It's ridiculous."

He was set off by the question and jumped to abstractions for answers. I wondered if he had been forced to defend his refusal to join the protests one too many times.

"Whenever someone gets shot," he continued, "it doesn't matter who they were or what they did. If it is a black man getting killed by a white cop, forget about it. Michael Ferguson. He was throwing that convenience store owner around like a rag doll—Mike Brown, that is. He was not a good guy at all. But all they want to talk about is how he was shot by police, all the while never talking about what he was doing right before he was shot. And that is not to mention all the occasions—what was it?—how many people were shot in Chicago on July 4th alone?"

"Um, I am not sure," I answered.

"Something like seventy-seven," he replied. "And these gangbangers aren't great shots, so most of them shoot and kill little kids playing in the street or parents getting into their cars—people who have nothing to do with gang activity." He did not mention the number of unarmed children gunned down by police that year. "But when one cop kills one of these bad guys, it's *suddenly* a national problem. Why don't they address the problems, the gun violence, within their own communities?" I was surprised to hear Mr. Johnson draw on a well-worn racist trope that is favored among conservative white men. "And then you have these protestors, these activist types, who just want to come in and make noise and shut things down, but they have no agendas, no plans, no willingness to sit at the table and work through things and actually try to make things better. They just want to make noise."

I had not been present for the first protests that he referenced, which were spearheaded by Ms. Reid and a few local organizers. But following the release of the prosecutor's blatant refusal to indict the officers, I felt how quiet—that is, how not noisy—the streets were throughout the area. One of the prosecutor's husbands worked as a corrections officer in one of the state prisons and was, according to multiple residents, "good friends" with Braheme Days, the shooting officer.

"Like the people who came in and protested the Jerame Reid case, for example. They have no community, no actual concern for black people. They just want to make noise and get famous. These people have no interest in making things better. They only want to make a lot of noise. And look, we all know there were a lot of question marks around the encounter, and how and why Jerame was pulled over, and the relationship prior to this case, and, LET ME BE CLEAR, Officer Days is NOT one of the good cops, but still. Do you think cops are maybe scared for their lives a little bit?"

"Yes!" Pastor Bert responded. "When the protests started, the mayor called me with concerns about the media attention and the kind of disruption they were going to make. And I told him: 'Hold on, wait, because after a little bit, all the noise will quiet down, and people will forget about the entire thing.' And, sure enough, within two weeks, everything had settled down and no one was worried about the riots anymore. They're just causing trouble to be famous."

"Like I said," Mr. Johnson picked back up. "We know there are bad cops. But when I get pulled over, I keep my hands on the steering wheel [he mimes holding a steering wheel at ten and two], I say, 'Yes sir' and 'No sir,' and I ask if it is 'OK to reach into my glove box, sir' [he mimes lowering his head and reaching into a glove box]. Bad things will happen; that's inevitable. My motto is: live to fight another day."

"I agree," Pastor Bert affirmed.

"We need to start worrying a little bit more about the violence in our own communities." He repeated the trope. "When we get that under control, the violence from the police will get under control also."

David Johnson and Pastor Bert are local leaders with wide influence throughout the social and political systems of the county and even across New Jersey. In the wake of Jerame's murder, they coalesced as two critical voices against the family members and other concerned residents who were organizing and protesting in the streets. Their shared approach to and motivations for organizing stand in contrast to what we learned from Ms. Reid.

Both articulate great concern with and motivation to silence what they determined to be noisy, unruly streets that were full of people who "have no community, no actual concern for black people." It remained unclear how they knew the motivations of the people who were protesting since they had not joined. Mr. Johnson emphasized that Officer Days was not a good cop and that there were a lot of "question marks" around the shooting. But he would not answer why these two factors were not enough to convince him of the need to lead members of his group to stand in the streets or to help facilitate educational gatherings with other organizers. In fact, he condemned "activist types" in much the same way that he condemned "gangbangers": as slurs for people who disrupted quiet and orderly streets. He judged "activist types" as having no plan, no concern for black people, and for only wanting to "get famous."

This is a moment where being an activist does not imply a monolithic experience or a shared political orientation. Ms. Reid wanted to hold police officers accountable as a necessary step toward the primary goal of building free and open streets for Jerame Jr. and the next generation. She pursued this through an on-the-ground activism, which was rarely captured in photo opportunities, talk show appearances, or Twitter remarks. She avoided the spotlight, but at any moment, one of her brightly colored wigs could pop from a drab street corner when least expected, and there Ms. Reid would be, arm in arm with others, evidencing collective life and lifting up a chorus for remaking the streets. David Johnson, on the other hand, reveals something more like a corporate activism, which is largely detached from the kinds of vulnerabilities a person might experience by placing their body in the streets with others—an activism that is funded through tax deductible donations and is reproduced through corporate media outlets. His power in this role is derived less from locking arms with people in the streets and more from sitting shoulder to shoulder with police unions, politicians, and financiers. His interests thus aligned in very similar ways with those of other powerful people. He articulated them as a pursuit to keep the streets quiet and as a concern for taking care of "the violence in our own [black] communities." That is, he articulated his concern the way police officers often articulate their concern: order.[1] For Mr. Johnson, when police officers kill black people, it is most likely because black people either did not behave correctly during the encounter or were already committing acts of gun violence against each other. It is rarely, if ever, a problem with the institution of policing itself. This position is not entirely surprising, given his twenty-two years of employment working as a corrections officer in a state prison. And one might also assume that his work in the prisons is where he learned to become concerned with stifling noise and enforcing order.

There was, however, one place where Mr. Johnson and Ms. Reid and a few other residents aligned: imagination. He offered "new imagination" as the key to reorienting the economy and for keeping people out of prison. Like Ms. Reid and Jon, he believed that residents must have not only the will but the imaginative capacities to build something besides another institution of confinement. I agree, though Mr. Johnson's own imagination appears deeply curtailed by these very systems of confinement that are already in place. In fact, the only idea he offered for emancipating confined people was the writing and passing of policies that would legalize cannabis growing and distribution. He did not offer a vision for how the streets might be remade as free spaces for celebration and life. He did not mention sitting with and listening to the voices of the prematurely dead. And he repeatedly expressed an abiding hatred for "activist types" whom, he was convinced, only cared about fame and getting noisy. He articulated little more than a vision that has been pounded into the narrowness of confinement. That is to say, it is a vision in service of reproducing institutions of confinement that can reproduce economic and political systems.

CHAPTER NINE

MR. CANTALE & THE COMMUNITY

I knocked on the screen door of Mr. Cantale's house, which was in an old neighborhood sandwiched between expansive farmlands and the city limits. After an extended pause, with shuffling and rustling, I pounded a bit harder. Finally, it opened. Mr. Cantale, a former high school math teacher and one of the organizers of the street protests that followed the Jerame Reid shooting, stood before me, bouncing a baby girl on his hip. Ms. Reid had connected us shortly after our lunch.

"Hello." Mr. Cantale kept the screen door closed between us.

"Mr. Cantale?" I asked. "My name is Heath, and I'm here to talk about the Jerame Reid killing with you . . ."

"Oh no!" he replied, warming. "Are we supposed to meet today? I completely forgot."

"No worries. I can come back another day."

"No, no, please, come on in." He swung the screen door wide.

Three children ran wild. In and out of the garden they went, back into the house and through the hallways, and circling around Mr. Cantale. He showed me through, room by room, into the basement and back out, around the first floor and then out the back of the house, past the chickens and the just-starting-to-pop spring vegetable garden before we slid into either side of a big wooden picnic table that was fading and chipping away its fire-engine-red paint.

"I'm sure your neighbors love the chickens," I laughed.

"Actually, they're all pretty cool, man," he replied, laughing.

Mr. Cantale lit a cigarette and kerplunked the lighter onto the table. I joined him. We sat in silence beneath the warm sun, white smoke puffs swirling around our heads while his children played garden superheroes with baseball bats and lightsabers.

"It's really peaceful out here. I like it." I scanned the big yard.

"Yeah, we like it, too," Mr. Cantale agreed.

"So, if it's okay with you, I'm going to record our conversation?"

"Of course." He waved.

"So, tell me the whole story. Or, tell me what you want to tell me," I began, setting my phone between us.

"Jilly Bean, can you get your helmet on, please?" Mr. Cantale turned to his daughter, who was tearing by on a purple and pink bike.

"I have one on!" she yelled over her shoulder, circling back.

"No, that's a hat. And a hat is not going to protect your head when you fall in the road, baby. Can you please get your helmet on?" he repeated.

"Yes, daddy."

"Thank you." Mr. Cantale leaned over—she fast-and-furious braked with a hard back pedal, quick-stopping next to the picnic table like a stunt driver—to give her a side hug. "Thank you," he repeated.

"We have a Toyota." She looked at me. "But Mommy took it to work."

"Cool!" I said. "I have a Toyota, too." I pointed to their driveway behind us. She raced off.

"So, I got the job while I was here for student teaching, and there was a contact who basically said, 'Look, we are looking for someone in the math department. Just put in your application and I'll make sure they look at it.' So, I put in my application, and they hired me. There was a board of education vote that I couldn't take part in, because I didn't live locally, so, I'm like, these are the people that are my bosses and determine my job, so I'm gonna move so I can have a decision in the town I am working in."

Jilly Bean handed me a crayon drawing.

"Thank you!" I said, holding it up and examining it. "I will put this in my office! So, your partner is not a teacher?"

"No, she is not. My experiences teaching in the high school were great—great people. The kids, I didn't have any problems with them. But the administration—the decisions that were made in administration bothered me to no end. Left and right," he said. "Some of us were more vocal about it than others. A lot of people just keep their heads down, and rightfully so. It's understandable. Who wants to put a job with pension and benefits at risk?"

I spoke with more than fifteen public schoolteachers, all of whom complained about the incompetence and corruption of the elected school boards, one of which has seven elected members, six of whom work as corrections officers in one of the state prisons.

"OK, so, from the jump, you are in open conflict with the administration and the board of education? And you started after the third and fourth prisons opened. So, what was your experience with the students? Because I think administrators and school board members across the country are pretty much anti-education. That's kind of an American value at this point, isn't it? But how did the prisons impact the students?" I asked.

"Well, a lot of the stuff we had to take care of discipline-wise was from the streets. And the stuff on the streets, I mean, I did do some reading—this was a booming town. And, basically, everything left, and everyone was out of a job and just had to fend for themselves. All the money left. It was just—it was abandoned as this poor town with a city status, basically. It's just an urban area; it's not a city, but it's got many of the city problems. And it's just so small that the problems are huge." Mr. Cantale lit another cigarette. "But it's working fine. It's not broken; it's fixed. This is how they want it."

I am reminded of Ruth Wilson Gilmore's idea of the "prison fix" for California's so-called surplus problems of the 1970s. Mr. Cantale is the first white person to agree with my read that the town and its prisons and its police are working just as they are intended to work. But prisons were not exactly a "fix." His own experiences would suggest that confinement has not been used to fix anything but instead continues to reproduce and maintain the context for contained and corralled life in the region. "Everything" did not leave. The productive system simply emerged through another form of confinement.

"Yeah, so you noticed that the disciplinary problems in school were somehow affiliated with wider problems outside of school?"

"You know—" He exhaled smoke. "I understood them. As a kid who grew up like these kids—I grew up poor, I got into a lot of fights. I have two cousins in South Woods State right now, just down the street." He pointed toward the general direction of the prison. "People are always talking about the fights at the high schools here. There's fights in every school. We *actually* reported the fights that happened. Other schools don't. But the kids that were involved in the fighting, more often than not, had family in the prison system 90 percent of the time or they were already in a gang themselves. Somebody said something two nights ago at a party . . . now it's brewing in the hallways . . ." Mr. Cantale trailed off.

"So, to make sure we have enough time to get to the Jerame Reid shooting—" I attempted to steer the conversation. "You were working in the high school, and you and your partner were organizing protests in the downtown . . . on Saturday mornings?"

"Sure. Um, so my wife teamed up with one of our old college professors, and they started a group called the Cumberland Justice Alliance. There was another young man who was shot downtown, at the intersection of Main and First, and, um, my wife donated a memorial garden." Mr. Cantale became noticeably uncomfortable discussing what followed. "Donated plants to it. Some volunteers came out, and they turned it into weekly block parties for education awareness on how to handle yourself in situations with police officers. Because the situation was pretty bad for the kid; the video shows the cops telling him not to move, he wants to get out of the car, he gets out of the car, even though the officer tells him not to . . . and the officer just opens fire—" He stopped the story midsentence.

"Is this Jerame you're referring to or someone else?" I asked. He blurred back and forth between the two police shootings.

"Yes. Um, we just do not support violence. It's—it shouldn't be a systematic thing. It shouldn't be something that some people have the power to control. It wasn't necessarily a Jerame Reid thing; it was the system, and, so, we really started trying to get out there to protest the system."

"And who is 'we'?" I asked.

"Jerame's wife was part of it for a little bit. But she stopped for some reason. His family—his brother was coming up from DC, his mom, Ms. Reid, was driving down from Newark every week."

"I had lunch with her!" I told him. "She seems like a relentless force."

"Yes, yes. I heard you spoke with her. And yes she is," he concurred. "But the whole thing evolved into trying to get people aware: if you find yourself in a situation, try to do this, or try not to do this, or try to do this, know your rights to this—that type of thing, trying to educate people. They work on a real problem: that citizens aren't educated about their individual rights. Even I fell victim to the same thing. If I'd thought my way through and knew exactly everything I had the right to, things would be a lot different for my family . . . I'd probably still be teaching." He stopped abruptly.

"OK, so before we get to what happened to you, exactly, what was the response like when you all were downtown every Saturday for protest and education classes?"

"Well, it definitely got local attention. Umm, the biggest thing was at the protests for Jerame, like, they didn't block off any of the streets, even though the police knew it was happening, so cars were driving through and stuff. And a man gets hit by a car—not hard, but he gets knocked down, and the police come in, and rather than helping, they start roughing him up. And he's getting angry; he's yelling and screaming, 'Well, he just hit me. Why are you coming at me?!' and the police threw him in the back of the police truck. His wife and kids are standing there watching it happen. They won't let him give them his keys, so his family can't drive home, and so my wife steps in trying to talk to the police, and the officers shove my wife in the chest. We would learn later, from a family friend who is also a police officer, that she discovered multiple pictures of my wife hanging on the walls of the detectives' offices in the police station before this happened."

White people have been driving their vehicles into protestors across the country.[1] And conservative politicians at the state level have been passing laws to protect (white) people who drive their vehicles into protestors.[2]

"Wait, what?! The police had pictures of your wife hanging on their walls? So, you're suggesting that they were targeting her . . . and you prior to your arrest?" I asked. "So, I mean, how many people were showing up to these Saturday events?"

"It varied from Saturday to Saturday, depending on what was happening, but I would say anywhere from like four to sixteen. Block parties might have as many as forty people," he said.

"OK," I replied. "And who besides Jerame's family attended these events?"

"I'd say I was the only white-colored person—the only white person there. My wife is Latina, but there were no other Latinos there at all, unfortunately. We are trying to get them involved, because they are part of the community," he said.

"And, also, they are targets of police officers."

"Exactly!"

"And, so, how did this spill into your job at the high school?" I pushed him a little bit. He proceeded to unpack a detailed step-by-step story of that day, which stirred up his anxiety. He lit another cigarette, and I joined him again. He told me that on his lunch break, three months after Jerame's death, which amounted to roughly ten Saturday protest meetings, he was paged into the principal's office. He sped down the hallways—I imagined his long and lanky strides making quick work—to find two police officers flanking the principal.

"Is everything OK?!" Mr. Cantale asked them, assuming something happened to one of his children.

"No, no everything is alright—everything is fine. You just have to come with us," one officer answered, and the other stayed silent.

Without handcuffing Mr. Cantale, the detectives walked him to the car and put him into the back seat. The short car ride to his house was excruciating, he told me, as he recalled begging the officers to tell him what was going on. "Are my kids OK? What's going on?" he pleaded from the back seat.

"Everyone is alright; no one is hurt. It's what we found in your basement," the same officer finally turned to tell him as they pulled up to his home.

"I can see all these officers moving around inside my house, where my kids are being held." Then an officer handed him a piece of paper. "What's this?" he asked.

"A consent to search," the officer responded.

"You already searched the house. What's the difference?" He did not bother reading the print on the consent to search because, he told me, he was frantic at the thought of his children being alone and held at gunpoint.

"The difference is, if you sign this, you can go inside," the officer replied. "Or, you don't sign it, and you stay out here for however long it takes us to get a warrant."

Mr. Cantale grabbed the consent to search, probably as haphazardly as I would if my kid was being held unlawfully by police, while two hulking officers blocked the door to his home and while his children sat somewhere inside, out of his line of sight.

"So, I signed it." He exhaled smoke. "That was my first mistake. No judge would have given them a warrant; they were already in there illegally without a search warrant, but I was worried about my kids' safety!" Leveraging the safety of children to manipulate people is a common tactic police officers use.

Earlier that day, the childcare worker was bathing the youngest daughter, and the oldest son tried to call Mr. Cantale at the high school and accidentally dialed 9-1-1. When a voice answered, he hung up. In the middle of putting new pants on the youngest child, the babysitter heard the *ding-dong* of the doorbell. She found two officers standing at the door.

"There was a 9-1-1 call from this address," one officer said.

"Oh, really? No, everything is fine. I think it was just an accident. It probably happened when Maisey [Mr. Cantale's youngest daughter] dialed the number and Jimmy Jr. [his son] was holding the receiver," the childcare worker said.

"We need to check the house," the officers answered.

"No, no, everything is fine," the childcare worker responded, holding the door firm.

"Ma'am, we need to come in and check the house." The two officers shoved the door and pushed past her—without a warrant—and walked directly down into the unfinished basement.

"Then they walked to the back corner and pried open a padlocked door. They didn't go through any other cabinets or drawers throughout the entire house or garage. I keep all my plants in that room with a grow light because it's important to get our vegetables started early. In addition to my fruits and vegetables, they found three six-inch marijuana plants with no flowers and half a gram of dried marijuana next to a glass pipe," he finished.

"They pegged you on half a gram?" My eyes must have been enormous.

"Actually, I lost my teaching license for possession of paraphernalia [the glass pipe]."

"Wow," I replied.

"I was the only white person that protested," Mr. Cantale repeated. "And that's when I got the call from Donna, our family friend who works at the police department."

"And what did she say, exactly?" I asked him to repeat.

"She stopped at the detectives' office and saw multiple pictures of my wife hanging on the wall a month before our house was raided." He smashed his cigarette into the picnic tabletop.

"Why? Because she was the organizer?" I asked.

"She organized, she spoke out at city council meetings, she got ordinances for the street protests. But from what Donna said, she was a primary target of the department."

Shortly after his arrest, an officer leaked to the local news outlet that they suspected, though did not yet have proof, that he and his wife had been physically (and insinuated sexually) abusing their children and that they were running a large-scale marijuana operation—growing, harvesting, and distributing cannabis to local high school students. They proposed these alleged suspicions to a media outlet based on three six-inch plants with no flowers, a half-gram of dried marijuana, and one glass pipe. To put that into legal perspective, Philadelphia, which is a one-hour drive away, issues twenty-five-dollar tickets to individuals publicly carrying (up to) thirty grams of marijuana, and Washington, DC, which is less than two hours' drive in the opposite direction, has legalized the recreational use of cannabis. Mr. Cantale possessed one half-gram in a padlocked room in the basement of his home and lost his teaching license, his job, his family's local reputation, and nearly his children.

"So, you can imagine what people think when they read that a local high school teacher has been arrested for intent to distribute to minors," he stated flatly.

Mr. Cantale had worked as a math teacher at the high school for nine years without a single disciplinary action or write-up. Within two months of publicly protesting the shooting death, the police had allegedly taken multiple photographs of his wife and plastered them across the detectives' office, and only one month later they would arrest him at his place of work.

"I'm really sorry you had to go through all of this," I replied, at a loss for better words.

"Yeah, thanks. Everything is done now. We basically did what we had to do with DYFS [Division of Youth and Family Services]. We had to take drug and alcohol classes, we had to go to AA meetings, and we had to pay lots of fines. But the biggest inconvenience was we had to have twenty-four-hour supervision with our kids. Someone had to be with us at all times, even when we were sleeping." His eyes sparkled with tears that formed tiny waterways creeping down his cheeks to his patchy beard. "We had about thirteen families sign up to do that with and for us. It was incredible. Like, the people that showed up for us were just amazing—in a town where everybody has to work overtime just to scrape by." Mr. Cantale hung his head in remembering the care he and his family received from the community, and we paused together in the warmness of the memory.

"I'm really sorry," I said again.

"They were after us before I even lost my teaching certification. The members of the school board wanted me fired before I was convicted. Of course, some people on the board are now under investigation for misuse of public resources. They have been allegedly using school maintenance workers and district equipment to do repair work at their own personal homes."

Jilly Bean squealed in delight a few feet away as she began circling the picnic table on her bicycle, pedaling as fast as her little legs would go, laughing more loudly each time she completed a revolution.

"I'm really sorry this happened to you," I repeated for the third time. "And I'm sorry to say that I'm not at all surprised to hear that the school board was leading the charge against your family. I have yet to speak with anyone who has something positive to say about the members of the school board."

"We are coping now."

Mr. Cantale is a resident who, in the span of only a few short months, experienced his first street protests against policing before experiencing the unending nightmare of becoming a target of policing. He and his partner were drawn into the street after local police officers killed multiple unarmed black men across a five-year span (two in ten months during my research). They never held interviews with media outlets, and they spent the bulk of their organizing time working with a university professor to craft education materials. Contrary to what someone like David Johnson claimed about them, Mr. Cantale, like Ms. Reid, articulated nothing to suggest that he and his partner were protesting because they were interested in becoming famous. They followed a tradition of quiet Quaker pacifism (though neither identified as Christian) and kept their condemnation of the situation aimed at the systemic level, fighting "against a system" that reproduces premature death. But Mr. Cantale soon learned that it is not only racism that motivates policing and other confinement technologies. It is also disorderly, noisy streets full of people demanding change or institutional accountability that will draw police officers out in full riot gear. Whether it is the World War II mayor complaining to C. F. Seabrook about "unruly" black people who live in the segregated part of town, or C. F. Seabrook slandering both black and white labor organizers for demanding fair wages and safe working conditions, or today's mayor snapping to Pastor Bert about "unruly" protestors (all of whom were black, save Mr. Cantale and his partner) disrupting the streets, police officers are weapons of the owner classes employed to stifle disorder and maintain silence in the streets.

We can now more fully understand how the streets remained so still, so quiet after the prosecutor's explicit refusal to indict the two officers. Because the streets were *made* quiet. I could not find anyone protesting after the nonindictment of Jerame's shooting because six months earlier they had been smashed, bullied, hit with cars, disemployed, threatened, and chased out of town. It is easy to assume that people simply go home after street protests end. The gathering comes to a conclusion, and the organizers who were standing in the street with blow horns return to their daily activities. But this is not always how the story ends. In big cities, officers might grab a protestor, like Ramsey Orta, and disappear them into a labyrinth of hallways and dark cells located in the belly of some beastly correctional facility. In small towns, police officers can do the same, perhaps even more strategically, since they have the distinct advantage of being able to identify each person who is out in the streets. Not every protestor gets to go home after the riot.

Mr. Cantale's position as a schoolteacher made his social standing more vulnerable to policing tactics, since they could leverage his public persona by moralizing something like cannabis use. And more widely, Mr. Cantale's situation reveals a blurry distinction between prisons, policing, and the public school system. Similar to the county's prisons, armed officers roam the hallways of the public high school, patting down students, surveilling entryways and hallways and classrooms, looking for anyone, even teachers, to arrest and confine. And the deepest connection between prisons and schooling manifests in the six school board members, including the board president, who work as corrections officers. In this region, there is no such thing as a school-to-prison pipeline. There is no need. The same officers run both institutions.

Again, though, we bear witness in this story to that which exceeds domination. There is a glimmer, however faint, of the alternative street corners that motivate Ms. Reid's organizing. Prior to Mr. Cantale's arrest, the primary goals of the weekend gatherings were to protest the killing of Jerame and to bring residents together to learn and teach one another the individual rights a person has when dealing with police officers. And on special occasions, they celebrated in the streets with music and food. For a few short hours, they transformed the streets into spaces where people could gather together, learn, eat, and even get down—no small task in a town trying to confine as many people as possible. These noisy gatherings in the streets flashed the spark of something different. With all kinds of people joining together to get loud in quiet streets, an unwelcome kind of space broke in and expanded, which triggered angry white residents to drive their vehicles into protestors and drew police officers out, dressed in full battle gear. But the significance of these moments cannot be distilled in the anger of racist white people or the militarized responses of police officers. The power is best felt in the care that came a few months later, after Mr. Cantale and his family had their entire lives upended by local police officers. When a few families who participated in the street protests came alongside the Cantale family to help them through—in shifts to watch after the children, in casseroles and side dishes dropped off, in help with utility bills and other expenses. As Mr. Cantale told me, in acts carried out by people who have to "work overtime just to scrape by," the family is cobbling together life on the other side. This is an example of a space produced by a tangle of meaningful relationships that the system of confinement simply could not figure out how to stifle or break apart. Police officers tried their best to turn the house into a war zone, armed soldiers pacing the grounds, separating and hiding children from parents, and bullying their way into every nook and cranny—all without a search warrant, which means all illegally. They desperately wanted to invalidate Mr. Cantale and to undermine the voices of people demanding an end to their deadly, unaccountable work behavior. But a small collection of people came around them to reclaim the house as a space where love, care, and support would flourish. The Cantale family, like so many families before and yet to come, paid a steep and unrecoverable price for standing face-to-face with police officers in riot gear, who will always work to trample these momentary spaces of life and relationships beneath their feet, since they despise when people are noisy, dancing in the street. But Jilly Bean will still ride her bicycle like the wind, helmet or no helmet, and squeal with delight long after they have gone.

CHAPTER TEN

FRED, KEN & INTENSIVE SUPERVISION

I sat across from Fred at Wendy's, scarfing my food before the Intensive Supervision Program (ISP) meeting started, which he has led with Ken for more than a decade. A state program that offers incarcerated people an option for early release, ISP is conditional on their ability to secure employment as well as an approved place of residence. Fred has lived in this region his entire life, outside his four years of college. Ken I have not yet met.

A month prior to this meal, I shared a dinner at Fred's mother's house, where I sat with B (his mother) and his grandmother (who was introduced as Granny) and listened to stories about how the family had been on this particular piece of land since World War II. His grandmother fled the Jim Crow South in the 1930s, when Seabrook Farms was the largest employer in the region. Eventually, she married, had B, and began working at the Illinois Glass factory, where she spent thirty-four years on the assembly line. She, like B, is quiet, speaking only in whispers and low tones, and only after Fred has coaxed her into a particular memory. She remembers that the factory was hot, very hot, and that the work was demanding, but it paid well enough to purchase a home and a little land and raise her daughter. When the company abandoned town to move its production south (where there were no labor unions), she found employment at a casino in Atlantic City, about forty-five miles due east. She commuted by bus, ninety minutes one way, for another fifteen years, attempting to recoup the retirement savings that evaporated amid the factory's closure. B has never left the area. After high school, she found employment as a corrections officer at Bayside State Prison, which is about twenty miles from the home. She was the first black woman to work as a corrections officer in the prison.

"It was rough," B told me between chews. "It was mainly two families that had run that prison since it opened decades earlier. All white men. All very racist. So, I was a black woman working with racist colleagues who did not like me because I was black and a woman. And I was overseeing people in prison who did not like me because I was a CO."

"Two families ran the entire prison?" I asked. "What does that mean?"

"In those days, there wasn't much state oversight all the way down here, and a lot of these COs were members of the Klan and had belonged to Klan families for generations." She seemed increasingly uncomfortable sharing. "But I was hired amid growing complaints about preferential treatment in hiring, and there were guards who were found guilty of sexually and physically assaulting prisoners. So, they hired me and one other black woman during this time, but it was rough and scary."

Bayside State Prison came to national notoriety on August 19, 1970, when George Wright, a member of the Black Liberation Army (BLA), escaped after being convicted of armed robbery and murder. He and four other BLA members boarded a commercial flight en route to Detroit from Miami and forced it to land in Algeria. Eldridge Cleaver sent a letter to President Houari Boumediene encouraging him to shelter them, writing, "In all humbleness and all sincerity, I think it would be consistent with the Algerian tradition of struggle and revolution to continue welcoming American revolutionaries . . . whether they come to your shores or your airfields, penniless or with millions of dollars." They were received. Four members continued their escape and were eventually caught in Paris. Wright made it to Portugal alone, changed his name to José Luís Jorge dos Santos, and purchased a small home on the shore where he lived with his family for the next forty years. In 2011, Wright's fingerprints showed up on an FBI database, and the police in Portugal detained him. Despite the United States' best efforts, however, Portugal refused to extradite Santos/Wright on the grounds that he was a citizen. Wright's four colleagues had been tried and found guilty decades earlier in French courts, though none served more than five years, and none were extradited to the United States. Santos/Wright remains unconfined.[1]

After college, Fred returned to the area and took a job as a social worker in the newly opened South Woods State Prison. It was the best employment he could find locally in those days. Growing up with a mother who is a CO had led him to the idea of prison abolition at a young age, but his need for money overrode his politics. He spent two years as a social worker in the prison, quietly helping incarcerated people to organize for better conditions. The warden and a few of the COs caught wind, however, and he was unceremoniously fired after only two years.

"My bosses were after me almost immediately," Fred told me. "They did not appreciate the way I listened to the prisoners, and they did not appreciate how I challenged the administration's authority or the planning I was doing to change the prison's programming, so I was fired without out reason. I could have sued them for wrongful termination, and I had an attorney who agreed to take the case, but at the time it seemed like a bad idea given how much power those folks have in a place like this."

Fred found work elsewhere and bounced around a few years before eventually landing at the county's community college. He now serves as a counselor, advising students as they chart courses on their way to an associate's degree and then placing them in colleges (often Rutgers University) where they can continue working toward a bachelor's degree. He also mentors students at one of the high schools every Friday morning (this will come up again in part 3).

"Hey, look, we better get over to the class before I'm up and late," he laughed, wadding the sandwich wrapper and grabbing his plastic Wendy's tray. "Look over there. The mayor, ignoring me, pretending like he doesn't see me sitting over here."

"Wait, you are beefing with the mayor?" I asked. "Why?"

"Yeah, because I have been organizing a group of people in town to unseat him and all his friends, since they ain't interested in doing anything for black people in this town. They're only interested in making money and giving favors to each other. And we ain't gonna have that. So, we put everyone on notice: either they can change, they can respond to the needs of the people in this town, or we are gonna put someone else in charge who will."

"I love that you put the mayor 'on notice,'" I laughed.

We exited Wendy's without saying hello to the mayor, and we made our way to the government building across the street, signing in after receiving a nod of approval from the security guard at the desk. We entered an open classroom that was bathed in fluorescent light over various shades of dingy taupe walls. Fred's shiny, colorful shoes that often matched his ties popped like fireworks against the monochromatic room, and when he entered, everyone else shushed. Ken was already seated at the head of the large rectangular table, where Fred would soon join. He also flashed fancy threads but of a younger generation. I am wearing the usual blue sneakers and black jeans. I grabbed the empty seat to Ken's right. Six other people were seated around the table chattering and joking.

"Alright, alright, let's get started," Fred began. "I brought my friend Heath today, and he's gonna ask some questions because he is here to write a book about this county and the impact that prisons have on towns and people."

Everyone perked up.

"You're really gonna write a book on this place? About us?!" one person laughed.

"Well, at least a dissertation," I laughed. "The book hopefully comes later. Is everyone OK with me recording this conversation?"

I had no idea that Fred would be turning the entire time over to me. I stumbled and then introduced myself again, repeating almost exactly to the word what Fred had just said. It was a stellar opening. But everyone appeared all too happy to share what they were charged with, their experiences in prison, and in trying to navigate life after prison. These kinds of programs are often spaces where people learn to openly discuss their prior "mistakes" in a kind of therapeutic or even salvific narrative form, and ISP's curriculum is no different, heavily emphasizing the need to accept responsibility for one's past life. I had to try and get below or behind that routinized storytelling. Of the six people scattered around the table, four were white, one was black, and one was brown, two were male and four were female. None had been charged with "violent crimes," each person was quick to tell me, since the violent crimes category essentially marked one as permanently ineligible for early release programs like ISP. One person was convicted of possession of a controlled substance and sex work. One person was convicted of growing and distributing a controlled substance (cannabis). One person was convicted of "playing with other people's money." He was a lawyer before his conviction. And three were convicted of various possession of controlled substances charges.

"So, I guess my first question is: Do prisons work?" I asked, laughing. The room groaned; they laughed and immediately became boisterous. Every person wanted to respond in detail about why prisons do not work. I lucked out. My initial question popped the lid off the program's formalities since it bypassed the anticipated focus on individual narratives in order to put the prison system itself on trial.

"There's a lot of supposed different reasons why we would imprison people." The former lawyer, sitting just to my right, began listing with his fingers, one at a time. "Deterring people from committing a crime, rehabilitation, protecting society, and so forth." He peered over his glasses at me, like a lawyer in a John Grisham movie might do. "In prison, you have some real badass characters who, no matter what you did to them on the inside, they're just gonna keep committing violent crimes, whether on the inside or outside. But by and large, the people I met in prison either were there because they had drug problems, and, really, prison was doing nothing to solve those drug problems, or they had made a mistake, and they were never gonna make that mistake again. But in terms of being rehabilitated or anything like that, prisons are a total failure—" He stopped short in what felt like the middle of a sentence and folded his hands down into his lap.

"I've been in the prison system since 2005, and now I'm paying for my crime, and the thing is, they like to keep you in the system because they make the money off you." Martha spoke next, pointing at me from across the table. "So, that's what I'm going through. When you're in county jail, they're making so much money off you every day. They're making money off me being on ISP. Even the people who teach the classes in the prison will tell you that you're only there because 'people are making money off you.' When I was on the run, they even charged me a monitoring fee for those four years they couldn't catch me. They sent it to collections, but I'm not gonna pay it."

Martha highlighted fees and penalties at the state and county levels, which local governments often use to offset mammoth budgetary deficits, partially produced by four consecutive decades of unending drug wars alongside perpetual tax cuts for rich people. In most states, failure to pay these fees, especially court fees and monitoring fees, often results in more jail or prison time. There are currently thousands of people confined in prison for the sole charge of failure to pay fees.[2]

Each person around the table, minus the lawyer, still had outstanding and continuing court and probation fees, in addition to the fees they were incurring for attending these weekly ISP meetings. For most people in the program, their fees would simply continue to pile and pile and pile.

But fees were not the only obstacle to avoiding a return trip to prison. A person must also have a robust network of family and friends (with clean records) who are willing to provide support and a place to live. And all of this is contingent on a person finding and holding a steady job that will be validated by the courts.

"So, then, how do you get a job?" I asked the table.

"You can find a job, and then you have thirty days to tell the employer," Martha replied.

"No, no, you don't tell the employer. Believe me! ISP sends them a letter," Janet rebutted, pounding the table with an open palm at each word.

"I found a job, and ISP told me I couldn't work there anymore, even though I was all happy, because the job paid me under the table," Sue said, smacking her chair forward onto all four legs.

"You know, it's a kind of gift and a curse when you have to disclose ISP to your work," Ken spoke for the first time, the way a professor might intervene in a classroom conversation. "To land in ISP, you must show the court that you really want to work, that you really want to get your life back on track. But to employers, ISP signals nothing different than you are still just a criminal. It's an impossible situation."

Ken highlighted the inherent contradiction of ISP as both gift and curse. Within the world of people being confined in prisons, ISP is a privileged position reserved for slivers of the confined population who can prove a history "without violence" and a network on the outside that is without criminal record and capable of housing them. But this gift also thrusts a person upon the mercy of employers who regularly discriminate against formerly incarcerated people. This means that a formerly incarcerated person's capacity to remain outside of prison is tied to a random boss's personal prejudices, biases, and whims.

"My manager is in recovery herself," Janet told the group. "So, it was easy to talk to her because she's dealt with people coming in and out of prison her whole life."

"Yeah, my boss is also my sponsor," the lawyer said quietly.

"Yeah, I mean, what ends up happening, realistically, is you start to reinvent yourself and to rebrand yourself." Ken steered the topic into a more constructive space. "That conversation at the initial interview is gonna be—it's gonna be easier and easier to have. I can remember, the first job I was applying for and interviewing for when I first got out, you know, when they got to the question—it always used to be question twelve or thirteen on the application: 'Have you ever been convicted of anything beyond a misdemeanor or traffic violation?'—and I can see the guy going through the application, question by question: 'Oh, you know, your resume looks great, blah, blah, blah,' and then he got to THAT question [Janet groaned loudly in agreement], and the interview just changed! You know, it turned into the 'We'll call you' moment, and you just know you'll never hear from them again."

"Yeah," the lawyer grumbled in agreement. His by-the-book response from earlier, detailing the alleged social and economic function of prisons, was subsumed by the materiality of his own experiences in and after prison.

At this point, though, I was lucky to have been recording the conversation. I had no idea Ken spent nearly a decade in prison. The news came as a shock to me, since my own social biases had led me to quickly categorize Ken as someone who had never been incarcerated. Ken, unlike Fred, was thus able to speak to people in ISP as one who had successfully made it to the other side of his prison stint. And he had a gentle way of offering advice in a tone that felt invitational rather than self-congratulatory or judgmental.

"And, you know, it just got to the point where it was just like, you know what? I might need to *not* be honest on the application to get in the door. But if you don't disclose it, when you get in the door, then it's a conversation . . ." Ken continued.

"I got caught by Wawa doing that!" Martha laughed.

"Then it's a conversation of 'Why didn't you tell us?'" Ken continued. "And, of course, then they say at that point, 'You know, if you woulda told us we still woulda hired you and worked with you, but you know . . .'"

"It's bullcrap!" Janet raised her voice. "It's total bullcrap." She waved and leaned back in the chair. I was glad to have made the first question about the system itself. It seemed to invite people to be honest about their experiences and to share their criticisms.

"It's all about you just have to rebrand yourself, you have to reinvent yourself, you have to do some things that make you a lot more marketable," Ken reiterated. "It's one thing to have a felony and no degree, and it's another thing to have a felony *and* a degree. Especially if you get the degree after you get the felony, you know, that's part of your conversation. You know, it's: 'Yeah, I do have a background, but since I've been out of prison, I enrolled in college, I received my associate degree, and am now working on my bachelor's degree, or I have my bachelor's degree. You know, this is what I'm doing to get myself on the right path.' It's about rebranding yourself, reinventing yourself, because you gotta think about it like this: the job market is horrible now, just period. So if you have a background, it's quadruple horrible!" Ken finished.

The back-and-forth conversation continued around the table while Ken unpacked in greater detail how he managed to get himself "back on track" after release. Recidivism rates are astronomical in the United States. According to the US Bureau of Justice, within three years, 67.8 percent of people who are released are arrested again. Within five years, that number climbs to 76.6 percent. This means that roughly half of all arrests on any given day are people who have already been confined in prison.[3] Ken was one of the few people that never returned. He credits heightened conscientiousness that he developed in prison, a strong support system when he got out, including his mother, Gene, and a commitment to earning his bachelor's degree and beginning work on his master's degree as reasons for his ability to stay out of prison.

The meeting concluded after about ninety minutes, and I walked into the parking lot with Ken and Fred.

"Your best question was asking if prisons work," Ken said.

"The first one?" I replied, laughing. "But I already knew the answer to that. It was more of an icebreaker question to get the conversation going."

"Yeah, but maybe the answers to the question were less for you and more for the people who were sitting around that table. I mean, you have to understand that so many people here have no way of imagining something different. We eat, drink, and breathe prisons," Ken explained. "This is not simply an interesting topic for intellectual curiosities. It is our—it is many people's existence! It is something that is so big it is just kind of beyond questioning."

"True," I replied. "It does seem that most people see prisons as a foregone conclusion around here. They certainly understand, at the very least, that this area's existence is predicated on confining people in prisons."

"If you've been in prison," Ken continued, "you know you're there because people are making money off of you. Everyone in prison knows that. It is people outside of prison who don't. Even at the individual scale, we know it. The commissary sells individual items that were purchased in bulk. It reads 'Not for Individual Sale' right on the packaging! I once spent seventy-five dollars on a single phone call, though AT&T is responsible for the markup on that one."

"Wow. I know some commissaries are priced like airport food courts, but I have never heard that they do it like that," I replied.

Ken proceeded to share a story about how he was thrown into "the hole" (solitary confinement) for a week after declining to purchase goods from the commissary. Not because he avoided the purchases, but because he led other people to refuse the purchases as a protest of the inflated prices. Within a month, the entire west wing of the prison was declining to purchase goods. The COs and warden launched an internal investigation to find out why prisoners were boycotting the commissary.

"They found out I was the first one," Ken said, shrugging his shoulders. "So, they dragged me out of my cell and threw me into the hole for a week. They accused me of 'inciting a riot.' Not purchasing goods from the prison commissary is considered riotous activity. It is not a secret to anyone who has been incarcerated that prisons are there to make money off us."

"That's why I'm getting these [formerly incarcerated] people to invest in private prisons," Fred jumped in. "Not because they are a good company—they aren't! But they aren't going anywhere. So, I'm trying to make it where we eventually own 51 percent of the stock of this company and can start changing the way things happen. I can get formerly incarcerated people making money off the system that was designed to make money off them."

"Yeah, I am intrigued by your plan [he had shared the plan with me a few months earlier]," I replied. "But I am not sure I can get on board. At the end of the day, I don't want to make money off a system of confinement, even if I think of myself as a better and more ethical person than the current people who are making money off it."

"It's more than that," Fred pushed back (as he did the first time). "It's more than about who is making money. What do you think a kid dreams about when they grow up literally in the shadow of a prison? With a prison in their backyard? And I'm not talkin' figuratively or metaphorically here. This is not statistics or likelihood or even the vague idea of systems. Kids around here grow up playing kickball, basketball, everything outside of prisons. Visiting a parent every week in a prison, listening to their uncle tell stories about his times in prison. What do we expect is gonna happen?"

Fred and Ken have committed themselves to the slow and steady work of fighting confinement from and at the local, individual scale. Between the two of them, they have personal experiences with many different labor positions directly produced by confinement. The conversation we had around the ISP table challenges some of the assumptions other residents expressed about incarcerated people, and it highlighted the profit motives of confinement from the perspective of the people who have been most directly and negatively impacted by it. It also affirmed the difficulty of disentangling from confinement.

That prisons exist to make money is not a revelation to anyone who has spent time confined in them or studying them. Part 1 tracked the consistency of this motive at the structural scale across many hundreds of years. But the stories of those who have spent time confined in a prison move beyond the structural scale to the personal, relational, and communal scales through which most people think and feel the possibilities and limitations of their life. In addition to state and federal money streams, and city and county fees, prisons nickel-and-dime the hell out of confined people and their loved ones for every service they can figure out ways to exploit. Sending or receiving telephone calls costs many dollars per minute. Purchasing junk food and other personal items from the commissary, or long underwear and warmer clothing for the winter months, all cost more than purchasing those same goods on the outside. Sending and receiving messages through the communication platform JPay costs thirty to fifty cents per email. And Ken's own story is an exclamation point to remind everyone that these inflated goods and services do not belong to a so-called free-market system. Incarcerated people are not permitted to choose if they will participate in the prison's market. On the contrary, the stories Ken shared suggest that refusing to participate in the prison market will eventually land a person in solitary confinement or worse. Prison Policy Initiative's 2016 study, for example, estimated that prison and jail commissary sales amounted to almost $2 billion a year nationwide, not counting digital sales of email and music platforms. A lot of corporations are making money from this captive consumer market. Incarcerated people are not only part of the wider profit-generating production process, they are also a population of confined consumers. Like Old Man Tilley's father, people and corporations have (always) found numerous ways to capitalize on a confined population.

The structural consistency of systems of confinement producing the economy, however, does not mean that the people who are currently or formerly confined are all the same. Someone like Carl might generalize the moral character of incarcerated people as violent and incapable of planning, while an organization like Sheepdog Seminars categorizes any person who is not a Shepherd, Sheep, or Sheepdog as a Wolf in need of confinement or death. And confinement itself functions as a kind of universalizing system for devaluing labor and producing millions of people who share disadvantages across a range of social, political, and economic metrics. But incarcerated people represent a vast mix of individuals, personalities, and life experiences that are as distinct from one another as people who are not confined. This is a fact consistently glossed over or treated as irrelevant by studies that remain abstracted and theoretically attuned only to populations and probabilities.

The vignettes of part 2 have revealed that a connection to confinement takes a person's life. It is obvious in the cases of the formerly incarcerated people who are sitting around Fred and Ken's ISP table. Confinement is sticky and remains attached to a person long after their formal sentence has ended. A Herculean effort led by a caring community with sufficient money (combined with a good bit of luck) is necessary for disentangling in any kind of permanent manner. The experiences of Ken and Mr. Cantale show this much. But people like Fred, and Ms. Reid, and David Johnson, who have not been incarcerated, also evidence the difficulties a person faces in trying to remain outside the hold of confinement. When Jerame Reid was killed by police officers, for example, Ms. Reid dedicated herself, her time, her energies, her strategizing, her relationships to fighting against the system of confinement. It has seized her life even if it has not formally confined her. Fred has been committed to prison abolition since he was a college student, and he has spent the bulk of his life, his minutes, his hours, his days fighting against the system of confinement through many different means. It is, in so many ways, his life's work. In one way or another, systems of confinement will capture a person's life, mind, body, and labor, permanently keeping them busy, distracted, and caught up, whether they are inside or outside the prison walls.

This is the reason for the focus on cultivating new imagination and dreams. The fight against confinement necessitates a rejuvenated imagination. The owner class of this region has been committed to expanding confinement across hundreds of years. And, according to Jon, the current elected leadership continues to imagine the same. They play in a dreamworld of confinement, and it's easy to see that many residents, even those who fight against it, have been dragged deep into this dream. Ms. Reid wants it to be fairer. Fred wants it to have a new board of shareholders. Mr. Johnson wants to change some of the laws that lead to it. These restricted visions are products of a context reproducing visions and imaginations that have been infinitely structured by systems of confinement.

RUTHIE AT LUNCH

I met up with Ruthie in the parking lot of the nonprofit she worked at, which occupied a remodeled factory a few blocks from the Spot. I hopped in her SUV and we raced out. The car swerved and U-turned and sped and braked through the streets, and I clung to the door handle, repeatedly stomping an imaginary brake on the passenger's side. Ruthie insisted on driving me to her old neighborhood, just a few minutes north, and then shuttling me around to random places before we stopped for lunch.

"So, you walked to school every day?" I asked, as she slowed the car and pointed out the elementary school that she attended with Millsy, her lifelong friend.

"Pretty much, yeah. We were too close for a bus or anything like that, so we walked. Here, I will drive you along the route we walked." Ruthie threw the car in reverse to take a hard right onto the narrow street she had just missed, driving us behind the school and past a long row of small homes with rusty fences and overgrown lawns. It reminded me of a street I had to cross to get to elementary school.

"Every day we would get in fistfights around here, run home, play over there . . . this was our spot. And this is where I grew up." She slowed the car, turning into an almost-empty parking lot with a large brown dumpster, half its lid flung open, rusting in the middle. "That's it." She pointed. "That first-floor apartment right there. We had a bunch of us in there," Ruthie laughed. "And my grandma still lives there!" Many of the windows in the apartment units were bare or half-covered by crooked sheets tacked to the wall, giving the empty parking lot an eerie, blinking feeling of exhausted abandonment. One kid, perhaps seven or eight, rode a bicycle in a figure-8 pattern around and around and around the dumpster.

"Wow. So, you spent your growing-up years in that apartment, huh?"

"Yep, and I will take you to Millsy's . . . right there." She pointed to another small apartment located just around the corner from her family's. "I had such an interesting childhood, because I lived with a bunch of my cousins and uncles and whatnot, who were always in and out of trouble, some of them. And many of the people I was in school with were only interested in fighting and doing drugs. So, I had to fight in these streets a lot just to survive," Ruthie laughed.

It is nearly impossible for me to imagine Ruthie—her infectious laughter and steady smiling—wrestling and fighting with other kids.

"I was tough. But then I had this other side of me, when I would go at night, or sometimes during the day, and hide in the closet to read as many books as I could get my hands on. Sometimes I would sit there in the closet with the door closed, flashlight in hand, and just read and read. It was my escape. It was my education. It was the only way I knew to get out of this place."

"I think I can relate," I shared. "I grew up in a similar neighborhood, and walked to school down a similar street, and had to dodge bigger kids who could make my life miserable. My mother had to petition the school board to allow me to use the middle school's library, since I read every book in our elementary school by the end of second grade."

"Yeah, I still love to read!" Ruthie concurred and laughed. "It is how I formed who I am as a person, by reading all these amazing stories about other people and other worlds. Now, listen." She became slightly serious. "These housing projects are the worst. I understand that you grew up in a similar place, but this place has a lot of activity, a lot of murders that happen . . . and most people who don't live here stay away." The apartment building was less than a mile, on the same road, from one of the state prisons. "So, you need to stay away from here unless you're with someone like me."

Avoiding the apartment complex was the same warning Shakes and a few other residents stressed when I first arrived. Mostly I followed these recommendations, save the few random times I was asked to drop someone off at one of the apartment units. Ruthie continued driving and pointing as we made our way to the restaurant, which was a few miles southeast in a pocket of the outskirts I had never visited. It was still unclear to me why she wanted to have lunch alone, but I was content riding with her and listening to stories. We arrived at the Olde House, which is a white-tablecloth-on-round-tables kind of restaurant, and took a table in the middle of the dining room. I plopped my recorder next to the salt and pepper shakers, and we continued chatting.

"So, thanks so much for agreeing to have lunch with me today. And please order whatever you would like. It's on me." She scanned the menu.

"Oh my god, thank you. You really don't need to do that. I am happy to—"

"Please!" She threw a hand up. "Don't argue with me. With the kids, I never get to have a nice meal out anymore, so, please don't even think about it," she emphasized.

"Well, thank you. That is so kind." I felt thankful and embarrassed at the generosity.

"So, you know that I was appointed to a school board position, right?" Ruthie asked.

"Yeah, you told me that was in the works the last time we spoke. So, that became official?"

"It did. That was the meeting I invited you to last week. It got so crazy, and I wanted to tell you what happened."

Ruthie unpacked a detailed story about how the school board president and two other members were being investigated at the state level for charges of corruption that included but were not limited to the misuse of state resources (primarily for sending school maintenance people to do work on their homes) and for falsifying multiple GEDs (to get family members jobs as school security guards who carry guns). Some members had been elected to serve on the school board for more than fifteen straight years. Ruthie was invited onto the board after one of those members being investigated was forced to resign, midterm, because of the growing fallout. The public meeting she invited me to the week before, when she was officially sworn into service on the school board, devolved into a public shouting match over members' loyalty to the school district (and superintendent) versus loyalty to other board members (and the board president). I am sorry to have missed it. But having to commute in and out each day, to stay safe from police officers, meant picking and choosing which evening events I could attend. Thankfully, by this point in the research, I had built relationships with enough people that the local events I did miss were often relayed back to me by multiple people who were in attendance. I heard four different accounts of the school board story Ruthie was about to unpack.

"Now, everyone is pissed at me for one thing or another. The person that nominated me for the position expected me to be loyal," Ruthie told me, as our entrees were delivered. "Each member is now calling me for meetings, because they are afraid my vote is going to buck the established order."

"Wait, they are upset because they assumed that you would vote along their party lines?" I asked. "I don't understand. What is the vote about?"

"Correct. But it is not party lines around here . . . everyone is a Democrat. It's lines that go way beyond party politics. At this point, there are only two board members that were not included in the state report, and they are the ones tasked with leading the action plan committee." Ruthie was speaking fast. "So, Tom stands up to give his report and—"

"Wait. Who is Tom?"

"Tom is one of the two board members *not* included in the investigation."

"But, I mean, who is he? What does he do besides school board?"

"He is a corrections officer."

"Wait, wait, wait!" I stopped her. "You're telling me the person who is leading the action committee that is investigating other board members who are COs is also a CO?"

"Correct," she emphasized.

"And, let me guess: they all work at the same prison?"

"Correct."

"Jesus. This place is just . . ." I stopped short.

"You got yourself into some shit in this place," Ruthie laughed. "So, Tom stands up and reads a report where he mumbles around, talking, 'You know, there were no criminal charges, so, you know, it made my job difficult, because we are trying to figure what to say and what to do so that nothing happens again . . . even though nothing happened in the first place.' Those were his exact words. And then Smith, the solicitor who also happens to be one of the largest campaign fundraisers for a certain political party in South Jersey, stands and agrees and tries to get the room to just move on. The room went into an uproar. Everyone was there—even David Johnson."

"Yeah?" I asked.

"Yeah. He is bad news . . ." Ruthie began and stopped.

"Yeah, I am familiar," I replied.

"Then Seymour Green stands up. He's no longer a board member, but . . ."

"You mean the corporate CEO Seymour Green?"

"No, that is Seymour's brother. Seymour owns a business that holds large state-money contracts for the entire school district. His company—"

"Wait, Seymour is also a board member?!" I asked.

"He used to be. But he is *really* close with all the board members who are under investigation. They make sure he keeps the state contracts with the school district, and he makes sure the party keeps them funded and keeps local voters in support of their efforts."

"Wait, what? I am so confused." I stopped writing notes and decided to rely on the recorder. I could not keep up.

"You have to run for election for school board every four years. These folks have won four consecutive terms. That's not an accident. So—"

"But what does a business guy have to do with school board funds?"

"We will get to that. Then Frank, a former board member and vocal supporter of the school system's superintendent, whose faction is directly opposed to the board's current faction, stands up and says, 'OK, we need to get back to the action plan,' because remember, this meeting was open to the public because of the state investigation, and so, he then says, 'Because this investigation has not been handled properly,' and at that Angie stood up out of her seat and started yelling, 'Whatchu tryna say?!' And he replied, 'I'm not trying to say anything. I'm saying it: things need to be handled properly. That's what's wrong with the board of education in this town. Kids have real needs. That's the problem with the school system. Y'all aren't handling ANYthing properly!' And then the superintendent stood up and said she agreed. Well, this exploded the entire meeting, with all three of them yelling back and forth while the rest of the room grew louder and louder."

"Holy shit."

"Then the superintendent stopped and made everyone not on the school board get out of the room, and that's when everybody had to leave. So, you should read the full report when it is released online tomorrow."

Ruthie had no explicit connection to prisons or policing but nevertheless had to navigate the context produced by the system of confinement. She agreed to sit on the school board because she wanted to be part of building a different kind of school system for her children and others. Occupying this position brought her into immediate conflict with the rest of the elected leadership, who were working as COs in the same state prisons.

By standing up to the school board membership, all of whom were employed by one of the state prisons, Ruthie learned how entrenched the vision for and commitment to confinement is among the local leaders who make decisions. She also learned firsthand that working to create accountability for elected leaders is a fast track to become a political target.

The division that Ruthie highlighted in this vignette, although tied to electoral politics, has nothing to do with partisan loyalties. Democrats have had long-term electoral success up and down the ballot in many of the towns throughout the county since the early 1990s. The political factions of the school board were not drawn by conflicting party lines. The division, instead, was created by the fight to create an oversight committee for school board members that would monitor activities and track the use of public school funds. The board members who worked as corrections officers were raucous in their arguing against an oversight board, and powerful residents like David Johnson and Seymour Green were yelling in support for that side. Ruthie (and others who were not loyal to the agenda of the COs) believed this was because the corrections officers had been stealing public resources and funneling state contracts to their friends. In short, the fear was that an oversight committee might tighten up the faucet of public money streams that were leaking into a few people's pockets. Since the school system's budget subsisted on a shoestring, there was a growing chorus of residents who wanted to implement the oversight committee. Ruthie found herself representing this faction as she stood against the overwhelming bloc of people who worked in the prisons.

As consistently shown, confinement does not produce a passive landscape. To participate in electoral politics is to support or to fight against confinement—there is no alternative to this if you want to hold elected office, given its necessity to the political economy. People who hold elected power must be loyal to their relevant system of confinement. Residents learned this, for example, when C. F. Seabrook overrode the board of chosen freeholders and other residents' concerns to transplant 2,500 Japanese Americans onto his farm. Jon learned this when he suggested an annual comic book festival as a way to build alternative money sources as well as a new cultural orientation. Mr. Cantale learned this after he started protesting in the streets. Ruthie learned this when she wanted to establish an oversight committee for the school board. This region was produced by confinement and, in ways both large and small, it continues to be reproduced by it. Doing anything to disrupt the systems of confinement and their many employees has always been strictly off-limits.

Ruthie, however, held her ground since, as a young kid long ago, fighting bullies and making her way, she had figured out how to find a break, how to locate or make another path—not by running away or escaping elsewhere but off to the side, where other worlds, hidden and unknown, would grow beneath the glow of a single light bulb. There, in that cramped closet, her imagination expanded and her visions of what could be took root until she learned to see beyond the horizons of confinement. This is what made her an enemy to those still comfortably ensnared in the murky depths of police wars and prisons and profits.

CHAPTER TWELVE

SEYMOUR GREEN & POLITICAL PARTY(ING)

I stood outside the Spot with Benny, laughing and chattering about random things. Seymour Green sauntered from around the corner, walking toward us, with a skinny cigar tucked behind his ear.

"Look at this motherfucker," Benny laughed.

"What up, man? What's good?" Seymour clapped hands with Benny.

"You know, just out here." He exhaled smoke. "Hey, this is who I have been telling you about. This is Heath." Benny elbowed me.

"What's up, man." Seymour reached out a hand. "You are here from Princeton to study some policing and corruption shit, right?"

"Uhh." I shook his hand, laughing. "I guess, yeah. At this point, I am studying something like that."

"Heath, this is Seymour," Benny continued.

"Well, let me tell you this right now," Seymour started. "I will give you stories that no one else around here can even begin to tell you. I know more shit on people in this town than you can fit into your little notebook," he laughed, elbowing Benny as they clapped hands. "It's nice to meet you, Heath."

The door opened and Shakes flopped down on his chair and flicked a flame across a cigarette.

"What's up, Seymour?" Shakes greeted him coolly. "What are you doing around here?"

"Ohh, man. You know, swinging through to see how things are, check in on my man. How's everything with the store?"

"It's good, man. Just doing things the *right* way. Trying to grow this business."

"That's good, man." Seymour smiled. "I'm glad to hear it."

"Man, yo, tell Heath what you told me last week." Benny was anxious to steer the conversation in a specific direction.

Seymour grinned. "Ahh, man. We might have to get somewhere else to talk like that."

"You're good here," Benny replied. "We talk about shit like this *all the time*, especially when Heath is around."

"When can you get together and talk?" Seymour turned to me.

"Well, I can get together basically anytime. I'm always around, just let me—"

"What about right now?" He grinned. "We can go over to my house, and I will tell you everything—won't hold anything back."

"Sure. What time works for you?" I asked.

"Right now, man," he laughed. "You can just follow me over to my house right now. You have a car here, right?"

"Yeah, yeah. OK, that sounds good. I need to talk with Shakes for a few minutes and then I'll head over to your place. What is your address?" I asked.

Seymour wrote his address down and then disappeared with Benny around the same corner he had arrived.

"Hey man. You need to be careful with him," Shakes exhaled, staring to the corner they disappeared around. "I don't trust that dude not one little bit. He's a *baaaad* dude."

"Really? What do you mean? Why don't you trust him? Should I not go?"

"I can't say if you *should* go. That's on you, but you *should* definitely be careful." Shakes stopped abruptly. "Don't trust him with anything. Don't tell him nothing."

"Well, I mean, I guess . . ." I became nervous. "I can probably just shoot him a text and lie and say something came up."

"Look, I'm not saying you should skip it. Just be careful." Shakes picked back up. "And don't tell him anything you've learned from your research. Don't tell him anything I tell you. And don't talk any of that library mess you come in here and tell me. Definitely don't tell him *no* names—nothing like that!" Shakes had never been like this about anyone.

"Damn, you got me kind of scared—"

"And leave your phone on," Shakes exhaled, and cut me off. "And call me when you're leaving his place, just so I know it's all good. Don't tell him anything." He picked up his chair and disappeared back into the Spot.

I pulled into the driveway of a two-story yellow home in a quiet neighborhood a few miles from the Spot. Two luxury sedans were parked in front of a two-car garage. I texted "here," hoping for no response, but the garage door began lifting up almost immediately, revealing Seymour in reverse: white sneakers, jeans, shirt, large grin, cigar.

"Come on in, man!" Seymour clapped hands with me and then pulled me in for a big hug. "I'm glad you could make it over. So, this is my pad." He raised his arms in a Y shape. "Come on, come on."

Seymour is always smiling. We entered the basement level, which has multiple flat-screen televisions, a pool table, a bar in the shape of a large L, multiple mirrors, a large leather couch, a mini basketball game, and the kind of dim lighting you might expect in an illegal poker room.

"Man, take a seat. Make yourself comfortable. Can I get you anything? Water, beer, something harder?" he asked.

"No," I replied, swallowing a few nervous energies that were still hanging around. "I am good, thanks. I still have to drive home."

"Where is home?"

"Well, Princeton is home for now," I replied. "But I grew up in Indiana."

"Indiana, huh? OK," Seymour replied, like he was piecing something together. "But I thought you were also living around here, locally? No?"

"Well, I was living here for, umm, like the first eight months or so, but three police officers took me into a locked room and kind of low-key threatened me, and I just, well, I decided to get the fuck out of here." I already knew about Seymour's recent run-in with the police, so I wanted to use my experiences with them to build comradery with him. "So, just to be as safe as possible, I drive down here from Princeton Monday through Friday, sometimes on the weekends. I usually rent a hotel room at least once or twice a week, just to ease the commute. But mostly—"

"You drive down here all the way from Princeton? Damn, man! It must be kind of a mindfuck to go back and forth between such different places," he laughed. "And the cops here threatened you? I didn't hear about that." This comment affirmed that residents had been sharing stories about me.

"Yeah. It's probably a boring story to you," I started, "but, the short of it is, they took me to the back of the station, shuffled me into a locked room with three officers, and then interrogated me for about forty-five minutes, trying to suggest that I had to give the names of every person I had interviewed." It was only thirty minutes, but I was nervous-exaggerating.

"Oh shit." He stopped what he was doing. "Fucking cops. Why did they do that?"

"I dunno." I fidgeted. "The best I can guess is that they thought I was an undercover FBI agent here to investigate the Jerame Reid shooting. I learned that the FBI has been here for almost five months now. Did you know that?"

"Of course I knew that. But you actually think the police thought *you* were FBI?" he laughed. "Seriously?"

"I don't know?" I laughed. "Someone who works in the legal realm of this town floated the idea."

"I've had my own run-ins with the cops around here. They're all fucking corrupt." He stood up from the couch. "I would bet they didn't actually think you were the FBI, but they couldn't figure out who you were. And probably some people were informing on you. You gotta watch who you talk to around here. Let me get you some water."

"Oh, thanks so much," I replied.

He plopped down again, much too close to me, which caused the couch cushion to depress, and, so, I slyly scooched away and straightened myself into the far corner.

"Hey, so, thanks so much for taking the time to talk with me—"

"Hey man, you wanna hit this blunt if I roll it up?" He was not ready to chat.

"Normally I would, yeah, but, like I said, I have to drive home today . . ."

"Right, right. No worries. You mind if I smoke, though?"

"No, not at all, I—"

"So, I was pulled over and arrested a few months back. They finally got me. Fucking cops. I had to call in some heavy favors to get out of that one and I still got a few hundred hours of community service and a bunch of fines." He nudged me with his elbow. "But I got a medical card last week, so I'm cool now. Found a doctor who would prescribe. Finally, these motherfuckers can't do anything to me anymore." He told the story while pulling at a flurry of green buds still attached to their stems, separating the flowers into a tidy pile of skunky aromatics. He ordered them into a straight line and then into a hollowed-out cigar, nudging them into place with his knuckle, smoothing them out, and then licking the leafy brown paper shut.

"Maybe I will just take a tiny hit." I leaned in, smiling. "I can always stay at the hotel tonight."

"Right on."

Seymour clicked on the central flat screen, punching a series of buttons to pull up eight video surveillance windows, two by four.

"See, no one can sneak up on me in this house." He looked over, smiling. "I can see every possible entry point on this property from this couch right here. Motherfuckers should try and break in. So, look man, you're just gonna have to tell me what you want to know about. I know shit about everybody, OK? And I mean ev-ery-*body* around here."

"OK. So what do *you* do?" I asked.

"I own and run the family business that my father started. You met my brother, right?"

"Yeah, we met a couple of times, but I never really had a conversation with him."

"And then I also own a few personal businesses."

"OK, and when did you—"

"Look at this." He cut me off and pointed to the screen, which showed someone pausing on the sidewalk to look up at Seymour's house. "I wish this dude would *try* to hop that fence." He looked back to me. "But look, what I really do, what I really get paid for in this town, is that political people pay me for my extensive contact list, especially of black people who live in this area. I get paid for my connections to poor people, basically. And then—" He raised both arms in the same Y-shape formation. "Look around. This is where we party when the day is done. Right here! People in politics come to my place to party. Women, drugs, you name it. If you even knew how many prominent New Jersey people had snorted cocaine right there next to the bar . . ."

"So, wait. You're saying—"

"Motherfuckers with money, who mostly live elsewhere in the state, pay me for my Rolodex. You know what I'm saying? These motherfuckers don't have connections to poor black people around here. Even the black politicians from *this* place don't have connections to *act*ual black people. Do you understand what I'm saying to you?"

"Umm, you're saying that you work for—" I did not really understand.

"Hell no!" He cut me off. "I don't work for anybody but myself. They *pay* me for what I offer them, but I do not *work* for them. I am explicitly off their books. You know what I'm saying? But many of them are on mine . . . if you follow me."

"Wait." I threw a hand in the air. "So, you're saying that you serve as a kind of mediator for getting black residents to vote?"

"In a sense, yes, that is part of what I do. Yes." He finally lit the blunt and puffed, cheeks sucked in like a deflated balloon. "That is a big part of what I do. But that's only one part. I make sure people are connected to voters. But I *also* make sure other people are taken care of. You know what I'm saying?"

"Not really," I answered. "What you're telling me is that you throw parties for people with money?"

He dragged deeply and passed the lighter up and down the blunt paper's seam before handing it to me. "Yeah. But, you know, *parrr*ties . . . not parties," he exhaled. He really appeared to be enjoying this bleary back-and-forth.

"OK." I hit the blunt and began coughing. "Damn!" I coughed twice more. I handed the cigar back. "You mean, like, you throw parties with illegal activities down here."

"Man, I throw parties from here to Cuba." He inhaled deeply, closed his eyes, looked up, held his breath, and exhaled an atomic bomb–sized smoke plume.

"Cuba, huh?" I laughed. "There's a lot of partying in Cuba?"

"More than you would ever think." He passed the cigar back.

"Like who?"

"Like someone you had dinner with when you first got here, to name one . . ." He looked coyly.

"Someone I had dinner with?" I inhaled and passed the blunt back, only coughing once on the exhale.

"You." He pointed at me with the blunt and leaned in. "He told me to look out for you."

"Look out for me?" My head was spinning. "What the fuck does that mean?"

He grinned and shrugged. "You know, look out." He exhaled. "The fuck do you think it means? Keep an eye out . . . beware . . . don't tell him anything."

"OK. Who said that to you?" I asked. My mind raced. More than a year's worth of dinners to account for.

"In fact, we are having a party here next month," he grinned. "That's how I paid for this place. I throw good parties."

"Can I come to your party?" I asked. "Who were you with in Cuba?"

He laughed. "No, you cannot come to the party." He squinted at me. "I don't handle the invitations part."

"OK." I was annoyed—and a little stoned.

"Look—" He passed the blunt.

"No, no, man. I am all good, thanks." I was pretending to write in my notebook in order to steady my thoughts.

"Look, look, this is how it is around here, man." Seymour assumed a kind of formal voice. "When someone is up for election, let's say, a person running for office that lives up north or way out in the suburbs or wherever and wants to make sure the right black leaders are encouraging their people to vote for the right person, then they contact me. They call me and ask: 'Who do you know that can get these people to vote for person X?' And I get certain people to mobilize *those* people to vote for specific people, like person X. Like I said, I get paid for the people who are in my Rolodex," he exhaled.

"Wow. OK. Like, who have you done this for?"

"Probably people you know. Like, senators that you know or at least have heard of."

"And then you throw parties for them in Cuba?"

He grinned and dragged deeply on the blunt. "In fact, just last month I was in Cuba. Have you ever been?"

"No, I haven't." I shook my head and smiled. Weed makes me smile. "But I have wanted to visit for a long time."

"Ohh, man. You have to. You have to visit whenever you can." Seymour became excited. "The weather. The food. You can't believe that shit. It's like—"

"Who did you go to Cuba with?" I tried to intervene.

"You can buy—well, anyways, man, it's a good place to unwind." He exhaled in spurts, staring at the ceiling, as if reflecting.

"You were down there recently?" I asked.

"Man, it's like nothing. Costs nothing."

"Were you there alone?"

"I was not. Not even a little bit."

"Who were you with? Senator [name omitted]?"

At this question he belly laughed as smoky bursts puffed out of his nose and mouth. "Honestly, you should stop asking. I am not going to give you anyone's name—not even a little bit." He coughed and laughed. "And you don't really want to know . . . trust me. Let's talk about other shit."

"El Chapo?" I grinned.

"Ha!" Seymour fake-laughed. "They have been scaring you with stories of El Chapo, eh?"

"Not exactly scaring me," I lied again. "But, yeah, lots of people want to tell me about El Chapo." I laughed and grabbed the blunt for one more hit.

"It's nothing to laugh about." He took the blunt back, pausing halfway to his mouth. "He's here."

"OK," I replied. "He was with you in Cuba?"

Seymour laughed. "Look, you should be careful who you say shit to around here. People don't take comments about politics or the suggestion of certain senators from up north being corrupt lightly, you know what I'm saying to you?"

"What people?" I was getting more irritated with his vagueness and the blunt was loosening my tongue.

"People in elected politics, people who can fuck your life up if they want to." He did not seem to be speaking in hyperbole anymore. "Much worse than the cops ever could."

"Wait. You're saying people in politics have alternative motives beyond protecting and serving their constituency?" I asked.

"I'm saying, watch what the fuck you say and to who you say it."

Seymour Green learned how to hustle around the economic system produced by confinement. Everyone seemed to know him—he could be seen circulating at a fancy dinner with people in suits or smoking in front of the Spot with people who spent time in prison. During my three years, I did not meet a single other resident who exercised this kind of stretch across the entrenched divisions of class and race. His abilities to earn money are predicated on his understanding that there is a fractured dynamic of local politics that is obscured by elected politicians who represent publicly as a unified and coherent national party. In other words, Seymour suggests that representation in electoral politics, like representation in corporate activism, is an outcome of masterful mediation—not solidarity. He knows this because he makes money as the person who can mediate between people who have money and power (and are seeking elected office) and people who vote for people who have money and power.

Following Seymour's stories, vague as they were, provides further evidence of how prisons are not only destructive and dominating but are productive and generative. His mediating work kept him well paid. He even suggested that these powerful connections kept him out of prison on felony drug charges. And while Ruthie and Seymour are on opposing sides, they offer similar claims regarding the blatant connections flowing between electoral politics, civil rights organizations, corrections officers, police officers, and the school board. It is the prisons that are central to all these distinct institutions. This is not hyperbole. It is an observation that the same people occupy positions across various institutions that otherwise appear to be at odds with each other. At what point, one might wonder, will the people getting paid as corrections officers start making decisions, for example, that explicitly undermine students in the public school system and make it more likely that they will wind up in prison? Or why would anyone expect some of the most prominent local organizers to stand up to police abuse or to fight against the prison system when their own paychecks are contingent on police officers abusing people and on the prison system confining people? It is not a contradiction that Seymour is both a target of police officers and a mediator for corrections officers and elected politicians, just as it is not ironic that David Johnson leads a well-connected civil rights organization while working as a corrections officer within the prison system. These are examples of the centrality of confinement to every other system, evidence of the individual power that is attainable for those who work in the business of confinement, to remain unaccountable, to create and manipulate the region's economic, political, and social systems. There is nothing explosive or revealing about any of these seeming contradictions. They are not scandalous. Because as long as people in power get paid, all manner of so-called contradictions are smoothed out. And Seymour understood exactly that.

CONVEYANCE II

The system of confinement perpetually finds ways to dictate or incorporate its own opposition. As we saw in part 1, different systems of confinement have been central to the reproduction of the political and economic systems in this region across four hundred years. In part 2, we see the different ways that people organize against today's system of confinement. And, along the way, we witness how the prisons shape organizers' politics, resistance, and what they believe is possible. That is to say, human confinement is not only the engine of political economy; it is also central to the many visions for a changed future in Cumberland County. Fred, for example, wants to "change the way things happen" by organizing with formerly incarcerated people to seize majority ownership of a private prison corporation. The drive for "change" does not actually come up against the prisons or their centrality to everything else. Instead, this vision for change converts people who are working to challenge prisons into people with interests in making profits from them. Similarly, Ms. Reid works tirelessly for a future with open, celebratory street corners that would also signal the end of premature black death. But her vision includes keeping the prison system in place and at times even utilizing it for the purposes of punishment. David Johnson, as well, articulates a vision for change that modifies the legal classification of cannabis but otherwise wants to leave the system as it is presently structured. Each of these visions, while potentially better than what currently exists, includes keeping the prison system in working order and at times even utilizing it for the purposes of punishment and profit.

These distinct struggles to change Cumberland County's future cast into relief two related insights: the significance of collective struggle and the incompleteness of collective struggle. Fred points to this when we are standing in the parking lot with Ken, discussing the physical presence of prison facilities dominating the visual horizon of children at play. Ms. Reid, too, is concerned with children being able to play freely and joyfully wherever they find themselves. Both can be heard as a callback to Mrs. Taylor cleaning the remains of death, left behind in the wake of yet another police killing, so that her children and others might be able to walk to school in peace. It is not enough to fight the domination of police officers on the block, or to collectively struggle for the reform (or end) of prisons. The domination of the current order must be attended to in the present moment so that children have the opportunity to walk into a different future. That is to say, collective struggle is incomplete unless it is entangled with collective care for the people who are caught up in the system. And, more specifically, care that includes efforts to remake the dominant order so that (especially) young people might be able to see and move differently through the present.

This is most evident in the communal response to the police aggression that nearly crushed the Cantale family. After weeks of organizing street protests and education meetings, Mr. Cantale and his family were targeted by local police officers and smeared by the civil rights organization led by David Johnson. They were then lifted up and held close by a swarm of people who took it upon themselves to create a different present, and therefore an altered future, for the Cantale family. From this vantage point, there is a distinct chasm between the corporate, delocalized activism of David Johnson and the rooted, locally oriented activism of the Cantale family (with Ms. Reid and others). In David Johnson, we see an organizing presence who is disconnected from the related work of care, even as he admits that the shooting was riddled with questions and that the officer was not a good cop. In fact, shortly after the prosecutors' offices issued their refusal to indict the police officers who shot and killed Jerame Reid, he appeared on social media as well as on his civil rights organization's website locking arms with police officers in various departments across the state of New Jersey, promoting a plan to bolster diversity training. His vision for the future remains dominated by the current system of confinement—not simply because he is involved in a corporate activism that is detached from the specificity of place and people, but because he is isolated from the work of care and support that is necessarily entangled with local organizing and fighting.

We see, then, in these distinct and competing examples of resistance, that life in a system reproduced by confinement does not necessarily mean life that is entirely dominated by it. And it does not have to mean a life that is perpetually organizing and fighting against that domination. The community that surrounded the Cantale family, like Mrs. Taylor did in part 1, shows us other possibilities and impulses at work, disruptive beats of alternative rhythms vibrating the dominant order, infectious laughter in muted moments that simply cannot be contained, cannot be captured or held down by confinement.[1] The impulse to fight against the system can easily get swallowed, smashed, shaped, or co-opted by the system. But there are so many other impulses beating out other beats. They are pulsing even now. They always have been. It requires only shifting our gaze, ever so slightly, off to the side, where the work of resistance meets the entanglements where care, support, and love take place. Or, better, where they make place.

TO-THE-SIDE

OVERLEAF Shakes in front of the Spot.

FRED & THE DECLARATION OF INDEPENDENCE

I met Fred in a parking lot of one of the local high schools. He stood alone, gripping an oversized brown bag from McDonald's. It felt early, and I was having flashbacks to morning meetings in high school when I would show up half-asleep with no interest in the day. The school building was large and in disrepair. After the recent school board elections, only five (instead of six) of the seven board members worked as corrections officers. People in academic settings are always quick to muse on the "school-to-prison pipeline." In this region, there is not exactly a pipeline. The cos help manage and steer the public school system and they also help to manage the prison system.

We entered through the glass double doors at the front of the building. All other doors around the building were locked, I was told. I removed my backpack to slide it into an X-ray machine and walked behind Fred, single file, through the metal detector while armed police officers stared at us without speaking a word. Another armed officer paced in the hall about fifteen feet in front of us. My high school installed metal detectors at the main entrance the year after I graduated, in 1999. I wondered if white suburban schools also funneled students through prison-style pat-downs and metal detectors. I slid my backpack onto my shoulders, and Fred gave the officers a curt "Thank you" as he grabbed the brown bag, and we moved on to the administrative office. We signed in as two additional armed officers lurked behind us silently.

"It's nice to meet you!" the person behind the desk said cheerily.

"It's nice to meet you!" I replied, shaking her extended hand. "Thanks for letting me hang with Fred and the students today. I didn't know if this was going to be allowed to happen."

"Oh, of course. I hope you can keep coming with Fred," she replied.

"Yeah, I hope so, too," I said.

We walked around the large oval administrative desk and into the nurse's office directly behind it. Fred dragged a couple of chairs in and placed them next to an old plaid couch. The room was cramped but cozy.

"This is the only place we can meet. I can't get permission to use a classroom or anything like that," Fred told me. "It's all I can do to keep this up every Friday." He uncrinkled the large McDonald's bag and peered inside. "I always bring sandwiches and hash browns to these meetings."

"So, what are you teaching them today?" I asked. "Algebra?"

"Just the Declaration of Independence and the amendments to the Constitution. Thirteen years in public schools and they don't ever learn any of this stuff. So, we are just going through one amendment at a time, each week." He fished a pocket-sized Declaration out of his pocket and tossed it across the office to me. "Check it out."

"The people who are running this school system want these kids to learn corrections," I said, flipping through the little book. "One side of the cell or the other; it doesn't matter."

"Not on my watch," Fred replied.

"Mr. Fred!" The first student arrived, snatching a sandwich and hash browns. "Who are you?" He turned to me.

"I'm Heath."

"Nice to meet you, Keith."

"H-H-Heath . . . like the candy bar or—"

"Oh, HEATH! My bad." He clapped hands with me.

"No worries," I said. "What's your name?"

"Ray."

The office soon filled up with five more students, each grabbing sandwiches and hash browns before squeezing onto the plaid couch. Every student slid the same pocket-sized Declaration from their pockets or backpacks. No one forgot it at home.

"Can I have another one, Mr. Fred?" one student asked, smiling, his cheeks shiny from sandwich grease.

Fred grabbed the bag and peered inside again. "We got two sandwiches and one hash browns, but we don't know if anyone else is coming yet, so let's wait."

"Alright, but first dibs!" he replied, elbowing the student next to him.

"He can have mine." Everyone looked at me. "I already ate, so he can have mine."

One more student entered the room at that moment and grabbed a sandwich before plopping onto the final couch space. The remaining sandwich was tossed to the student who called dibs and the meeting began.

"Alright, alright. Let's get going before the bell rings on us. This is my friend, Heath, and he is joining us today and maybe some other days. So, before we begin, let's go around and say our names, our grades, and what we want to do after graduation."

There were seven male students squeezed into the room. Five were black. Two were brown. Five were seniors. Two were juniors. Three of the seniors had already signed contracts with a branch of the US military. One of the juniors elaborated on his situation.

"Yeah, they have been recruiting me, too," he added. "They were after my older brother, but he wasn't with it. Now they are after me. But I'm just not sure I want to be in the army."

"Why not?" Fred asked. "What do you want to do instead?"

"Well, because I think I might want to be in the Air Force!" he responded.

Fred shot me a *see-I-told-you-so* look before moving on. Fewer than 10 percent of this high school's graduating seniors would go on to college.

"I want to play in the NFL," the last student responded.

Six of the seven teenagers wanted to be a uniformed soldier. Fred began reading the Declaration out loud in the small room. The bell rang five minutes later.

Less than 10 percent of the high school's seniors go on to attend university. Fred had witnessed, year after year after year, the countless students who went on to careers in military, policing, and corrections—students who became soldiers carrying weapons for pay. This is not surprising since almost every space across the wider region is dominated by people carrying weapons for pay. The easiest way to escape life as a target in this context is to become a person who is paid to target others, to become an armed soldier—an occupation that pays extremely well, better than any other occupation in the area, and carries the added bonus of driving the fastest cars (for police officers), providing protection for family and friends, gaining the possibility of political access and even power, and existing mostly above legal attention, accountability, or punishment. University training could not offer any of that. At least not immediately.

But this did not deter Fred from carving out a tiny space off to the side, in the nurse's office, where, for a few short minutes, he could invite a handful of students into a short break with the rhythm of confinement that dominated the rest of their school days and, often, their outside-of-school days. He ditched the more individualistic curriculum of ISP to make time and space for sitting and listening to a few teenagers who were trying to navigate a brutal context that was perpetually drawing them into confinement, on one side of the bars or the other. He led them through simple lessons about the US Constitution and the amendments. But the true lessons he smuggled into that nurse's office, from my perspective, came in the form of him not carrying a weapon, of tiny questions that might disrupt and worm into their thinking, of ideas that might lift their imaginations, of simply laughing with them as if they were people who might be worth laughing with. When he closed the door and everyone huddled around that fading plaid couch, an altogether different rhythm came to life, where young people were able to locate another beat, where they could receive and give care, attention, and support. Many of the students would still become soldiers. Some would become people controlled by soldiers. But some students he spent time with, however few, managed to get out and not become soldiers. And for Fred, those few students who did not wind up entangled on one side of the cell or the other were worth all the years of McDonald's sandwiches, constitutional lessons, and crummy plaid couches.

CHAPTER FOURTEEN

HERC & PRISON ON THE OUTSIDE

> Now, why does a person have to wait
> until prison to read a law book?
> **DOUGHBOY**

I pulled up to the Spot in the late afternoon. Doughboy and Shakes were chattering out front.

"My man! What's good?" Shakes hollered from his folding chair.

"Oh, you know, just making my rounds," I yelled back.

The Spot was the only place in the region where I felt comfortable enough to stretch out and let my guard down. Early on in the research, I began to organize my interviews and archival work during the mornings and early afternoons so that I could spend a few hours at the end of each day sitting with Shakes and whoever else happened to be around. The regulars treated me like something of an odd friend, or at least a quirky acquaintance, rather than strictly as an outsider. I came to appreciate, like many other regulars, the stories, the joking, and the laughter as an essential part and necessary release from the stresses that had compiled during my own workday. Since the region is quite small, some residents knew me, or at least knew of me, and were immediately hostile toward me. Or, worse, they entered our meetings with well-rehearsed opinions. Nothing at the Spot was previously rehearsed.

"Catching up on reading and emails and a few random meetings. What are y'all getting into this afternoon?" I asked.

"Man, you know. We're just here trying to make things happen. So, did you find anything interesting today? Were you in the archives or interviews?" Shakes asked.

"Yeah, around here, I am always finding interesting things, but I am more focused on the archival research at this point," I answered. "I have been sitting in the office that holds all the land deeds going back to the beginning. I am just about finished scrolling through the microfiche of the *Evening News* stored in the library. I began before World War II and have been slowly trying to skim through every page. And I gave you all the first-person narratives of Japanese American people who were confined on Seabrook Farms. But the land deeds are my primary focus at the moment."

"Really? Hmm. The land deeds? Where do you find those—?" Shakes started.

"What have you been finding out?" Doughboy cut him off.

"Well, for one thing," I started, "the land that South Woods sits upon was originally a bunch of individual pieces of land owned by different farmers. In the mid-1980s, two lawyers from New York City purchased multiple plots of land until they had a contiguous piece of property that was more than one hundred acres. They then sold it to the county for exactly twice what they paid. Then it was sold to the New Jersey Department of Corrections for one dollar."

"*ONE DOLLAR?!*" they replied in almost unison.

"Stop," Shakes continued.

"Yep, one dollar. And basically the same thing happened a few years later for the land that Fairton Federal is on," I continued. "It's all there in haphazardly stored documents located in a small room on the first floor of the county courthouse. People in the know already knew the prisons were coming long before they arrived—like, almost a decade before they opened—and so a few people made large sums of money from the purchase and sale. My suspicion is that it was spearheaded by William J. Hughes, the congressman for this district for twenty-some years. How else would wealthy people from New York City have the foresight to purchase more than one hundred acres of land all the way down here? And a decade before the prisons would open? But I can in no way prove any of that."

"Well, what does William Hughes have to do with—" Doughboy began but was cut off.

"Just what I thought!" Herc yelled from across the street, walking toward us, wearing a black, puffy ski coat that was far too warm for the weather.

"What are you getting back from?" Shakes asked.

"Had to do what I had to do today," Herc answered, clapping hands with everyone. "How's your book research coming?" He turned to me.

"Oh, it's good. Slow. You know. But good," I replied.

"And who are you talking to?" he asked.

"I am trying to talk to everyone," I said. "The most important thing to me is to hear from a wide range of people who have different relationships to the prisons and to policing."

"Yeah?" Herc replied. "But who, specifically, have you talked to?"

"Oh, I can't say names or anything like that," I replied. "Just like I don't tell anyone I have been talking with y'all."

"Hmm," Herc frowned. "You can't see this shit in Princeton, huh? They are sending kids down here to figure out what the fuck is going on?!" He clapped hands with Shakes again.

"You can't see this shit in Princeton, no," I replied. "But Princeton is just as overpoliced as this place is. Maybe more so."

"Look—" Herc took the lead. "You really wanna know how it is around here?"

"Turn on that microphone!" Shakes tapped me excitedly.

"My daddy taught me: we are the strongest men on this earth," Herc began. "This is how it's supposed to be."

"OK." Doughboy leaned toward him. Everyone did.

"There is nothing on this earth we can't do." Herc tapped his chest.

"Right, OK," Doughboy nodded.

"Your mind is the strongest thing connected to this earth." Herc pointed to his head. "Not your body, but this earth. Because this is Mother Earth, and we are just living in it."

"OK." Doughboy tilted his head.

"And if we are living in it, we are cohabitating with our people." Herc gestured widely with his arms, forming a Y. "So, guess what?"

"Tell him," Shakes urged.

"You ain't got no money. *He* got some money." Herc pointed to Doughboy. "He got some money." He pointed at me. "*I* got some money." He tapped his chest. "Guess what? You hang with us, we are supposed to pull a dollar out of our pockets and make sure you are good. And guess what? You are gonna grab your little buddy that you hang with. And guess what? You pull money out of your pocket for *him*! Now we are all hanging. He gets the pizza. We get the soda. He gets the chips. Now we are all cool. We are all fed. We still got a little money in our pocket, right?" Herc paused and looked around the circle.

These prefatory remarks followed a very normal rhythm outside the Spot. One person slowly unpacked their views on a particular subject, any subject, or relayed a juicy bit of gossip, and then paused for affirmation from the group. Then someone asked a follow-up question or simply offered an affirmative "That's right." It was a delicate back-and-forth to keep the conversation lively without devolving into chaos, where everyone was speaking at once, or narrowing into monologue, where one person was simply mansplaining the afternoon away. And there were always moments for release, when a well-timed joke or clever response produced group laughter. Each conversation, irrespective of the topic, was brimming with laughter. These spaces, when multiple people stood in front of the Spot, were precious. They were the reason people made their way to the Spot after work or after hustling or after a late lunch. They were the reason I spent so much time there. And Shakes sat as the center of gravity. Rather than inserting his presence as the leader, or the boss, or the owner of the store, even though he was the owner of the store, he sat in the middle, like the sun, helping keep everyone warm and circling together.

"So, that's how it's supposed to be, you say?" Doughboy assumed a professorial tone, leaning away from the conversation and assessing the landscape.

"*THIS* is how it's supposed to be," Herc picked back up.

"Oh, OK." Doughboy resumed his listening posture.

"Understand it." Herc slowed and repeated, "Understand it." He pulled apart his coat and patted his belly. "Our era, the '80s–'90s era, when there were jobs around here, it was fluctuating, yes, but everything was good. Our city was our city." Herc had not been present a few moments earlier when I told them that parts of and around *their city* were being sold out from under them in the 1980s and '90s. "It was alright. But it changed. It progressed. Jobs started leaving, and guess what? They had machines to do work that a man could do. So, now, we don't need those thirteen hundred people right there because we have seven hundred machines. So, now, guess what? That caused those people to go and do what they needed to do. Whether they sold some ass, shot guns, robbed motherfuckers, alright. Fine. Now, we got more robbers, jackers, car thieves out here, and boom!"

Herc said that people living here were left with nothing and had to "do what they had to do," which was how he described his own activities for the day. It was a way of recognizing that his work situation, and therefore the context he had to navigate to earn money, were outcomes of decisions made by people with no concern for the life possibilities of regular residents. Herc patted his belly when he began and within a few moments was analyzing the structural conditions produced by capital becoming more technologically advanced and efficient.[1] No matter how theoretically expansive the conversations became, they were always grounded in what it meant, in what it felt like to live in the area, to live in the area as a black man, with highly constrained options at hand.

"OK?" Doughboy asked.

"But if you take the same people and teach them something else, they won't do that!" Herc emphasized.

"If *who* takes 'em?" Doughboy asked.

"It's all about progress. Progress . . ." Herc continued.

"If *WHO* takes 'em?" Doughboy asked again, raising his voice.

"If the black people take them, whoever takes them, whoever teaches them. It's each one teach one. I can teach *him* something!" Herc moved to throw an arm around both of my shoulders and then jostled me before the group. "It's a white man! But he's still a person. Understand that!" The group erupted in laughter.

Whenever I was around, I was the primary target for most of the jokes. Three teenagers walked from the corner and moseyed up to the group. They started smoking and joined in the joking for a few minutes before continuing down the sidewalk, laughing and jeering. Herc and Doughboy were far too deep in conversation to let them or anyone else fully intervene.

"So, what's your point?" Doughboy pushed back.

"My point is this: we put ourselves in this goddamn hole. They didn't do this to us. Go find another goddamn job," Herc emphasized.

"Who is *they*? I'm just trying to understand what you're talking about," Doughboy asked.

"The black people of this place," Herc stressed.

"Did what, exactly?" Doughboy asked.

"We put ourselves in this hole," Herc repeated.

"Hmm. You believe that?" Doughboy turned to me. "Do you believe that?" he repeated and nudged my shoulder. Everyone paused and looked at me.

"No, I don't believe that," I hesitated to answer.

I prefer not to outright disagree with ideas. But while standing in this circle, honesty is expected over artificial agreement. There is enough trust and mutual debt among the regulars to disagree in love. They do not have to posture. They do not have to bite their tongues to feign false consensus. And they do not have to shout disagreements like a sports talk show. They simply talk it out. They give one another the room to stretch and explore with the same grace and abundance that they give anything else. They are, in a certain sense, collectively or mutually indebted to one another because each is constantly giving without calculation.

"You don't believe that?" Herc re-placed his arm around my shoulder. Our disagreement did not produce division.

"There are all kinds of schisms that add to a situation." Doughboy took over. "But a community is built on *inter*dependence. You understand?"

"I understand," Herc nodded.

"They divide us to make us not be codependent on one another," Doughboy continued, tapping his own chest and then elbowing mine.

"That's right!" Shakes affirmed.

"*You* understand what I'm trying to say." Doughboy looked to me and then to the group. "He understands: *inter*dependence means *co*dependence. That means he depends on me and—"

"Hold, hold, HOLD UP!" Herc interjected.

"I depend on him. He depends on me. I don't care what color he is," Doughboy continued.

"Now listen." Herc inched closer to Doughboy. "Herc Nelson is a very smart person."

"Mmmhmm," Doughboy nodded. "Yessir."

"Intellectually . . . outspoken, yeah. But when you say something, I understand what you are saying," Herc pushed back.

"OK, that's why I ask questions," Doughboy replied, "because if we don't ask questions, there will be a misunderstanding, and then we will get nowhere."

"That's right," Shakes agreed.

"Right," Herc replied. "So, speak on then." He threw his hands in the air. Everyone laughed.

"You are alright, man," Doughboy laughed and clapped hands with Herc.

"Listen, I'm gonna tell you something going back." Herc took over again. "I laid back in my couch, smoking my Dutch." Everyone laughed again as he mimed leaning back and smoking. "I said, 'Yooooo! He's the one that used to be in the back . . . you!" He pointed at Doughboy.

"Who?!" Doughboy asked.

"*You*! In the back of the Hill [the apartment complex I visited with Ruthie in part 2]!" Herc emphasized.

"Oh, yeah, all over the Hill," Doughboy laughed.

"'Cause you used to be next to our house, hiding your drugs," Herc laughed.

"Oh, you were peeking out the window at me?" Doughboy asked.

"Yeah," Herc laughed. "You put that little white box—what's the name?—you used to hide it back there." Herc mimed a small white box.

"Yeah, I hid back there."

"You ever miss a package?" Shakes laughed, "HE GOT YOU!"

Everyone was laughing at the insinuation of the teenaged Herc stealing drugs from the young Doughboy.

"Never. *NEVER!*" Herc replied. "Because my daddy would say to me, 'Don't touch that shit; mind your goddamn business!'"

"It's something, man." Doughboy nodded his head.

"It's the truth, what y'all fellas are saying about 'can't get a job.'" Shakes took the floor. "I went up to Wawa, maybe about twelve to thirteen years ago . . ."

"Wawa," Doughboy nudged me. "Think about it. Wa. Wa."

"You gotta have three interviews," Shakes continued.

"Right." Doughboy was also familiar with the hiring process at Wawa.

"I sold it in two," Shakes bragged. And we all knew it was true. "The lady said, 'Come back up and give me my third interview.' But by the time I got up there, she had told corporate that she was hiring me, and corporate said: 'No you're not; he's a felon.' And I wrote on my application, 'Five years' probation for CDS [controlled dangerous substance].' They ain't hire me because of that! It was right there on my application! The very first time I went in. You know what I mean? Boyyy, I was *UP*set. I ain't gonna lie."

"You got CDS charges?" Herc asked. "Just imagine me! I got gun charges. I got CDS charges. I got armed robbery charges, kidnapping, all types of shit." He listed on each finger. "My jacket is from here to moth-erfucking North Newark!"

Everyone laughed.

"You got kidnapping charges?" Shakes asked. "For what?"

"Hell yeah," Herc replied. "Listen, if I pick you up and take you from here to there, that's a kidnapping charge. I never knew that shit. I had my baby's momma with me, in the street, when I got pinched, and the police officer said to her: 'Did he take you under duress?' She didn't respond, so he asked another way: 'Do you want to be here right now?' And she was like, 'No, I don't want to be here right now.' Boom. They got me with a kidnapping charge. I said to the cop: 'What the fuck?!' My bail was a million-and-a-half dollars," Herc emphasized.

"You went to prison didn't you?" Shakes already knew the answer.

"Fuck yeah!" Herc replied. "They gave me twenty years."

"How much of the twenty did you do?" Shakes asked.

"Ten," Herc replied.

"Mm, mm, mm." Shakes nodded his head disapprovingly and pulled another short from the pack of Newports.

"I was in the law library for the first eight years, though," Herc said.

"You gave ten of that back, huh?" Shakes asked.

"Damn straight!"

"They let you out!" Doughboy clapped Herc on the shoulder.

"Hell yeah!" Herc was excited.

"And you ain't been back since!" Shakes testified.

"Hell no!"

Everyone was laughing and clapping.

"I have been home for eight years, man." Herc took over. "And I'm still going through that mental change in my mind: getting up every day at 5:00 a.m., going to their motherfucking chow, eating mess in their mess hall, getting up and going to work for them for twelve cents an hour."

"See what I was telling you?" Doughboy nudged me.

"Listen. I know I made forty-four thousand pairs of boots. I made thirteen thousand T-shirts because that's on the . . ." Herc was counting.

"You say you made thirteen thousand T-shirts—?" Doughboy began.

"*T-SHIRTS!* Hell yeah!" Herc answered.

"In ten years?" Shakes asked.

"And got paid how much for it?" Doughboy asked.

"Twelve cents an hour," Herc answered.

"Alright," Doughboy hyped. "Do the math on it." He repeatedly elbowed me.

"Where were you held?" I asked.

"Rahway, Trenton State, South Woods." Herc pointed north. "Northern State, wherever the fuck. Name one. I'm there."

"So, they moved you around?" I asked.

"Man, look, this is how it is in prison," Herc started. "Ms. Ruiz, a co when I was at Northern State, my first bink [prison], and she accused me: 'Yo, he pulled his dick out!' Because I was in the bathroom and she was in the bathroom sucking this other boy off. So, guess what? I saw it happen. So, they had to get rid of me."

Herc's story came on the heels of the arrest of eight corrections officers who worked at the Cumberland County Jail, which had followed an external investigation led by the Department of Justice after multiple people had committed suicide while awaiting trial or sentencing. The findings charged that multiple cos had been physically assaulting and sexually abusing incarcerated people and then sharing pictures on their phones and members-only Facebook groups. Herc claimed that he was moved from his first prison because he inadvertently witnessed a sexual encounter between a co and an incarcerated person.

"Whatup, Stevie!" Shakes threw a hand in the air and hollered at a guy who was honking his horn while leaning over the roof of a car that was idling in the middle of the street. He drove off waving.

"They had to get rid of me!" Herc continued. "Ain't no words to be said. So, now I'm sent to Rahway. And that motherfucking tag shop in Rahway, making motherfucking license plates for cars. Then guess what? They said to me, to all of us: 'Yo, if you don't make seven hundred of these in an hour, bitch, you are going back into iso [solitary confinement]. You are going to be locked down. We want seven hundred from each one of you motherfuckers.' There were about sixty of us working on them."

"You better write that down, man." Doughboy pushed me to make a note of the authoritarian work conditions forced onto Herc and other people who are confined in New Jersey prisons—work conditions that continue today.[2]

"I'm'a tell you something, bro." Herc crossed the small circle and stared directly into my eyes, a few inches from my face. "This is some real-life shit. Get this shit *REAL CLEAR*."

Everyone was laughing.

"Rahway. Trenton State. South Woods. Bayside. Fairton. They are all just a monopoly to keep the black man down, to keep the black man from being in power. They put a black man in charge to make us say: 'Oh, we got a black president!' HA HA HA!" Herc fake-laughed. "But guess what?"

"What about President Obama?" Shakes asked. "He did something for me, man!"

"What?" Herc turned. "He gave you some fucking healthcare?!"

"I got insurance!" Shakes laughed.

"Kudos, motherfucker!" Herc replied. Everyone laughed and laughed. "Kudos! But did he help you get up this morning?"

"No."

"Did he help you open up this shop?" Herc asked.

"No."

"Right," Herc emphasized. "Why the fuck does this town look like this? You tell me?" Everyone semi-leaned in and became church-mouse quiet. "Because Obama was just a stunt dummy. He can't make any laws without the Senate, without Congress. The president ain't nothin' but the leader of the White House and the twelve acres around it. He doesn't run America. We black men are the strongest men on earth, and we don't need no motherfucking president to represent us." Herc was now steamrolling. Whether he intended to invert Nas's lyrics remains unclear.[3]

"Talk into the mic!" Shakes pointed at me.

"FUCK THAT MIC!" Herc replied, pointing.

Everyone laughed and laughed. Herc repeated his initial claim by reversing how the logic unfolds. He began with a structural analysis: prisons, like presidents, are designed by the owner class for one purpose: "to keep the black man from being in power." He argued that President Obama had no actual power outside what the other branches of government allowed, and he then returned to the exact spaces they were forced to navigate ("If he does have power, why does this town look like this?") before concluding with Shakes's own belly ("Did he help you put food on the table?"). If critical and structural analysis does not have anything to do with people getting fed and allowing them to live secure and safe lives in the company of those they love, then analysis is useless. Herc believed, as Marx also argued, that the point of analysis is to change the world.

"This shit is real," Herc continued. "Listen. Every day I live prison on the outside. That's minus the bars. And that's real fucked up. If you ain't been to prison, you can't speak about this shit, because this shit is real."

"I ain't never been." Shakes rubbed his hands. "I can't speak on it." His plea bargain with prosecutors kept him from serving a prison term (he only spent time in county jail).

"I take my hat off to anybody that's doing life . . . to all the young boys." Herc removed his beanie. "I don't give a fuck what they did or what they didn't do. 'Cause guess what? Life is real. That means any motherfucker can get life. That means you can't have no girlfriend unless you fucking a man, or paying one of them cos three to four hundred dollars for two to three minutes a fuck."

"That's all I got anyway!" Doughboy laughed and clapped hands with Shakes.

Everyone erupted.

"Say THAT into the mic!" Shakes laughed.

"Listen, listen." Herc quieted his voice. "Back to what I was saying. I'm'a tell you some real-life shit, 'cause ten years in the bink will make anybody think differently when they come out here. It'll make you think irrational. It'll make you think wiser of the things that you did. And it'll make you think more harshly. Because I'm not gonna let no man hurt me, none, not one whatsoever, never again. Before, I didn't carry no guns. Never. Not one. Now, I'm trying to shoot police because this shit is in my veins, in my head." He pointed to his head. "And I know how this shit works now. My next dollar comes from the trap, from the motherfucking trap. That means: I sell goddamn drugs. I'm a drug dealer. And I gotta be a drug dealer because I can't get no job. Why can't I get a job? Because they forced this shit on me. And this shit is being forced on 99 percent of black youth in America. From prisons to presidents, it's all a monopoly to keep us down. It's nice you get to go home at the end of all this and write your goddamn book, back in Princeton. Make your goddamn money. Get your goddamn job. But my next dollar comes from the trap. I won't see nothing from that book."

"You're alright, Herc," Doughboy said. "Sounds like you got some things figured out."

"Reading in the library to know your rights, huh?" Shakes added. "Reading to know how things work out here."

"Damn straight. And I ain't been back to prison since," Herc answered.

"Isn't that interesting?" Doughboy turned to me. "Isn't that interesting?" he repeated. "Now, why does a person have to wait until prison to read a law book, or to study, or to show himself improved mentally? Why's he need to wait to go to prison to do it?"

"Because he ain't got time on the streets," Shakes answered. "'Cause he's living fast."

Hanging out in front of the Spot was sometimes like the adult version of cramming into the nurse's office. It provided a break, off to the side, where people could stretch out and enter a different rhythm. Fred was helping to produce a break in order to connect with teenagers before they became ensnared by one side of the system or the other. The Spot was where people went after they were on the other side of being ensnared. And it was powerful. Of all the formerly incarcerated people (six total regulars) who regularly made their way to the Spot, who entered its rhythms, who participated in its culture and practices of interdependence, not a single person had been reincarcerated—a truly staggering fact, given that more than 70 percent of people who are released from prison make at least one return trip within seven years.[4] The year-in-year-out consistency of recidivism in the United States is an outcome of the social conditions we have already seen, which are part of a context that revolves around relying on confinement to reproduce political and economic possibilities. This is part of what Herc means when he says every day he lives "prison on the outside."

Herc begins his theory for a better world by highlighting the relationship that each person has with the planet, naming the interconnectedness, the contingency of all life. This interconnectedness is an essential point for establishing the socialist values of his ideal community, where each person is giving of what they have so that none are in need. He juxtaposes an interdependent community with an abstracted "they" (the owner class) that, from his perspective, sit greedily atop political scheming and capitalist development. He pats his belly to emphasize the significance of collective sharing that meets the material needs of the individual person. This enables him to interpret the idea of capitalist progress that is controlled by an owner class as little more than technological advancements that increase profits by displacing and devastating both people and place. This march of progress was the reason that residents like himself had to find other ways to scrape a life out of the area.

Interdependence is the value, the philosophy for life, the daily practices with others that can materialize mutually dependent and supportive relationships and enable the conditions that might bring about other possibilities and alternative contexts. Herc was not fooled by empty promises of elected politicians or by powerful leaders who shared his racial category. The system, as he saw it—from the county's prisons to the president of the United States—was designed in order to target, control, and depress black people. Herc was not tricked by the false promise of representative politics because he paid close attention to the realities of his own context. He patted his own belly. He listened to others' experiences. Unlike the rabid Sheepdogs of part 1, Herc had clarity; he looked at reality in its cold, hard brutality, unflinching, and so he understood the actual conditions of life in a place with this many prisons. He knew that the way to escape, to avoid the entanglements of confinement, was not by electing better leaders, or passing more robust policies, or constructing stronger institutions, but through interdependent relationships that did not simply reproduce the domination of those same contexts in different forms. Herc knew that politicians who happened to share his racial category, once they got into office, would do very little to alter the conditions of life for people in Cumberland County. That is to say, he knew that nonwhite politicians behaved mostly the same as white politicians. Herc, Shakes, and Doughboy knew that the real work, the on-the-ground work, the slow and steady work of carving out interdependent life to the side was the only way to break out of the speed of the streets, the only way that a few people might find another beat.

CHAPTER FIFTEEN

THE LAWYERS & THE AMISH MARKET

I arrived early at the Amish market, which was way out in the middle of nowhere. It was big like a Walmart. I squeezed my little car into a space between two beefy pickup trucks with aggressive bumper stickers. Millsy sat alone, rocking in a chair by the front doors, looking like she was lulling herself into a quick nap.

"Millsy!" I yelled. "You awake?"

"How are you?" she startled and laughed.

"I'm good. I have never eaten here before." I leaned in for a hug.

"What? Really?!" she answered. "We eat at this place all the time. They have everything."

Indeed, the market boasted *everything*. Restaurants and random food stands were packed in like a jamboree, as far as the eye could see, peddling candies and breads and lunches and honey and jams and ice cream and crab cakes and all foods fried.

"Let's save this table." Millsy set a notebook and pen onto the twelve-person table. "I'll meet you back here after we grab our food."

I wandered from restaurant stand to restaurant stand, looking for a meal without meat.

"Heath!" Henrietta yelled. "It's good to see you." We hugged.

"I can't believe we have never eaten here before?!" I repeated.

I set my tray in the middle of the twelve-top table and took my seat. There were seven women, five of whom were attorneys. Everyone has lived in this area their entire lives outside of time at university and law school. The conversation was lively and loud, and elderly white people sitting at other tables were consistently glaring in our direction. No one at our table seemed to mind much. I had been meeting regularly for lunch with some version of this group for almost four months.

"Do you enjoy hanging out with all these women all the time?" Annie, Henrietta's mother, asked, laughing and looking at the people at the other tables who were looking at us.

"Yes, of course I do," I laughed. "It's great. I don't get to listen in on conversations like this anywhere else."

"Really?" Annie asked. "You really want to sit here and listen to our conversations?"

"Really," I said. "And yes. I mean, pretty much everyone around this table has experiences and stories that are super relevant to what I am here to study, but it's also just as much the case that, given the jokes and enjoyment, I would come and hang out even if the conversations weren't relevant to my research," I answered.

". . . but that *is* racial profiling!" Henrietta replied to Millsy. Annie and I tuned in to the unfolding conversation.

"*How* is that racial profiling?! They found drugs on him?" Millsy pushed back. "The police were able to identify someone because they were doing their jobs well. If anything, your case is the perfect example of racial profiling actually doing what it's supposed to do!"

"Look—" Henrietta turned to me. "I have this client I am defending right now, who was riding home on his bicycle, not doing anything illegal, and—"

"Mmm," Millsy interjected. "He had just left a known drug house."

"*Not* doing anything illegal," Henrietta emphasized again, "when the police pulled him over on his bicycle, made him get off, and then patted him down. It was an entirely illegal search, from the beginning to the end."

"Patted him down before finding *drugs* on him," Millsy emphasized again.

"Yeah, I got that part," I replied. "They found drugs on him after they illegally patted him down."

"How are you going to defend an illegal search like that, Mills?" Henrietta turned back to Millsy.

"Seriously!" Lyn jumped in. "If this was your case, Millsy, if *you* were defending some wealthy white person who was illegally pulled over and then his car was searched, before officers found drugs on him, I know you would be singing a different tune." She sided with Henrietta.

This is not surprising since Lyn and Henrietta are both public defenders who work in the same office. Millsy is a private attorney and a part-time prosecuting attorney.

"How are you gonna act like arresting someone with drugs is not an example of good profiling?" Millsy refused to budge.

"Good profiling?" Henrietta pushed back. "Not according to the Constitution. It doesn't matter what he had on him. He is protected from unlawful search and seizure. So, they needed to prove reasonable suspicion, which they did not, or they needed to obtain a warrant, which they did not, before pulling him off his damn bicycle and searching him."

"He was breaking the law," Millsy repeated.

"OK," Henrietta scoffed. "So, that's how it is? You think officers should just be allowed to pull over and search any person they want, whenever they want, based on nothing more than whatever racist hunch they have at the moment?"

"No, but I think if we expect police officers to do their jobs, we need to assume they are *good* at doing their jobs, that they spend enough time watching and surveilling people and neighborhoods and houses to know what's going on and who is doing what." Millsy continued to stand firm on the side of supporting police officers using racial profiling. "That's the system we have, for better and for worse, and that's the system we have to work within."

"That's the system *you* have to work within." Henrietta raised her voice slightly. "I don't assume officers are *ever* doing their jobs well or correctly or with*in* the laws." Lyn was nodding in approval. "And I'm trying to change the system, because the system is *bull*shit."

"Standing outside the system, throwing rocks, yelling, and all that is *never* gonna change the system for the better." Millsy shrugged, cool and confident.

"Who is standing outside the system?" Henrietta snapped back. "I am more Malcolm than Martin, that's true, so I don't have *any* loyalties to an antiblack 'justice' system like the one of the United States. But I am trying to help people who are caught up in the system *and*, at the same time, I am trying to change the system to be better."

"What do you think?!" Lyn turned to me.

"Who me?" I replied, like a guilty person on the stand, laughing. "Oh, well, I like to hear y'all speak as legal experts who live here, who work in town. My opinion doesn't really matter all that much."

"It does to me!" Henrietta retorted. "It matters to *me* what *you* think."

"Well, I don't think police departments should exist." I hesitated. "Or prisons. Just period. So, of course, I do not think officers should be allowed to racially profile residents, no matter what they allegedly found on them . . . or planted on them. I'm not interested in any idea or program that gives any more power over to individual police officers. How can you be sure the officers didn't plant the drugs on the person they pulled over, Millsy? Officers are not exactly good neighbors or contributing members of the community. They are mostly power-hungry dudes on power trips who consistently abuse residents and operate like a crime syndicate, except with less accountability. And I think most people intuitively know that to be true, even if they won't say it out loud. Princeton, where I live when I'm not here, is every bit as overpoliced as this place, but the officers ride around in blacked-out vehicles and spend most of their time pulling over nonwhite motorists at the two edges of town. But Princeton's police department is just as invested in racial profiling as any other police department, this place included . . . probably more invested. It's only that white residents of Princeton hide their commitment to racism and segregation behind their liberal yard signs advertising that everyone is welcome and no one is illegal and science is real and blah, blah, blah. From my perspective, what's needed isn't better policing. There is no such thing. Or, if there is, how about some evidence? Isn't that what police and lawyers are all about? Evidence? Where's the evidence that policing can be anything other than what it is? From my perspective, what's needed—not just here but everywhere—is a new vision for how we might live collectively on this earth. Claiming we need better policing is like arguing that the eighteenth century only needed better plantation owners and slave patrollers. No. What's needed is people with better visions of and for the world." I stopped and everyone was staring at me. The only thing missing was an awkward cough from someone at another table.

"See," Henrietta thumbed at me. "Heath gets it."

"You don't think police departments should exist?!" Millsy leaned in while belly laughing. "So, well, what are we supposed to do? You've been hanging around this town long enough to know there are bad people here who actually need to be locked up."

"Yeah, most of the leadership needs to be locked up, from what I have seen," I continued. "Residents don't need more people locked up. They need all kinds of other things. But since this place is structured to prohibit access to the most basic of needs for a great majority of the population, their attempts at satisfying those needs often produce entanglements with police officers. Because what is the evidence that more policing and more prisons improve a town or a state? Or, how about improving a person's life? Do you have any, Millsy? To me, the assumption that policing and prisons are necessary is just that: an assumption. What is the evidence for that assumption? Y'all are the lawyers. You tell me? Give me one example where militarizing the police force produced a healthier and more robust community."

"You were steady prepared for that answer!" Millsy laughed. "Talking about evidence."

Everyone else laughed. The lunch conversation moved on. Arguing about abolition. Talking about shopping. Rehashing the most recent episode of *Power*. Poking fun at Annie's new hair style. The lunch winded down, and everyone hugged and exited. I was always sad to depart from these gatherings.

"Do you want to walk around with Lyn and I before we leave?" Henrietta asked.

"I'd love to!"

The Amish market was still hustling and bustling, with vendors vending all manner of goods. I had already spent a lot of time conversing with Henrietta, but I was talking more in depth with Lyn for the first time. We walked slowly, picking and teasing at random items around the market.

"I love honey." Lyn held up a jar of yellowy, golden, lava-like paste. "My girlfriend loves honey, too. I should get her this as a surprise."

"I bet this honey is super delicious," I agreed.

"Did Henrietta tell you what's up?" Lyn turned awkwardly to me. "Like, did she tell you what's going on with my situation? Or why I have been gone the last few times we had lunch? Why I haven't been able to meet up with you one-on-one?"

"No." I stopped to meet Lyn's eyes. "What's up? I had no idea anything was wrong."

We walked away from the homemade honey stand and continued meandering, fiddling with trinkets and putting them down. Lyn bought us three oversized cookies.

"I told my parents I am gay." She stared at me.

"OK," I responded. "Thank you so much for the cookie, by the way. And, from the sounds of it, that conversation with your parents did not go well?"

"Like I expected. Not too great." Lyn looked away.

"Damn," I replied. "I'm really sorry. Your parents told you that they have a problem? Or that—"

"Uhh, yeah." Lyn looked around again and lowered her voice. Henrietta leaned in closer. "In a big way. They told me they didn't want me coming around the house anymore. Not for holidays. Not for Sunday lunches. Nothing. I'm a grown-ass woman. My girlfriend is also a professional in this town. They talked down to me like I was a kid, like I was a kid who would be eternally judged in hell. They said they don't want to see me as long as I'm 'living in sin.' And that was basically that."

"Oh my god," I said. "I'm so sorry. Not that there's anything I can do, but if there is anything I can ever do, obviously, please just let me know."

"Thank you." Lyn looked at me. "Yeah, I really appreciate that. Thank you. Just to hear someone say something as basic as that is actually comforting. But that's not really the news I wanted to share with you."

"Oh, OK?" I replied.

"I just can't handle being here anymore." Lyn looked back down to the floor. "Living in this place and not being able to see my family anymore, not being able to go to my church anymore, I just can't stay here. I accepted a job with ICE, as a defender for incarcerated youth, down in Texas. I'm moving in two months. I've already put my notice in at the defender's office and found an apartment."

"What?! Seriously?" I was shocked.

"Can you believe that?" Henrietta said in deep sadness. I felt how hard she was taking this news.

"Wow. No, I can't believe it. It's really strange to think about. So, you're going to be working for . . . ICE? As in, ICE, ICE?"

"Yeah," Lyn replied, managing a half-smile. "I will still be defending minors, like I do now . . . just not here, not in my hometown. Plus, I've basically been here forever, except for college and law school, and so it will be nice to experience what it's like to live somewhere else."

"Gives me a place to visit in . . . *Tex*as, I guess," Henrietta laughed.

When Henrietta, Lyn, Millsy, and others gathered for lunch or dinner or drinks, a different kind of rhythm emerged and enveloped those who were present. Like the people at the Spot, or the teenagers in the nurse's office, or Mr. Cantale's family, the collective effervescence produced by people who were committed to building meaningful relationships broke open a different beat. The other guests at the Amish market were not staring at our table because we were being all that noisy. They were staring because people who are laughing, debating, and carrying on in public is a rare occurrence. And, so, a table of people doing that was a compelling scene to want to enter into. I think if we had stayed long enough, a few other diners would have slowly made their way to the side and joined in.

The debate between Henrietta and Millsy that unfolded tunes us into an important lesson regarding the primary factor that was predictive of a person's opinions on policing: proximity. Race, class, and gender categories are rarely predictive of a person's views on policing or the prisons. But proximity was seldom wrong. People who were abstracted from the daily practices of policing (owner and professional classes) were almost uniformly supportive of policing. People who were connected to the work of policing were divided: those whose jobs were dependent on policing (prosecutors, judges, prison employees, politicians) defended it as necessary and mostly good. Those whose daily activities and work were targeted by policing (black and brown residents, poor residents, people without US citizenship, public defenders who represented these categories of people) often viewed policing as violent, unaccountable, reckless, and brutal. The conversation between Henrietta and Millsy casts a spotlight on the difficulty in finding common ground between residents who live in different proximities to policing. Being targeted by police significantly changes the way a person is able to experience life in a place.

Henrietta's and Lyn's work defending residents, though, is not aimed at abolishing the police departments or at changing state and federal legislation. Their daily work, which required them to stand shoulder to shoulder with and defend residents who were primary targets, shaped their understanding of policing and the prisons they filled. Both understood that changes to state and federal policies do very little to alter the actions of police officers on the ground. Millsy spent a lot of time arguing for technologies like body cameras or institutional practices like civilian review boards (this part of the conversation was not included)—technological modifications that have no evidence of bringing about so-called positive change, aside from the dramatic increase to police budgets.[1] Instead, the disconnect between legislative impact and a person's experiences on the ground is similar to what Lyn experienced when she told her family that she was gay, which happened only a few months after the Equality Act of 2015. Politicians passing federal legislation that is designed to establish marriage equality has very little bearing on what it means or feels like to live, work, and build relationships in a place like Cumberland County. It was not federal policy but meaningful relationships with Henrietta, Millsy, and others that supported Lyn and provided her with the love, care, and friendship that she needed as her own family and Christian faith community cast her out. And it was this commitment to relation-building, I knew, that Lyn would carry to ICE in Texas, as she took up the mantle of standing shoulder to shoulder with minors who were targeted by the vicious practices of border policing.

CHAPTER SIXTEEN

THE SPOT IS AN ALTERNATIVE SPACE

I arrived at the Spot much earlier than usual, just before lunchtime. I forgot my rain jacket at home, and the sky was pouring buckets. I ran from my car and ripped through the front door like a soaked cat.

"My man!" Shakes's voice boomed, laughing at me. "Getting wet out there, huh? I'm heading out to grab some fish sandwiches from down the way . . . do you want one?"

"Oh yeah," I replied. "Do you want me to take your order so that I can go and grab the sandwiches while you stay here to keep the store open?"

"Nah, man," Shakes said. "How about you stay here and run the store while I grab the sandwiches?"

"You want me to run the store?" I asked. "By myself?"

"For starters, you aren't alone," Shakes replied, the way a seasoned coach might encourage a bench player who was entering the game for the first time. "Timmy [Big Tim] is across the street. And second, you have been in here more than anyone else but me. It's about time you start paying your dues," he laughed. "But seriously, you watch how I treat customers, when I offer deals and discounts, and, plus, I'll be back in no time, you won't even have a single customer during this time of the day—especially with the weather like this!" he assured me, already walking out the door, which *dinged* as the sales floor became empty with quiet. I had never been in the shop alone.

I dragged a chair next to the register, since it felt odd to sit behind it, plopped down, and began scrolling through my phone.

16.1 Photo of the Spot after Shakes left me to run the store on my own for the first time.

The door *dinged*. A person entered and shot me a surprised look.

"How much are your XL jeans?"

"Our . . . well—" I fumbled.

"Where is Shakes?" the person asked.

"He just ran out." I considered texting him. "But he'll be back in a few minutes . . ."

The door *dinged*. Another person walked in.

"Hi, I'm looking for socks. Can you—"

The door *dinged*. A third person walked in.

Not a single item in the store had any price tags. Shakes had memorized each item's cost and then adjusted a selling price in real time, depending on who was purchasing. I told the three customers that I needed to grab something from the storage room. I raced to the back of the store, ducked behind a stack of boxes, and sent Shakes a panicked text. One customer followed me.

"When will Shakes be back in?" the person asked again.

"Umm." I looked down at my watch, even though I was not wearing a watch. "He should be back in about fifteen minutes . . . at the most."

"OK, I'll just come back later. Tell him I stopped by." The door *dinged*. They were gone.

"Wait, what is your name . . . ?"

The door *dinged*. Another person walked in. Is this a joke? Over the last two years, I had never once seen more than two customers shopping at the same time (of course, lots of people regularly spent time hanging out together, but nobody was purchasing anything).

"Do you have these in an eleven and a half?" The second customer held a shoe before me.

"Umm, let me check . . . one second," I answered.

The door *dinged*. I jerked my head around. I was ready to lock the front door.

"Cynthia, let me help you with that." Shakes smiled. "What size would you like these in?"

He handled the customers, answered all the questions, ran to the back, and gave a couple of hefty discounts. I took the money and bagged the items at the register.

"You know what," Shakes told one person, "those pants are actually going on sale next week, but I can go ahead and give you 15 percent off right now."

"That's great," she smiled. "Tom can never find pants around here that fit him."

"Well, we always carry big and large sizes," Shakes reassured her.

The store emptied. Shakes placed the Styrofoam container of fried fish and white bread on a stool between us. We both dumped hot sauce on top and smashed.

"How much do I owe you for lunch?" I asked.

"Mannn, please," Shakes answered. "Just eat."

"Thank you," I replied. "You don't have to—"

"Man, I know I don't *have to*. I want to."

"Thank you. I really appreciate it."

"You're welcome," Shakes chewed.

"That was wild, man," I laughed. "Right after you left the store, like, a hundred people showed up wanting to spend money, wanting to ask questions I had no answers to. I'm just glad I didn't mess anything up."

"Man, look. I want to surround myself with good people." Shakes paused his chewing and took a slightly more serious tone. "I'm trying to get up out of this place of always being in some kind of state of emergency, you know? Like, it's always something—a bill, a friend going to jail, a parent dying, a kid needing money, whatever. You have been a good friend to me and, you know, I want to surround myself with people like you, like Doughboy, like Earl, because I'm trying to do something here. And I've been meaning to tell you: grab those shoes you've been eyeing over there. They're on me."

"What?! No!" I protested. "No way. I will buy them. I want to support your store—"

"Man, why not?!" Shakes retorted. "If I say I want to give you a pair of shoes, and I own the store, then that means I can give you a pair of shoes." I had hurt his feelings by initially rejecting the gift.

"Thank you," I replied. "I didn't mean to, well, you know, I'm not very good at receiving gifts from people. But thank you so much. I don't really know what to say."

"You don't have to say anything." He gathered the empty Styrofoam and hot sauce packets into a pile to throw away in the dumpster behind the building.

The door *dinged*. Doughboy entered, already halfway through a story.

"MY MAN!" Shakes yelled from the back of the store.

"Trying to get these purses stitched up before tomorrow!" Doughboy yelled, dragging a chair to the corner and dumping a mess of unstitched purses onto the floor.

I dragged my chair to his corner, unwrapped a purse, and began stitching—down, through, up, around, and back—trying to copy his motions.

"Tell me if I do anything wrong," I said.

"Yeah, you have to get the stitches right or the purse won't look right," he replied. "It's the most important part." He corrected me and went back to his own purse.

"I'm all thumbs," I fiddled.

"It takes time," he laughed. "So, I read your paper," he said, looking down at a purse and stitching in rhythm. "I wanted to talk to you

16.2 A shoe display in the Spot.

about it a few weeks ago, but this is the first we've overlapped when it was quiet."

Shakes clicked on a large boom box to a radio station with a gospel/ R&B mix.

"You did?!" I stopped stitching. "Wow. Which one? I think you're the first person around here to read one of my articles," I laughed. "So, what did you think?"

"It was on point, man." He stopped stitching. "I read the white supremacy one.[1] I really liked it. What does white supremacy feel like? It's an interesting approach to that, man."

"Thanks. I appreciate you reading it." I was no longer pretending to stitch. "Do you want me to keep doing this? I feel like I am fucking up your inventory."

"Yeah, I really dug it. But I didn't read your article for you," he laughed. "You don't have to thank me. I read it to make sure you are cool, to make sure you are who you say you are. So, now that I get what you're about when you write, tell me more about your personal life. You got any siblings?"

"Two. A younger brother and a younger sister."

"And what about your parents?"

"Yeah, a few of those, too," I laughed. "Both of my biological parents are remarried, and—"

"HE DON'T SPEAK TO HIS FATHER," Shakes yelled from the back. "He ain't spoken to him in years," he added, carrying a wobbly stack of shoe boxes to the front.

"You don't?" Doughboy paused, mid-stitch. "Why not?"

"Not really, no." I was white-knuckling the unstitched purse in my hand. "We never really got along, ummm, since for as long as I can remember."

"Do you hate him?" Doughboy continued stitching, methodically, rhythmically, pacing his stitching to his questioning. "Do you forgive him?"

"Hmm, well, no, I don't hate him," I replied. "But I'm not that interested in some kind of abstract forgiveness or whatever that even means."

"Why do you want to hold onto this, though?" He was not dropping it.

"I am not holding onto it!" I snapped. "Staying in a relationship with someone just because they are biologically related to me would be holding on."

"OK, man." Doughboy stopped. "I just don't want you to hold onto something like that. Anyways, it's cool. We don't have to talk about it. What does your brother do? How old is he?"

"He's, ummmm, thirty-one? Yeah, thirty-one," I laughed. "I have a hard time remembering my own age, much less my siblings'. He coordinates shipments for this huge trucking business in the town we grew up in."

"In Indiana? What is it, Marion you said, right?"

"Yeah, Marion."

"And where did you do your research for the paper that I read . . . Hamilton?"

"Huntington. Huntington, Indiana."

"Right, right." Stitching. "And what about your sister?"

"She's a social studies teacher at a public high school, also in Indiana— in a school for students who have been kicked out of their home school so many times that her school is their last stop. They leave her school and go back to their home high school or they leave her school and go to juvie."

"Wait, and you're how old?"

"I'm thirty-five."

"So, you're the oldest sibling? You've been in school a long time, huh?" he laughed at me. "Your younger siblings are already working their careers and you're still in college?!"

Shakes laughed loudly from the register. "Man, that's COLD!"

"Are you close with your siblings?" Doughboy went on.

"Hey," I laughed along. "I took a longer route. I flunked out of college on my first try. Moved to Colorado. Moved back to Indiana to work in an automobile factory. I demolitioned houses for a few slumlords in my hometown. I was learning other kinds of shit—nonacademic shit, you know?!"

"OK, OK." Doughboy smoothed the conversation with both hands in the air, like a person calming an upset horse. "You flunked out and now you're in Princeton. I get it."

"Life is weird," I laughed.

"And, you're close with your siblings?" Doughboy continued.

"Yep, we are all close," I answered. "Also really close with my mom and stepdad."

"What does your mom do?"

Shakes dragged his folding chair past us. The door *dinged*. He plopped down to smoke.

"She works in a mental healthcare hospital in Muncie, Indiana."

"And your stepdad?"

"He's an economics teacher where I graduated from," I replied. "Marion High School."

"OK." He dropped his purse to the floor. "Let's go outside with Shakes. I wanna show you something else."

"Yep," I replied. Anything to get out of stitching. I laid the purse I was pretending to stitch onto the chair. Two stitches completed and roughly a million to go. "This post-rain air is warm. It's nice."

"Man . . ." Shakes breathed deeply. "Sure is."

Doughboy was already twenty feet down the sidewalk, sliding his minivan's door fully open. I followed and stuck my head inside to find him sitting on the middle row bench, wearing a pair of sunglasses.

"Now, look here. This is a case of Ray-Bans that look like yours, the Wayfarers." He opened a pair and handed them to me. "This one over here is full of aviators. The next time you want to buy a pair, just let me know and I'll hook you up."

"Thanks, man." I tried them on and handed them back.

He unfurled a collection of purses, wallets, sunglasses, and even a line of men's denim. When he lost a steady factory job of eleven years, the one his brother's close friend had secured for him, he had to figure something else out. He had spent a decade behind bars before working in the factory, but his options remained limited because he still carried a list of felony charges. At that time, he began selling various clothing items out of his van and, according to him, had "not missed a beat." He stepped out, swooshed the door closed, and we joined Shakes under the awning.

"Hello, fellas," Earl greeted us, crossing the street from his pickup truck. His black goatee has piercing white stripes like a skunk's back, and he always wore wraparound sunglasses. He never smoked, and he never swore. But he came around often to gab.

"My man!" Shakes greeted.

"Now, where did you say you travel here from, Heath?" Earl asked.

"He's down here from Princeton!" Shakes answered.

"Princeton?!" Earl was shocked. "Wow. Things must be getting *really* bad around here?" He laughed, repeating almost exactly what Herc had said in a previous conversation. "You know it's not right when they have to send Princeton kids to try and figure this place out!"

Everyone laughed. Learning that I was from Princeton conjured predictable reactions. People with professional jobs wanted to treat me to dinner. People with policing or corrections jobs became suspicious. Pretty much everyone else responded with a combination of amusement, curiosity, what-the-fuckness, or sometimes, like Earl, acknowledgment of the wider social, economic, and political dynamics at work. Namely, Princeton is the kind of place that ships privileged kids around the world to document so-called problems like "violence" or "inequity" or "racism" or, even better, to found NGOs.

"Y'all hear about Will?" Doughboy asked.

"Hear about what?" Earl asked.

"Yeah, he got roughed up by the police last week, just past midnight. They left him bleeding out on the sidewalk," Shakes answered. "Just left him lying there in the middle of the night."

"Did he get into any trouble? Did anything happen to him?" Earl asked.

"Nah, man," Shakes answered. "They only put some hands and feet on him and moved on. Nothing happened."

Police officers in this area terrorize residents so regularly and so intensely that when someone says "nothing happened" it can mean that police officers "only" physically hurt a person and left them bleeding on the sidewalk.

"Man, did you see they got Malik just *last* week?" Shakes exhaled his cigarette.

"What?" Earl replied. "Nooo. You mean Joe's son, Malik? No. No. No."

"Yuup," Shakes answered.

"Who is Malik? And Joe?" I asked.

"Joe's older son, Abdur, was murdered last year, a few months before you came around. The investigation turned up zero leads. Abdur was turning thirty-five the following week." Shakes scratched his chin. "Just your age. It ain't right."

"Living fast," Doughboy shook his head.

"But Malik is the younger boy, Joe's younger boy," Shakes said to Doughboy. "And he can't be more than twenty-five. He was the one arrested on a murder charge, and they're trying to hang three more on him. They set his bail at half a mill, to be paid in full. Claiming he was out for revenge for his brother's murder. Man, he's a good kid, deep down. I just wanna help him out."

"He ain't never seeing the light of day again," Doughboy lamented.

"Nope," Shakes exhaled. "Now that they have him on this one charge, it will be easier to 'solve' a bunch of unresolved murders by hanging all of them on him. Happens all the time."

When a person is charged with a crime, especially when the person is young, the impact extends far beyond the immediate family. Shakes, Doughboy, and Earl expressed a collective sorrow for their friend's son. They were angry thinking about him sitting in prison for the rest of his life. I became angry, too.

"Whatchu been up to today?" Doughboy asked Earl.

The murder charge hung foul in the air.

"Finishing up this job for Ms. Reems. Fixing her cabinets and plumbing in the kitchen and bathroom. Man, I'm busier now than before I retired." Earl obsessively combed down on his goatee with all five fingers.

"You got more work now?" I asked. "Who are you working for?"

"No one," Earl smiled. "Retirement means just that. I take the jobs I want to take. I quit when I want to quit. I started a little LLC, but it makes it harder to compete when the Mexicans are here and not paying any taxes. I'm not against nobody coming to this country to earn a living. I'm all for it. But do it even with the rest of us is all I'm sayin'."

"You know that's right." Shakes rubbed his hands.

The wider region had a growing population of residents that had moved in from Mexico and Central and South America.

"This time of year always has me thinking about Bump, though, man." Earl's neck muscles tensed.

Shakes tapped another Newport into his hand. "Yeah, man. Me, too."

"I remember old Bump walking around, steady pulling a knot of cash from his pocket big enough to choke a horse," he laughed, miming the knot of cash. "I'd say to him, 'Bump, you can't be flashing *no* knot like that . . . not around here!' But he didn't care."

"Man, I miss him every day," Shakes laughed.

"Who is Bump?" I asked.

The group silenced and turned to me.

"Man, Bump is why I started this shop," Shakes began. "Everything here is a testament to him and what he did for me, what he taught me."

"I just remember those parties, man," Doughboy said.

"Bump was murdered about six years ago," Shakes continued. "No witnesses. No leads. The investigation turned up nothing . . ."

"Seems to be a theme around here," I said, biting my disgust at the all-too-familiar story.

"He was found in his apartment, face down, both hands zip-tied behind his back, and the cash still in the house . . . still in his wallet! The groceries were standing upright in the trunk of his car," Shakes exhaled.

"What?!" I nearly yelled. "Why were his hands zip-tied?"

"There was foul play somewhere," Shakes replied. "Someone with some kind of something didn't want him alive."

"It ain't right." Earl rubbed his goatee. "It ain't right."

"Bump gave me a job when no one else would," Shakes continued. "After the Wawa rejection, I was depressed. So, I went to him just to ask for advice on how he recovered, how he turned things around after prison, and he hired me right there on the spot. For ten years I worked at Bump's spot, just around the corner . . ." he trailed off.

"Just around the corner from where?" I asked.

"Right here, man." Shakes pointed around the corner of the closest block to our right. "His store was just like five stores down from this one, just around that corner." He was pointing.

"I can still hear his voice," Earl said.

"Man, I went to work early in the morning, like usual, with my coffee and my sandwich in hand, and there was yellow police tape all around the store, with police cars crammed all over the block, and Bump's wife was there . . ." Shakes told the story slowly and with long pauses.

"Maggie was there? That morning?" Earl asked.

"I didn't ever trust Maggie," Doughboy shook his head. "She was always after his money, I thought. I told him. But . . ."

"You know, she came around here one day," Shakes started back up. "Shortly after I opened this store, asking for money so she could get a fix. Mannn, all that money that he left her, and she was run dry in a year. It's not right."

"This town is too small for someone not to know what happened," Earl pondered.

"So," Shakes began again, "I hopped out of my car, and no one would talk to me or tell me anything, so I got back in and drove to his house. More yellow tape. But a few friends were standing around outside, and I knew it before they told me. All that store, all the merchandise, the shelving, the cases, everything, man, ev-ery-thing was just gotten rid of. I started this store in honor of him. Had to start from scratch. But everything I learned from him I used to build this store. I worked at Burger King for eighteen months saving up," Shakes intensified. "Can you imagine that? A grown-ass man flipping burgers at Burger King? But . . ."

"You were determined!" Doughboy helped to turn the painful memory into a testament of hard work and the significance of supportive and caring relationships.

"I paid rent on this building for almost a year before I could afford to open the shop," Shakes said proudly, making his arms into a Y. "Flipping burgers and saving money, buying a stock of merchandise. 'Faith does not make it easy; it makes it possible.'" He often liked to riff on the first chapter of Joshua in the Judeo-Christian Bible.

"Mmm, mmm," Doughboy agreed. "Makes ANYthing possible."

"Yes, sir," Earl agreed, combing his goatee.

The Spot is more than an alternative rhythm that opens up a space to the side. It is also a living memorial, like Mrs. Taylor's flower garden, where the voices of the prematurely dead continue speaking to those who listen. Bump had provided safe and stable ground for Shakes after his felony charges. He also imparted to him a set of practical skills for running a successful clothing store in the area. Following his death, Shakes was lost and confused about what he should or could do next. The relationship that had supported him, that had mentored him into another way to live and relate and work, that had held him tight when everything in his life loosened and spun out of control, was snuffed from this world like a candle on a cold night. But in the whispers of a warm wind, Shakes soon learned how to tune into the timbre of Bump's familiar and unwavering voice. The others also heard his voice. Sometimes I thought maybe I heard it through them. Learning to listen for his voice, though, did not begin and end with that single relationship. The lessons learned from his voice produced the Spot, and extended the practices of listening, the commitment to care, support, and love to all those who gathered there.

In this way, the everyday practices of the Spot multiplied the reach of interdependent values and efforts beyond the singular category of resource distribution. Interdependence encompasses a wide range of practices of sharing. Sharing grief over Joe's sons—one murdered and one charged with murder—channeled a collective lamentation over the missed opportunity to help them, to bring them into the protections and support of the Spot, where they might have been less available to the clamping jaws of confinement. Shakes sharing his own sales floor with Doughboy removed any potential obstacle of competition that could grow between their businesses, and it also created a de facto community during his workday. Sharing fish and bread got me fed, of course, but it also strengthened and deepened the bond between us as we dreamed and chatted and laughed. Shakes had learned from Bump how to convert the tools and trash of confinement that divided, isolated, and destabilized life into connective tissues that forged horizontal bonds of love, care, and support. Interdependence enabled people to keep bread in their pockets and in their bellies, it invited people into resilient, challenging, and honest relationships, and it allowed numerous people who were vulnerable to be less available to the devastating outcomes of the system of confinement.[2]

With this perspective of the culture of the Spot, my somewhat uncomfortable conversation with Doughboy suggested more than the simple niceties of learning another person's work and family history or trying to understand their political orientation. Doughboy wanted to understand my most intimate and long-term relationships, how I tended to them across time and distance, who I relied upon and who relied upon me, and the kinds of values that informed and maintained these connections with others. It was more than resource distribution, more than just having money in my pocket to share, as Herc had discussed in an earlier conversation. It was a targeted probing to discover whether or not I was capable of and prepared to enter into interdependent relationships with others who wanted the same. This is the philosophy for collective life that people at the Spot were working so hard to cultivate. This is starkly different from someone like Old Man Tilley, for example, whose life was made possible by his family's possession of land and resources across time. Doughboy's life was made possible through values and relationships that crisscrossed the boundaries between life and death, between formerly incarcerated and locked up, between being fed and being hungry. His life was an outcome of and a testament to the interdependent relationships that both preceded and surrounded him, as well as those that would most certainly follow. The Spot harbored, fostered, and grew these kinds of interdependent relationships and, in a sense, harmonized them into new rhythms that did not reproduce the familiar beat of confinement.

HENRIETTA & ANNIE
FORTY-FIVE MINUTES FROM LIFE

I arrived at Henrietta's house, located on a country road a few miles from the nearest downtown. Three family houses lined a large chunk of land. The winds were warm but howling. I knocked twice.

"C'mon in!" Henrietta yelled from somewhere inside. "Hi, hi!" I entered to find her standing over the stove, stirring, moving, smelling, tasting. "I'm just getting this chicken ready."

"It smells delicious," I said as we hugged. "How is everything?"

"It's fine. I'm just in this fight with a prosecutor," Henrietta began, as if already in mid-argument.

"Like usual, I guess?" I replied.

"Yes." Henrietta turned from the chicken. "And they are trying to force my client into a *plea bargain* . . ." She pointed at me with her wooden spoon, speaking rapid-fire technicalities about legal defense. "Because she knows he will feel like he's better off signing and not taking the case to court, given all his priors. It's total bullshit." She turned back to the stove. "Gracie . . . GrACIE!" she hollered into a distant room. "Come in here and say hello to Mr. Heath." South New Jersey has a distinctly southern feel to me, especially when it comes to titles and manners, and most residents view their region as the rural south to the industrialism and elitism of the northern parts of the state. This sunk in over time but is best exemplified by a snatch of conversation I once overheard between two residents walking into a restaurant: "Yeah, well, that's because this isn't like North Jersey. Around here, people are kind and polite to you no matter how they actually feel about you [laughter]. In the north, they just say 'Fuck you' if they are thinking 'Fuck you' [laughter]."

"Hi, Gracie. It's very nice to meet you." I leaned down to shake hands.

"Mom, can I go back and watch TV now?" Gracie whispered to Henrietta.

The front door swung wide open. A person I had not met pushed Henrietta's grandma's wheelchair from the porch into the entryway.

Henrietta introduced us. "Hey, Grandma. You remember Mr. Heath."

"Hello, Grandma." I leaned down. "It's so nice to meet you."

"Remember, I told you he has been hanging out with Shakes at the store, Grandma, since he started doing research here last year," Henrietta was yelling. Grandma strained to hear.

"He's what?" she asked, in a whisper.

Henrietta leaned closer. "He's doing RE-SEARCH about the PRI-SONS."

"It's so nice to meet you," Grandma hushed, pulling me down and hugging my neck.

The front door swung wide open again.

"Hey, Uncle, this is Heath," Henrietta introduced. "And he's doing research here on prisons and things like that . . ."

"Hi, it's nice to meet—" I stretched my hand out.

"Do you play Ping-Pong?" Uncle asked, fist-bumping my open hand.

"Do I play Ping-Pong?" I repeated. "Yeah, I mean, I—"

"Yeah?!" He paused. "You do? Well, are you any good?"

"I'm OK. I don't know what your definition of 'good' is." I was laughing and he was not.

"Fifty cents a game, next door, if you wanna come over." He was halfway out the door.

"Not sure, since I have to drive back home tonight and, usually, I don't really gamble, especially on my Ping-Pong skills," I laughed.

"We will be next door if you change your mind." The front door closed.

"So, most of the family lives right around here?" I turned to Henrietta.

"We have always believed owning land is the best way to assure the family will be OK. We've been on this land for almost one hundred years. We have another forty-five acres about ten minutes from here, too."

"Wow," I replied. "That's a lot of land."

The door swung open and Annie, Henrietta's mom, walked in. "Hi, Heath! How are you doing today?"

"I'm good." I stood for a hug. "Excited to finally eat dinner at home with y'all!"

"I hope you like it." Annie walked to the oven and nudged Henrietta out of the way with her hip, grabbing a glass dish. "I wanted to make something special, so I soaked the chicken in peaches all day."

"Peaches?!" I asked. "I've never heard of that."

"Me neither," Annie laughed. "Hopefully it's edible!"

"I was just getting ready to tell Heath about Gracie's father," Henrietta cut in.

"OK," Annie said. "So, what have you learned so far for your book?"

"Well, if I tell you what I have learned—" I was already laughing. "Then you won't have any reason to buy the book!"

Annie laughed. "Do you think you'll actually write a book? About us? About this place? I mean, you think there will actually *be* a book?"

"Oh, well, definitely there will be a dissertation," I laughed. "And if I happen to get a university job, then writing a book is the only way to get tenure and keep that job. But who knows if I will get a job?"

"But you're at Princeton!" Annie replied. "It must be so easy to get a job when you graduate from a school like that."

"Yeah, if you want to work in tech or finance, but not necessarily if you want to work in a university. I mean," I continued, "it's true, it's definitely an advantage to hold an Ivy League degree, but it's very far from a guarantee in any way."

"Where did your parents go to college?" Annie asked.

"Mine?" I asked. "Neither of my biological parents went to college. My stepdad did. He's a high school teacher."

"Really?!" Annie's eyes grew wide. "Where are you from again?"

"I'm from Indiana . . . a place that feels not so different from here, actually. I called my mom after the first time visiting and told her, 'You won't believe how similar this place is to Marion,' and after all this time, I still think that."

"Really?" Annie repeated.

"The reason I wanted you to come over here for dinner tonight," Henrietta cut in again, "is because I wanted you to be here when Gracie's father calls from prison. He calls every Wednesday, so I thought it might be cool if you talked to him when he calls tonight."

"Gracie's father is in prison?" I had no idea. But after almost twelve straight hours of work, talking to a parent who is hoping to speak with his daughter did not sound like a good idea for either one of us.

"He had problems when he was younger," Henrietta began. "He was arrested for homicide, and initially the plea deal was for five years, which he would have served three to three and a half of, but he wouldn't take the deal because he said he never killed anyone, and he refused to admit to something he didn't do, so he took it to trial and lost. He was sentenced to the max: sixty years," Henrietta replied, speaking so fast I could barely keep up.

"Wow. Holy shit," I responded, for lack of something better to say. "I can't believe he got max from an initial five. God, that's so . . . wow. Sixty years."

"There was, apparently, an anonymous call from an '*articulate* woman,'" Henrietta continued, making scare quotes with her hands, "that supposedly tipped the defense off to evidence of his innocence, that they of course dismissed, and then I was called in and questioned by the prosecutors who were trying the case."

"You were a lawyer already?"

"Yes, and I told them, 'No, it wasn't me. You want my phone records? If I have something to say, I'm going to say it to your face. What?! Am I the only ar-tic-u-late black woman who lives in this place?!' You know what I'm saying?" She turned to me. "See, like, when my brother was murdered, we are still working through all that bitterness, but—"

"Wait," I interjected. "Your brother was murdered?" I stood up from the stool, a bit woozy from the flood of new information about a person I had already spent a lot of time with. I had no idea Henrietta had experienced so many different aspects of the terror produced by the system of confinement, and it shook me.

"Yeah," Henrietta paused. Annie looked down. "He was shot by someone who was trying to shoot someone else in a Burger King parking lot when we were still in high school." Annie exited the room. There was a resounding quiet in the room, like the ringing in your ears after a bullet pops.

"I'm so sorry to hear this," I apologized. "I really don't know what to say. I'm so, so sorry. God what a horrible string of—"

"So, that's another thing I wanted to talk to you about." Henrietta moved on, the wooden spoon lively in her hand. "We've gotta change this town. I've been thinking of joining the local civil rights group [the organization led by David Johnson]." Annie walked back in. "Because it's time to stop sitting around and letting these people destroy the town and everyone in it."

"Why would you join them, though, if you want to change the town?" I asked. "Is it because you think a bunch of corrections officers are interested in ending policing and prisons?!" I clasped my hands over my mouth. "Oh my god. I can't believe I just blurted that out. I'm sorry. I shouldn't have said that. It's been a long day and I am really tired and . . ."

Another quiet settled over the room before Henrietta and Annie exploded in laughter.

"NO!" Henrietta was still laughing. "You *definitely* should have said exactly what you just said. In part, we had you over for dinner to see what you've learned, to see what side you were on, after living here this long. Now we know a little better what you're about. But look, David Johnson's group is what we have, so if good people join, then maybe we can also push for change with*in* first." Henrietta and Annie, like Doughboy and Shakes, did not open up to me until they felt they knew me and what I was about.

"Maybe," I recovered. "But those are some powerful people around New Jersey, fully backed by statewide political parties and fully in bed with the police departments. No one's giving up power easily, I can promise you that. They control the reins of that organization and they plan to maintain that control for many years to come."

"Yeah," Henrietta continued. "So many more people would be involved if there was different leadership." Annie nodded in agreement. "But we all have to come together through our differences and try to build something better. I've been dealing with that bitterness lately inside of *me*. I connected with the man who murdered my brother. He got out of prison last year and contacted me to apologize and ask for forgiveness. After twenty years, I still wasn't ready to forgive him, but after thinking about it and praying about it, I decided building a relationship with him was the right thing to do. Justice, at the time of my brother's murder, for me, was putting a bullet in his head for what he did to my brother. But after time, it changed. I started to believe that I need you and you need me. Until we get to that place of recognition, it will never get better around here. He and I want to start something, so we are going to start meeting for coffee or food regularly, to figure out how to fight this racist criminal justice system."

"Wow," I replied. "I can't believe you are doing that. I really don't know what to say. So, what are you two doing, exactly?"

"Well, it's still very early," Henrietta explained. "And we have not met in person yet. We are still getting to know one another over the phone. We know we want to do something that highlights the problems with the system but, even more importantly, we want to build a group that protects people who are being abused by this system, something that can provide a safe place for people. This place is so isolated from programs like this, and we think with our own personal experiences and expertise, in addition to the unique history of our relationship with one another, that we can draw some attention and then hopefully build something that can help people who are facing this system."

"Yeah, this place is very isolated in certain ways," I agreed. "And your story is *definitely* one that people will want to hear. A story people should hear."

"This part of New Jersey is *so* isolated!" Annie agreed. "When I went away for college, I lived on campus and only came home on random weekends, but even all the way back during *my* time, it started to feel more and more isolated around here. At least we have Philly and DC and other places that are close to get away to, you know, forty-five minutes or so away by car. Whenever you're down here, you are *always* forty-five minutes from life."

Henrietta is fighting against the system of confinement on multiple fronts. Her work as a public defender places her squarely inside the jaws of the system of confinement, standing shoulder to shoulder with people who are facing the potential of time (often significant time) confined in a prison. This means that she regularly works in an oppositional professional position to some of her oldest and closest friends, which, as seen earlier, can sometimes create arguments or even conflict that spills into social life. This is distinct work from what she will do if she and Annie join a civil rights organization to more explicitly plan with others against the system of confinement. She also has learned to balance the difficult space of her family, which has been cut through and in certain ways shattered by various facets or effects of the system of confinement. But the commitment that stands out most prominently is the slow and steady work happening off to the side, where she is reconciling with the person who murdered her brother twenty years earlier.

Like Fred, Shakes, Herc, and Doughboy, Henrietta places extreme value on meaningful and supportive relationships that stretch across time and place. Many of her family members were unhappy that she was connecting with the person who murdered her brother. But she saw this relationship with him as the best way to bring about meaningful change that would last. She identified open community as the best way to protect and support people and to keep them out of the purview of patrolling police officers and a prison sentence. Henrietta came to this conclusion by turning the critical lens onto herself, rooting out her own "bitterness," disconnectedness, and feelings of revenge, which gave her the space to empathize with a person she had hated and even dreamed of killing for two decades—feelings I knew that many other people could understand and relate to. "I need you and you need me" is the core value, the organizing principle that she believes is capable of upending a context that has been perpetually reproduced by systems of confinement—not simply because the person who murdered her brother needs social and economic help and wants forgiveness from her but because she recognizes that she, too, needs connection, needs his friendship, needs his support and care. She, too, needs help in letting go of the bitterness, of redirecting her desire for revenge. Henrietta believes that their relationship will produce interdependent ("I need you and you need me") life for both of them.

Annie's remark about always being "forty-five minutes from life" thus carries multiple meanings within this social and conversational context. Geographically, it means that a person can drive to a bustling city in under an hour. Annie, like many other residents, viewed Philadelphia and DC as places to escape. Of course, this capacity to escape is only applicable for residents who are not incarcerated (and for residents who have automobiles). Within a context produced by confinement, "life" is also a common idiom for receiving a life sentence confined in prison. Many residents live life daily trying to avoid various traps or obstacles that could bring about the possibility of a "life" sentence. And, finally, it could be interpreted as recognition that connecting meaningfully with another person—especially a person whom the system has abused, confined, and then spit out—is life. Any resident who is committed to building meaningful bonds with other people is always close to life, because life is the outcome of interdependent relationality that produces not only friendship but love, care, support, and safety. Life in interdependence is the path through which a context produced by systems of confinement can be remade.

CHAPTER EIGHTEEN

SHAKES & THE PACE OF CONNECTION

I entered the Spot, surprised to find a millennial white man speaking enthusiastically with Shakes. It must have been the same kind of surprise most people felt when they entered to see me running the register. He was peddling a federally subsidized loan program mediated through a local nonprofit that was designed to make credit available to formerly incarcerated people. Shakes qualified to apply since he still carried the felony charges. The loan was presented as a gift that would enable Shakes to stabilize his monthly operating budget and possibly even expand the footprint of his business. There was one catch: he had to come up with a $7,000 down payment in order to secure about $50,000 at very high interest.

"If I had the seven, then I wouldn't need the fifty!" Shakes retorted, swiftly ushering, almost shoving, the nonprofit banker out to the *ding* of the door.

We followed with our folding chairs in hand.

I was glad to have witnessed the exchange, but it enraged me. In all my time in Cumberland County, I did not meet a single person who was formerly incarcerated that successfully secured one of these small-business loans. I began to fantasize about waiting in the nonprofit's parking lot. I would bump into the director, who would be stepping into a mid-tier luxury vehicle to drive to their suburban home that was no doubt located somewhere else. I would confront them with my blistering anger. I would belittle them for trying to ensnare already economically vulnerable residents with high-interest loans. Get in debt to save yourself—the slickest capitalist trick in the book. But also, perhaps more poignantly, I felt the sting of seeing my own reflection in the enthusiasm of the nonprofit banker. I may have spent three years seeking out strategies of resistance and communities of care, but I was no doubt also participating in a specific kind of capital capture during those very same years. Earl, Herc, and many others had pointed this out to me in numerous ways.

As Shakes lit his cigarette, a scrawny, scruffy white man in an oversized winter coat made his way slowly up the sidewalk in our direction. He stopped before us, smiling widely and patting his jacket one, two, three times, as if to threaten and alert us to the fact that he was carrying a gun at his waist.

"Never walk around this place without some fire." He burst into cackling laughter and flung open his coat like a mobster from the 1920s. I flinched. And he revealed a half-emptied bottle of MD 20/20 (generally called Mad Dog 20/20) tucked in his belt, which caused him to double over in laughter. He pointed at me, "HE THOUGHT I HAD A GUN! HE THOUGHT I HAD A GUN!" He looked to Shakes and then back to me. "You think I would show *you* if I had a gun?"

"Man, I don't know what you have or what you would show me," I replied, salty as hell.

"Let's go knock over that armored car." He pointed over his shoulder at two security guards emptying an ATM. "We could grab the cash, and no one would ever be the wiser." He continued the high-pitched cackle.

"We're good, man," Shakes told him. "And we don't want none of that mess around here. If you wanna sit down and drink your Mad Dog, and share a smoke and a chat, then take a seat. Otherwise, move on."

"Alright, alright, alright, alright." He threw both hands in the air, like he, too, was trying to slow down a wild horse, and snatched the bottle from his waist and said, "We're cool."

He sidled up next to me, leaned against the wall, and slid down until he was seated on the sidewalk like a disheveled yogi. He glugged hard from the Mad Dog bottle. Then he stood back up to use his hands in order to act out a story about a liquor store clerk around the corner who stole his money and never handed over his liquor. He wanted more cash from us. I emptied my wallet and handed him some money. He apologized for the joke earlier. Two police vehicles creeped onto the street and parked near the Spot. Four officers got out and walked silently toward us. With his back to the officers, he continued telling his story in great detail. Two of the officers positioned themselves twenty or so feet away. Two more closed in. No one said a word. They got close enough to grab his shoulders and walk him to the building, squishing his face hard against the rough brick.

"You are under arrest," one officer said.

He did not squirm. He put his head down and clutched at his Mad Dog. They walked him twenty feet to our right and stripped off his coat. They patted him down. One officer grabbed the Mad Dog out of his grasping hands, now flailing more fiercely, and held it above his head, just out of his extended reach, like an older brother teasing a younger sibling. The man begged and spit for his bottle.

"HEY! I bought that, that's mine," he repeated. "I paid that clerk."

The officer untwisted the cap, poured the pinkish-red liquor onto the concrete, and tossed the bottle into the trash can. Both officers guffawed in the man's face. The other two stood a few feet back, watching the scene unfold before slowly returning to their vehicle. The second officer grabbed the cash I had just given him and stuffed it into his pocket. They shoved him into the vehicle and drove off.

"Man, he'll be back out by tonight. Those dudes ain't got nothing to do, so they are just driving around and looking for people to pick on," Shakes said, shaking his head. "It ain't right."

Shakes did not exchange a word with the officers. Neither did I. Their banal cruelty made me feel nauseous and angry. First the nonprofit and now the police. A lively afternoon of white power surrounding the store.

"Tonight? You think so?" I asked. "How do you know that?"

"Because he ain't have nothing on him." Shakes lifted his hand in the direction where the poured-out Mad Dog still puddled on the sidewalk.

"He had that money the cops just stole," I replied. "Wouldn't have given it to him if I knew it was going to help them roll up on some fuckin' donuts."

"Man, stop!" Shakes laughed. "Roll up on some donuts."

"Hey!" Henrietta called from down the street.

I waved and stepped inside to grab a third chair. Everyone hugged. Shakes and Henrietta share a maternal grandparent. Occasionally, she swings by for a chat and a few laughs when her casework ends early, since her offices are only a few blocks from the Spot.

"What have you been doing today?" I asked.

"Defending someone against some illegal searches by police officers." Henrietta shook her head. "The prosecutors are trying to bully my client into signing a ridiculous plea."

18.1 Sitting in front of the Spot with Shakes as police officers bully and then arrest a person we were in conversation with.

"Again?" I asked. "I guess that's what you mostly face since something like 95 percent of all cases eventually plea deal out of court, right?"

"Always," she answered. "But that was this morning. Now I'm just coming from my first in-person meeting with Jay."

Shakes twisted his head. "Jay who?"

"Jay that—"

"What? Him?" Shakes replied, cutting her off.

"Who is Jay?" I asked, expecting it to be her daughter's father, who is confined in prison.

"The guy who killed my brother," Henrietta said.

"Wait, you met with him? Today?" I asked.

"Just now. Yep." She smiled.

"I cannot believe it! So, you actually ARE starting a reconciliation program with him?" I said. "You're like a real-life Jesus or something."

"Look, I've seen too much violence already in my life." She slowed down. "Too many people who think prisons are the answer, or their destination, or just a good industry for this town. But if we keep reproducing the same kind of hatefulness of each other, the same kind of judgment of each other, the same divisions from each other, which is basically what the justice system itself reproduces, then things will never change around here. I don't want my daughter to grow up in this environment. And we haven't started a program yet. We are taking it slow, getting to know one another."

"Trying to change the system, huh, cuz?" Shakes exhaled smoke, nodding his head.

"I see myself politically as more X than King," Henrietta laughed and elbowed me. "Heath and I already got into a fight with Millsy about this . . ."

"Ahh, man, Millsy," Shakes laughed. "She didn't agree with you? What did she say?"

"Well, it's true," Henrietta laughed. "I do work from within the system, and I do have to work for change from within *that* system. But those of us who are in the system must also fight to change it just as much if not more than those who are supposedly outside the system. I'm trying to do what I can to protect vulnerable people. I feel like that's one of the most important things I can do personally within the system."

"That's amazing," I repeated.

"We are still in the early stages. And some of my family is not too happy with me for establishing contact with him. But what good does it do any of us to keep holding onto that? To stay angry with him?" Henrietta asked.

"Got to forgive," Shakes agreed.

"Yeah. That's tough, though," I said. "Forgiveness is easier to talk about than to live out."

"That's the truth," Henrietta nodded. "Just taking it slow right now."

"That's beautiful," Shakes said. He nudged me and handed his phone over. "That's my little girl, right there." He smiled widely. A two-year-old with perfect braids smiled on his screen.

"Really, wait, what?" I asked. "I didn't know you had a daughter that young?! Why don't you ever bring her into the store?"

"Not my biological daughter, man." Shakes took his phone back, tenderly staring once again before pocketing it. "Her parents got into a little trouble and had to relocate in a hurry to another state."

"Huh?" I asked. "They relocated and left their daughter here?"

"Man, not permanently," Shakes said. "But they had to leave the state, trying to stay safe from the cops and all that mess, and so they left her with her grandma who is, you know, she's . . . like . . . my girlfriend." Shakes blushed and laughed and turned away.

"A girlfriend?!" I asked, nudging him and laughing. "How am I just now hearing about this?"

"Yeah, man," Shakes said, laughing. "They had to get out of town in a hurry. So, each day, after I close the shop, I head over to her grandma's house. And we make some dinner, put on some cartoons, and then we put her to bed."

"You do that every single day?" I asked, still shocked it had never come up earlier.

"Every day," Shakes repeated. "I love her like she is my own daughter."

"That's . . . wow. Seriously," I fumbled. "I mean, just imagine what could have happened if you and her grandma weren't around?!"

"I know, man. I know." Shakes looked up. "Too many people have exactly that story around here. Too many people."

"I can't believe you haven't told me this yet," I said. "It's just kind of blowing my mind that y'all are taking care of her like that," I repeated. "I mean—"

"Taking care of *her*?" Shakes twisted his head around to look at me. "Mannn, please! She's taking care of me. I need her just as much as she needs me."

"You know that's right," Henrietta said, laughing.

Shakes and Henrietta enrich and expand our understanding of what interdependent life looks and feels like on a daily basis. Their commitment to building relationships with people who are the most targeted and vulnerable puts them more at risk for the many entanglements that are produced on the streets. Most residents, if they were able, avoided any and all potential encounters with people who spent time in prisons, and they stayed far away from the county's various downtown city blocks. This allowed residents to feel protected from unruly others and safe from perceived dangers. But from the perspective of Henrietta, Shakes, and others who spent time at the Spot, this physical and social distance also inhibited them from meaningful relationships that could aid in the wider efforts to bring about substantive change. That is to say, Henrietta, Shakes, and others (like Fred) believed that systemic change was not possible without building, multiplying, and strengthening person-to-person bonds of care that stretched across the strict divisions of race, class, and legal status that were, as we have seen throughout the vignettes, perpetually reproduced and enforced by the current system of confinement.

When police officers arrested the man with the pink-colored Mad Dog, they exemplified the kinds of interpersonal connections that mark life for so many people in this region. There was no conversing—much less supporting, empathizing with, or relating to—because the four officers had no interest in any of this. They were not paid or promoted to build relationships with people who lived in Cumberland County. They were instead regularly seen bullying, teasing, and arresting residents because, according to Shakes, they were bored and had nothing else to do—and because that kind of behavior is in line with how police officers treat economically vulnerable residents.[1] The county is stuffed with armed men just like this, who drive around in battle-ready automobiles looking for people to harass or arrest. When I began keeping tabs on the number of police vehicles I would see while hanging out at the Spot or any other downtown location, the daily total often climbed into the double digits. Like hungry sharks in the water, they were always circling, sometimes slowly and sometimes at high speeds. From the perspective of Shakes, Henrietta, and others we have met, there is only one way to disrupt this context: interdependent relationality. It is not a form of intervention that is predicated on one privileged person coming to the rescue of one so-called needy person. A hierarchical dynamic reproduced, for example, in Old Man Tilley's attempt at "returning" the recovered artifacts to current Lenape residents. It is a form of relationality energized by the recognition that each one of us is a person who needs the support and love of others. Some are more explicitly teetering on the possibility of social and economic devastation, while others are merely isolated or disconnected, perhaps wrestling through feelings of bitterness, hatefulness, or even revenge. Or, at the very least, they are exhausted by the countless conflicting demands that stretch them to the point of breaking.

But through the recognition that each and every person is in need comes the possibility that each and every person can give love, care, and support to others. Interdependence is not about gritting one's teeth, pulling up one's bootstraps, and resolving to fight until absolutely nothing is left. It is about finding renewal, life, joy, and beauty in the humble act of submitting oneself to others as they submit to you, and in doing the slow work to collectively build a space where these kinds of relationships can happen regularly. The Spot fostered this kind of relationality for many different people throughout the area. Finding, fostering, and feeling life in this way does not rely on first reforming or abolishing the system. Nor does it rely on fleeing the system. It can happen (and is happening) off to the side, beyond recognition that is generated by social media posts and in excess of the attention of police officers or local organizers alike. Shakes and others taught me these lessons. Day in and day out, I learned, I witnessed, I experienced, like so many others who found love, care, and support at the Spot, that each of us is always forty-five minutes from some kind of life.

CONVEYANCE III

Interdependent relationships as the grounds for the system's eventual undoing is a confounding point. These relationships do not fit into the leftist landscape of strategic acts of resistance that eventually build enough momentum to topple the established order. Nor do they exemplify a kind of false consciousness naturalizing the forces of domination and one's place within them. Instead, these relationships grow and are nourished off to the side, moving and morphing in unpredictable directions. And it is here, rooted in the rich soil of person-to-person relationships, that the flowers of an alternative world are nurtured until the day they fully bloom. An alternative world where street corners are spaces of celebration. Where premature black death is a history that is told rather than a future that is promised. Where bellies are full and laughter rings loud. Where one who has killed becomes one who can comfort.

To work collectively to create a space like the Spot is to continually put down the hollowed-out visions derived from solutions-oriented goals and to perpetually put on the embodied practices necessary for meeting another's needs. For Herc, as for many, there is no relief or change coming from the top. He understands, as many do, that the current context is already an outcome of decisions made from the top. And that the false categories that break apart the possibility of meaningful relationships—racial difference, economic status, legal standing—are eternally reproduced by the outcomes of these top-down solutions. Interdependent relationships, in contrast, bind people together in such a way that the impact of domination is mitigated and the solutions to their current struggles are found in the horizontal flow of giving and receiving without account. It is these kinds of relationships, which flourish in the Spot, that have been largely responsible for the profound reality that the six regulars who carried multiple felony charges (five of whom spent significant time incarcerated) had each avoided return trips to prison.

Participating in interdependent relationships, however, does not have to mean the rejection of other modes and forms of resistance to the system of confinement. Fred and Henrietta, for example, both value and participate in myriad approaches to the long-term fight. But both also align with Shakes, Herc, and Doughboy in the belief that people must work just as diligently to forge relationships that are strong like steel. To take the time and to expend the energies to cultivate spaces where other values, relationships, and practices can grow. Because the system of confinement, as we have seen, is well-positioned to maintain order by smashing to bits any resident who fights against it, as in the case of Mr. Cantale and his family, or by co-opting and incorporating any resident who cannot be smashed to bits, be that through a life behind bars or a life being paid to monitor people who are behind bars. But when residents refuse to cooperate and refuse to engage in constant battles, they also refuse to participate in the system's given order, which at times includes the resistance to its own order, and thus the landscape of domination reveals something like small but growing cracks—perhaps not in ways that will immediately bring about its dissolution or downfall, but in ways that make and keep people unavailable to its greedy reach, in ways that open spaces for people to keep fighting, tooth and nail, while also tending to the core of one another's humanity.

The brutal work of fighting against a system of confinement that has been central since the beginning, which has appeared and reappeared throughout the centuries in multiple forms, can be undertaken through means that mimic the system. To be engaged in constant fighting, to study, plot, dream, and imagine unceasingly about how to exploit the weaknesses of the system of confinement, to spend all of one's energies and time moving in this direction, is to tiptoe along a tightrope of tactics and relationships that are part of the very system itself. But there are other ways to undermine domination. I learned this lesson during my time in Cumberland County, when I began my research hell-bent on finding others who were fighting against whatever part of the system they could. Shakes and

Henrietta, Fred and Doughboy, Herc and Mr. Cantale, Mrs. Taylor and others taught me, showed me, invited me into other ways and other rhythms. They retuned my pulse to something like a socialist impulse, bringing me into an altogether different song. They put my hands into the soil, orienting me to a different kind of work. And hearing that tune, feeling that pulse, smelling those flowers, finding that beat, might just be the best hope for collectively overgrowing the systems of confinement and changing the rhythms of the streets.

EPILOGUE

Leaving this zone at night was always a mixture of relief and sadness. Sometimes I imagined the orchards at the edge of the county, with their uniform rows of apple trees as far as the eye could see, waving goodbye to me. Other times I imagined them melding together to hem in the people I had come to care about. All times the distinct vibe of Herc's "prison on the outside" grew more pronounced. But I was able to leave, to go to a home where police officers were not following me, to catch relief in the safety of my own bed. On these drives home, I began turning my phone's recorder on to ramble about whatever popped into my head. Most evenings this meant dumping raw emotions—anger, tears, joy. Whatever was there. Sometimes it meant musing over a theorist's ideas intersecting with a word or story a resident gave to me. Other times it meant imagining, dreaming, or theorizing about politics, power, prisons, and the radical im/possibilities of life.

I wonder if the socialist impulse, or the alternative spaces where interdependent relationality is happening, can be thought of as something similar to the trees, plants, animals, insects, and humans that are (re)building interconnected life in Chernobyl's zone of restriction. There are numerous ways to try and bring about a more vibrant and healthy social system, with a political economy not produced by and reliant upon systems of confinement—plotting, protesting, and fighting with aims of burning everything to the ground; sharing petitions and working to influence state and federal policies with aims of substantive reform; even detaching and founding a separatist colony with aims of anarchist utopia. I believe strongly that horizontal, demilitarized, degrowth socialism is the best and only way for our plants, animals, and planet to continue. And I like to imagine that beautiful day when a socialist form will grow bountiful from the toxic remains of capitalism's unending fallout zones. But what if the socialist impulse is even now alive and well, beating in nooks and crannies, hollers and havens across the planet? What if global capitalism and empire do not need to be overthrown before building a flourishing, unruly socialism? What if tending to spaces where the impulse of interdependent life still beats is an effective way to disempower systems of confinement and grow a new social piece by piece, from the ground up?

I started this project hoping to connect with others who were working to bring about the dissolution of the US system of prisons and policing. I found people doing something else entirely. Those I met and built relationships with taught me the necessity of interdependent relationships. They taught me how to better care for life, my own and others', while remaining attuned to the many fights being perpetually waged against any and all systems of domination.

As promised at the beginning, there are no answers in this conclusion. Nothing to inspire better policies. When it comes to the US system of prisons, and the eighteen-thousand-plus police departments, and the tens of millions of people whose lives have been decimated by one or both, the path before us feels dim, hopeless, perhaps even downright impossible. And some days, if I am being honest, that dim and hopeless path is the only one I feel capable of finding. But on my best days, I remember to lean on the lessons learned from Henrietta and Shakes, from Fred and Herc, from Doughboy and Mr. Cantale and so many others, and I remember that confinement is not the only beat—far from it.

I hope this small study can be a wellspring for people who are exhausted in whatever fallout zone they are in, for people who, like me, might forget that tending to the spaces—however small and fleeting, where love, joy, support, and care can flourish—is every bit as important as tending to the organizing meetings that lead to direct political action. The socialist impulse is everywhere all around, steadily beating out other beats for anyone willing to find it and tune themselves in. One day, the current system of confinement will burn to ash. That is inevitable. And along the way, more people will find the socialist impulse, and more and more, and as the fire rises higher, so, too, will the resounding rhythms of many feet dancing in many streets. I can't wait to see you there. But until that day, I conclude with the words of my friend and collaborator, Nathan "Freedom" Gray, who was recently released from a two-decade stint in New

Jersey prisons. Freedom mailed me a book of handwritten essays that he had been working on and protecting for nearly a decade. These are a few lines about his friend Xemo (who was incarcerated with him), in which he describes the significance of their relationship and the inevitability of radical social life, even in the heart of a fallout zone:

While I write this, I'm on the second day of a 4-day fast with a native comrade of mine. He told me he was going to go on a fast for a few days, to set things in order with himself and that he'd talk to me in a few days. I said, "Hold on, I'll do it with you." So, here I am on the second day of this fast, trying to stay strong and focused, no talking, no eating . . . and trying to keep negative thoughts out of my head. My native comrade Xemo has his reasons for going on his fast, which are mostly spiritual, and I have my reasons and objectives.

I'll have to admit that this fast isn't really for spiritual purposes for me, other than sacrificing my food, conversation, urges, and desires to will myself to endure and overcome anguish, pain and torment, and I'm doing this to prepare myself for future hardships. Those are my reasons for taking up this fast . . . dare to make War with the beast? Xemo tells me stories, sings me songs in Crow, sings me songs in Lakota, sings me songs in Shoshone. His love for the eagle is great, he sings songs about the bear, he talks about the determination of the wolf. He even taught me a song about healing. He tells me something good about the coyote, he says a coyote can adapt to any situation. You can take a coyote in Africa and the coyote will find a way to survive. I will always remember that . . . like a prisoner—we survive this graveyard!

APPENDIX I

LOCAL HISTORY OF CONFINEMENT WITH ARCHIVAL PICTURES

The earliest system of confinement began in 1665—amid the genocide and removal of the Lenape population who had occupied the land for centuries[1]—when white men were enticed to settle in New Jersey through a program that awarded seventy-five acres of land for each enslaved person they brought with them into the state.[2] The amount of free acreage diminished with each passing year, but the land was ordered, populated, and put to work through the state-incentivized establishment of slavery. Privatized land distribution tied to enslaved laborers of African descent is the first system of confinement to drive the region's political economy.

The second system crystallized when 2,500 people of Japanese descent were transported from internment camps in the US Southwest to labor camps on Seabrook Farms (based in the county but totaling 54,000 acres [84 square miles] that stretched into Pennsylvania and Delaware). Here is a letter from one of the local mayors to C. F. Seabrook, written in 1944, that illuminates the region's unapologetic reliance on organized confinement for economic survival as well as the embedded racial hierarchy of the region's politics (see figure app. 1.1).

The stated prejudice against people of Japanese descent was not without aim. The need for nonwhite labor was essential "to grow and produce the necessary foods required by our Armed Forces," even though the mayor and city council "[do] not welcome the American-Japanese . . . he realizes . . . [they] would be law-abiding and would cause the local police authorities no difficulty." He references a high school basketball game shut down by angry white parents because their children were sharing a court with Japanese American children (see figure app. 1.2).

May 6th, 1944

Deerfield Packing Corporation,
Bridgeton, New Jersey.

Attention: Mr. C. F. Seabrook, President.

Dear Mr. Seabrook:

In furtherance of our conversation had yesterday in your
office relative to various statements made by Mr. A. Lewis Turner, President of the Bridgeton City Council to several Field Representatives or
Officials of the War Labor Board in connection with the securing of
American-Japanese citizens for labor and employment with your enterprises,
this is to advise you that I immediately, upon my return to Bridgeton,
contacted Mr. Turner and discussed thoroughly the matter with him regarding said statements, which said statements apparently left some doubt in
the minds of the Government Officials of the War Labor Board as to the
desirability and advisability of American-Japanese coming to work in the
vicinity of Bridgeton.

Mr. Turner stated to me that while he informed the Investigators that he personally did not welcome the American-Japanese,
however, he could not speak officially for the other six members of City
Council. However, he stated to me that he advised the Investigators that
he would prefer Government investigated American-Japanese citizens to
work in connection with Deerfield Packing and the Seabrook enterprises,
rather than the undesirable southern Negro labor; his reasons being that
the southern Negro farm labor are undesirable because they frequent the
local saloons in the colored section in town, become intoxicated, become
unruly and are continually causing the local police considerable difficulty by fighting and continually behaving in a disorderly manner; that
he realizes the American-Japanese would be law-abiding and would cause the
local police authorities no difficulty.

He further stated to me that he would prefer that all the
additional imported farm labor at Seabrook Farms this summer were to be
American-Japanese rather than the undesirable southern Negro labor that
have heretofore been working at Seabrook Farms in the summer, particularly
last summer. He did mention the unfortunate incident involving the
American-Japanese this past winter in a basket ball game in our local high
school gymnasium. In his words he stated that it was most unfortunate

APP 1.1 Image of a letter from Mayor Bertram Aitken to C. F. Seabrook, May 6, 1944. Held (online) at RUcore: Rutgers University Community Repository. Last accessed November 7, 2023.

Deerfield Packing Corporation   - 2 -   5/6/44

that the situation arose and of course I explained to him that the matter
would never have happened had certain officials at the Farms, while you
were absent in Florida, taken my advice not to let these American-
Japanese play in the game and of course the incident would never have
happened had you been at home.

He also stated that he did make reference to the investigators of an incident wherein imported Negro farm labor, last summer in
the month of July, caused quite a disturbance in our City at and near a
saloon located in the colored section of our town and he felt that the
police of Seabrook Farms did not assist in the correction of this situation.

Mr. Turner further stated that he was sorry that the investigators misunderstood his views in connection with this situation,
that he was merely only explaining to them his personal feelings in the
matter.

As I have said, Mr. Turner is of the opinion that if Deerfield Packing Corporation requires additional labor in order to grow and
produce the necessary foods required by our Armed Forces, that he would
much prefer government investigated American-Japanese labor than he would
the undesirable southern Negroes who come into Bridgeton during their
leisure time and cause many disturbances.

If I can be of any further assistance to you along these
lines, please advise.

Very truly yours,

Bertram R. B. Aitken

A:C

Police Halt League Game In BHS Gym

Use of American-Born Japanese Players by Seabrook Farms Team Brought Speedy Action

Bridgeton police intervened last night and halted a scheduled game between Seabrook Farms and the Glass Bar in the City Basketball League because American-born Japanese were about to play.

The action was ordered by Inspector Norman Fletcher who said he had been informed that there "might be trouble" if the Japanese played.

After a lengthy discussion in the dressing rooms between the managers, Sergeant James McGowan and league president, Michael McCallick, the game finally started, although the Japanese boys were not in the lineup.

With the game under way only a short time, Manager Addison Behling of Seabrook Farms, walked over to Sergeant McGowan and said: "I'll save you the trouble of stopping the game - I'm taking my team off the floor."

Jap Player Inserted

Later, however, he put his team back on the floor, this time with a Japanese known as "Eiji" in the lineup.

Sergeant McGowan went out on the floor before referee Larry Powell could toss the ball and halted the game. There was no disturbance, and the final contest went on as scheduled.

Before the game Manager Paul Behr, of Glass Bar, said his boys were somewhat "sore" about the use of Japanese, but after consulting his team, agreed to go on with the game.

Manager Behling said it was a "test case" to see whether the American-born Japanese could play in the league. He protested against the interference of the

Their horror of atrocities inf when this group of Japanese donor center in Denver, Colo ma...

Fourth War I Turns on C

All Persons Who Purcha Theatres Entitled to Showing of Be Acquaintan

While War Bond workers mai tained their efforts to atta Bridgeton's quota of $1,500,000 the current campaign, the and

APP 1.2 "Police Halt League Game in BHS Gym," *Evening News*, February 1, 1944. Picture taken of an archived newspaper held in a public library in Cumberland County.

He then concludes his letter, stating that the distrust and dislike of interned Japanese Americans are nevertheless preferable to the employment of black people: "In connection with the securing of American-Japanese citizens for labor . . . [there is some doubt] as to the desirability and advisability of [them] coming to work in the vicinity," but, he writes four times in two pages, "[We] prefer Government investigated American-Japanese citizens . . . rather than the undesirable southern Negro labor . . . because they frequent the local saloons in the colored section in town, become intoxicated, become unruly and are continually causing the local police considerable difficulty by fighting and continually behaving in a disorderly manner."

A lot is learned about the region in this short letter. There is a hier-archical racial order that determines where nonwhite people can live, work, eat, and drink. Police officers are expected to patrol and enforce the boundaries of that order. Out-of-town Japanese Americans confined as prisoners of war are more privileged on the hierarchy than segregated black residents. And using confinement as well as police officers to con-trol labor and enforce order is not up for debate—it is assumed, given, run of the mill. The dilemma for the mayor and city council does not have to do with using thousands of laborers who are being confined with-out due process. The dilemma revolves around adding more nonwhite people to the local population. This is the second system of confinement to drive the region's political economy (and, following the mayor's letter, to bolster the US war efforts).

The third system of confinement is today's network of prisons, half-way houses, police, and sheriffs whose workforce has also long included people who are linked to white supremacist membership.[3] In the years leading up to World War II, Ku Klux Klan membership exploded in the region (and throughout New Jersey), quickly becoming a densely popu-lated hub of organized white supremacy.[4] Their presence has continued through the century, and there are firsthand accounts about the two Klan families that ran the region's first prison (Leesburg State, renamed Bay-side State in 1988), which opened in 1970. Leesburg was part of a network of New Jersey prisons that began using incarcerated people as almost-free agricultural laborers to produce food and dairy for other prisons across the state—an institutionalized system of explicit labor exploita-tion that continues in the region and throughout New Jersey today.[5] In 1983, Southern State opened, sharing a land border with Leesburg. Fairton Federal and South Woods State opened in 1990 and 1997, respectively. As Carl, the baker, matter-of-factly chuckled: "There is a lot of corrections going on." This is the third system of confinement to produce the region's political economy.

This sketch overviews the continuity of confinement across four hundred years. And it simultaneously betrays that these systems will inevitably break down, destabilize, and perish. The rise of each new system implies as much. But it is not simply that systems wear away, as the instruments of production always do.[6] It is also that people ensnared by these systems reveal their inherent entropy through an accumulation of daily acts that do not conform to or reproduce the logic and practices of confinement. My attention to this twinned historical perspective was shaped by Cedric Robinson, who wrote extensively both on the certainty of capitalist systems breaking down and the persistence of what he named "the black radical tradition," which identifies "an accretion, over generations, of collective intelligence gathered from struggle."[7] For Robinson, confined people are never controlled nor dominated as fully as the given system (and its ideological conceits) would like everyone to believe.[8]

In New Jersey, for example, some people confined by slavery did not wait for politicians to grant freedom from on high. They made their own way, fleeing when able, breaking tools and other forms of property, working slowly, and even going as far as physically harming planters.[9] This was happening across the country, in fact, as people forced an unsteady wobble throughout the system. W. E. B. Du Bois refers to this swarm of individual acts as a "general strike," which he credits for delivering the decisive blow during the Civil War: "The slave entered upon *a general strike against slavery by the same methods that he had used during the period of the fugitive slave. He ran away* to . . . safety and offered his services to the Federal Army. So that in this way it was really true that . . . *this withdrawal and bestowal of his labor decided the war*."[10] Enslaved people forced the national system's dissolution because they knew the weak spots, the gaps and breaks, of their own place of confinement. It was local knowledge about their specific context, which accumulated into a system-wide takedown.[11]

Similar acts transpired before, during, and after World War II. In 1934, years of strikes and disruptions precipitated "a series of disorders" that brought Seabrook Farms to a grinding halt for more than three straight weeks, leaving thousands of acres of fruits and vegetables rotting in the sun.[12] C. F. deployed police officers to crack skulls and try to force people back to work, before eventually relenting and installing a labor union (see figure app. 1.3).

The arrival of Japanese Americans and other prisoners of war, ten years later, provided him the opportunity to fire those earlier identified as disrupters and strikers and to use labor that could be more tightly controlled. But despite the extreme clampdown, there are numerous accounts of people building community and undermining the farm's productive capacities: sharing food, dousing crop bushels in water before weigh-in, redistributing yields so everyone passed quotas, assisting others to make sure no crops were left behind ("One Bean Johnny" was an infamous foreman who made sure the children picked every plant

APP 1.3 Photo of deputized security officers physically assaulting a union organizer at Seabrook Farms, July 1934. Image courtesy of "Invisible Restraints: Life and Labor at Seabrook Farms," as part of Rutgers University's digital exhibits. Last accessed November 7, 2023.

clean), and even skipping work altogether to snooze in the shade.[13] As the end of the war brought about the end of legally interned labor, Seabrook Farm's capacity to stay profitable dwindled. Within a decade, the brand and the land were sold.

Leesburg State opened thirteen years later. And almost immediately people escaped. Most famously, George Wright, a member of the Black Liberation Army, escaped on August 19, 1970. Wright, who changed his name to José Luís Jorge dos Santos, remains unconfined today, tending his garden, living with family and among neighbors, in a little white house on the Portugal shore.[14] A few years later, in 1977, people in Leesburg organized a work stoppage.[15] Firsthand accounts of strikes and disruptions in the prisons appear in part 2.

The primary point in this two-sided sketch is that there is no life outside the context that confinement has produced. To live in this region is to live in, around, beneath, behind, and through systems of confinement. And at the very same time, confinement is in no way total. To live in this region, for many, is to build life that exceeds, moves away from, on top of, around, and beyond confinement.

APPENDIX II

DEMOGRAPHIC DETAILS OF PEOPLE IN VIGNETTES

ANNIE .... Lifelong resident, black, female, mid-sixties, social worker (retired)

'BIGFOOT' .... Lifelong resident, white, male, early seventies, police detective (retired)

BIG TIM .... Lifelong resident, black, male, late thirties, Shakes's son, owns barbershop, formerly incarcerated

BUMP .... Lifelong resident, black, male, deceased, owned a men's clothing store, formerly incarcerated

CARL .... Resident, white, male, mid-sixties, owner of Waking Bakery

DAVID JOHNSON .... Lifelong resident, black, male, late fifties, corrections officer, leader of Civil Action Committee

DORIS TILLEY .... Married a lifelong resident (Old Man Tilley), white, female, early eighties, teacher (retired)

DOUGHBOY .... Lifelong resident, black, male, early fifties, formerly incarcerated

FRED .... Lifelong resident, black, male, mid-fifties, academic advisor at the county community college, director of Intensive Supervision Program

HENRIETTA .... Lifelong resident, black, female, late thirties, public defender

HERC	Lifelong resident, black, male, mid-forties, formerly incarcerated
JERAME REID	Resident since teenager, black, male, killed by police in mid-thirties, formerly incarcerated
JIM CANTALE	Resident, white, male, late thirties, teacher, local organizer
JOHN 'THE CHIEF' JONES	Lifelong resident, white, male, mid-seventies, police chief (retired)
JON	Lifelong resident, black, male, mid-forties, director of housing authority
KEN	Lifelong resident, black, male, late thirties, manager in corporate business, director of Intensive Supervision Program, formerly incarcerated
LYN	Lifelong resident, black, female, late thirties, public defender
MAYOR	Lifelong resident, black, male, mid-fifties, mayor, director of a nonprofit
MILLSY	Lifelong resident, black, female, mid-forties private attorney, part-time prosecutor
MS. REID	Newark resident, black, female, early sixties, mother of Jerame, organizer for People's Organization for Progress
OFFICER DAYS	Resident, black, male, late forties, Cliptown police officer
OFFICER WORLEY	Resident, white, male, late forties, Cliptown police officer
OLD MAN TILLEY	Lifelong resident, white, male, early eighties, owner of a farm, a natural gas company, and a pharmacy, bank president (retired)
PASTOR BERT	Lifelong resident, white, male, late thirties, pastor, professor, director of Feed the Sheep Initiative
RUTHIE	Lifelong resident, black, female, late thirties, administrator at a nonprofit
SHAKES	Lifelong resident, black, male, mid-fifties, owns the Spot, formerly incarcerated

APPENDIX III
HAND-DRAWN PICTOGRAPHS OF ARGUMENTS SKETCHED PRIOR TO WRITING THE BOOK

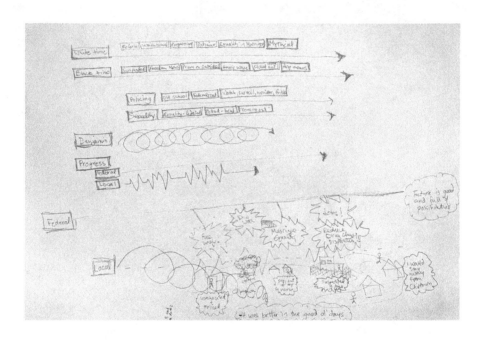

APP 3.1 Draft sketch to conceptualize different modes of time intersecting a single geography.

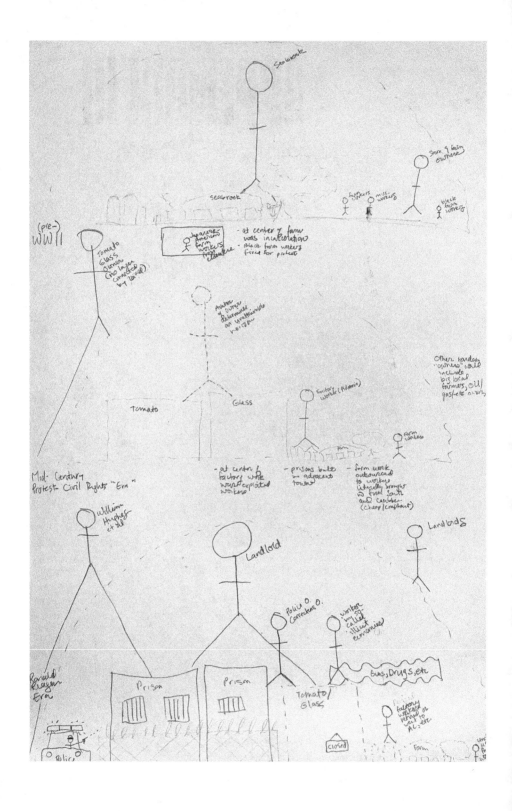

APP 3.2 (*opposite*) Draft sketch to conceptualize the changing means of production and the continuity of ruling-class hierarchy.

APP 3.3 Draft sketch (1 of 6) to conceptualize multiple vignettes at once.

APP 3.4 Draft sketch (2 of 6) to conceptualize multiple vignettes at once.

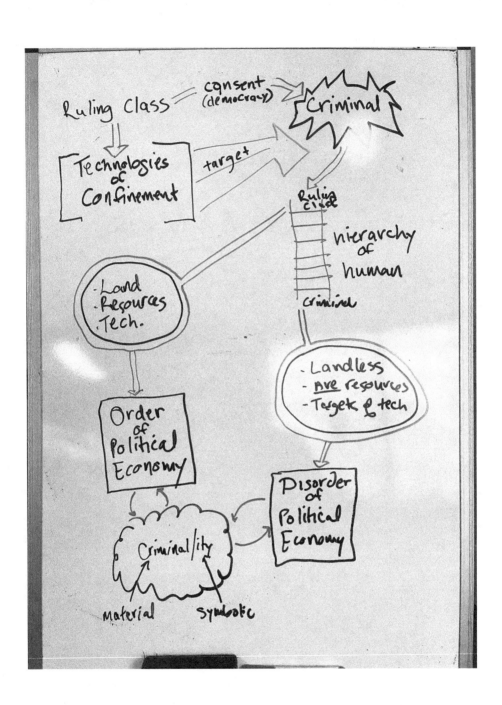

APP 3.5 Whiteboard sketch of the relationship between order, hierarchy, technologies of confinement, and land.

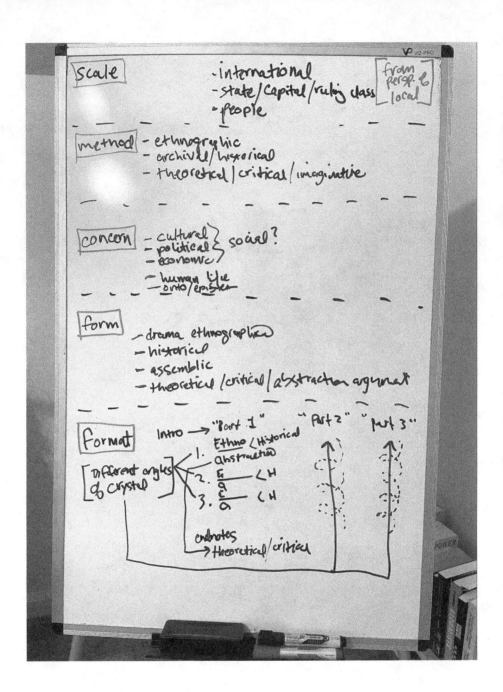

APP 3.6 Whiteboard sketch of the correlation between form and method.

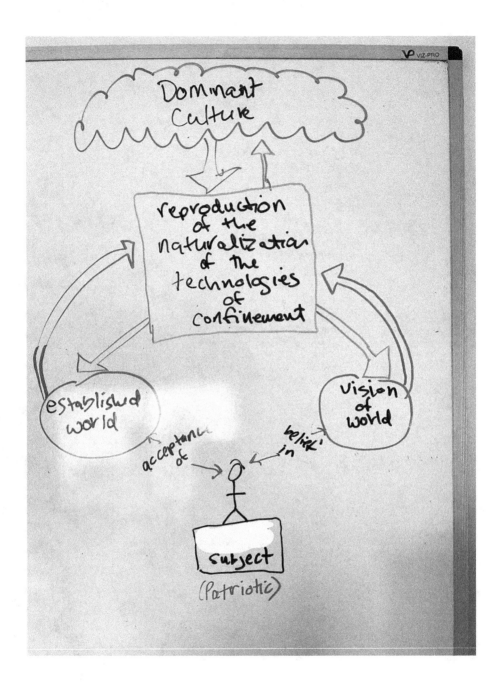

APP 3.7 Whiteboard sketch of the relationship (material and ideological) between domination, the reproduction of confinement technologies, and the person.

NOTES

INTRODUCTION

1   Cumberland County Jail, Cumberland County Juvenile Detention Center, South Woods State, Bayside State (formerly Leesburg State), Southern State, and Fairton Federal.

2   Of 154,000 total people, 45 percent are white, 18 percent are African American, 0.9 percent are Native American, 1.2 percent are Asian, and 34 percent are Hispanic or Latino. Figures are taken from the 2020 US Census. See https://www.census.gov/quickfacts/fact/table/cumberlandcountynewjersey,NJ/PST045222.

3   "Occupational Employment and Wage Statistics," US Bureau of Labor Statistics, May, 2022, https://www.bls.gov/oes/current/oes333012.htm.

4   Kelley, *Race Rebels*, 5–9.

5   Li, *Land's End*, 84–149.

6   At this time, there was also an increase of people moving into town from Central and South America.

7   Kelley, *Race Rebels*, 1.

8   Kelley, *Race Rebels*, 3–4.

9   Kelley, *Race Rebels*, 7–10.

10   Robinson, *Anthropology of Marxism*, 122–24.

11   For a more detailed history that includes archived letters, newspaper clippings, and land deeds, see appendix 1.

12   The vignette form of this book is deeply influenced by Zora Neale Hurston's *Mules and Men*.

13   Moten, *In the Break*, 85–169.

14   In *The Paradox of Relevance*, Carol Greenhouse defines the discourse of solutions that drives ethnographic imagination as the "aligning [of] social description with the discourse of federal political debate" (142). Greenhouse picks apart and analyzes ethnographies written in and about the United States to highlight the consistent practice of using specific life stories and personal narratives as ambiguous resources for generalized public use with aims toward the production of policy recommendations that might "make things better." Greenhouse argues that "the discourse of solutions prevails when providing solutions

for social problems is the precondition for anyone's interest in the experiences of men and women who live at the margins of recognition as neighbors, citizens, and human beings" (157). The drive toward solutions shapes and warps ethnographic research that enters the field, with a priori rubrics not only of who people are, based on national and federal categories, but also of what the alleged problems "those people" struggle with based on national and federal discourse within their particular locale. This approach to ethnographic fieldwork and the production of more generalizable knowledge is always already in danger of reifying racialized and classed differences by functionalizing people as their categories in order to use their experiences and ideas as representative examples for the purposes of intellectual analysis, social surveillance, political capture, and legislative recommendations.

15   Pearson, "Work without Labor," 167–92.

16   Woods, *Development Arrested*, 76–81.

17   Gordon, "Theory and Justice," 99–101.

18   In "Knowledge of Freedom," in *Stolen Life*, Fred Moten explores the "recidivist fringe [that] just won't act right no matter how much the power of judgment tries to make it 'well behaved'" (1). Moten writes to break out of the dialectic that holds freedom as a static abstraction that is conditional on the productive capacities of capital, be that through the emancipated self-realized self or the crumbling death of political economy as the condition of existence: "Its diplopic print is not marked 'before and after' but shows up as smudge, bend, ecstatic shift, common and impure" (1). There is a space in which freedom is known before the before of its unknowingness and impossibility, off to the side, away from the prior to or following of a "side step in apposition" (79), where what has been noncarceral before carceral was the given state of order. The smudge, the rhythms that beat and pulse to the side of rhythmic times, what Fanon refers to as a "blurred mass" (8) in *The Wretched of the Earth*, where that which is and breathes and lives and stretches is not responding to nor strictly speaking before but is speaking as that which is and is not. The Spot figures as something like this kind of space, where people, most specifically black middle-aged men who are both lifelong residents and formerly incarcerated, choreograph life together that is in excess of and outside the dialectic of domination or resistance, pessimism or possibility. It is a place entirely unrecognized by any person who has not already figured out how to find it and enter it. It is a place beyond the value of value, neither devalued nor valued, unimportant enough to surveil and insignificant enough to support. After a dicey three-month stretch, in which Shakes was wondering if he would have to close the doors, I

approached a nonprofit CEO whose building is across the street from the Spot and whose mission is to serve the community by meeting needs and connecting resources in real time, with special attention to formerly incarcerated people and their families. The first floor of the nonprofit's enormous nineteenth-century building was entirely empty, with massive street-facing windows. I thought it would make sense to invite Shakes to run his clothing store from there, since it aligned perfectly with his immediate needs and the nonprofit's stated goals. But the CEO looked at me as if I had been speaking in tongues. The support offered by meeting needs meant finding ways to incorporate people's needs beneath the nonprofit's leadership structure (similar to how prisons incorporate their own resistance). It meant getting in the way to provide support—not providing possibility and getting out of the way. The people at the Spot did not see themselves as emancipated products of the prison system nor as people needing support from nonprofit saviors. They saw life as exceeding what prisons tried to capture, control, and confine as capable, not simply of surviving the devastations of carceral capitalism but of sounding out beats that put the smooth rhythm of confinement out of sync so that they might be about and move about some other beat altogether.

19   Moten, "Knowledge of Freedom," in *Stolen Life*, 1–2.

20   Orisanmi Burton highlights a similar mode of life that happens inside prisons, when "captive men . . . develop deep and meaningful social ties based on mutual support rather than hierarchy." Burton, "Captivity, Kinship, and Black Masculine Care Work under Domestic Warfare," 622.

21   Here I am inspired by Cedric Robinson's *An Anthropology of Marxism*, which takes the "capitalocentrism" of Marxism to task for ignoring the thousands of years of socialist antecedents that predate the rise of capital. For example, Avery Gordon is fond of highlighting how the acts of the apostles "turned the world upside down" (*Anthropology of Marxism*, xiii), which is based on an earlier passage from the same scripture: "No one claimed ownership of private possessions, but everything they owned was held in common. . . . There was not a needy person among them" (Acts 4:32–34). The socialist impulse can often be seen where people mass together to meet needs, share resources, tend to the soul, and sometimes respond forcefully to social injustice. It can be spotted in the Haitian, Mexican, Russian, Chinese, Algerian, Cuban, Nicaraguan, and Iranian Revolutions, all of which preceded or exceeded Marx's historical materialist conceits (119). And it can be witnessed in a clothing store in the middle of a landscape teeming with prisons and police. In the future, it just might grow and

gain ground from the smoldering remains of capital. But it certainly was there, beating and clasping hands, long before capital. It is here even now, all over, everywhere people are found, for those with eyes to see, ears to hear, souls to feel.

22   Mahmood, *Politics of Piety*, x.

23   Robinson, *Anthropology of Marxism*, 1.

CHAPTER 1. OLD MAN TILLEY & THE LAND

1   Perhaps this mirroring of values and practices that were "biblical" had more to do with the fact that the US military was pointing rifles at them after stealing their homes and possessions.

CHAPTER 2. BIG TIM & MRS. TAYLOR

1   "As I sit in heaven and watch over you everyday [*sic*], I try to let you know with signs I never went away. I hear you when you're laughing, and watch you when you sleep. I even place my arms around you, to calm you as you weep. I see you wish the days away, begging to have me home. So I try to send you signs, so you know you're not alone. Don't feel guilty that you have life that was denied to me. Heaven is truly beautiful, just you wait and see. So live your life, be free and know with every breath you'll be taking one for me." Author unknown.

CHAPTER 3. THE CHIEF & BIGFOOT

1   See Arjun Shankar's introduction in *Brown Saviors and Their Others*, where he builds on Sara Ahmed's "sweaty concept" to explore the significance of nervous, sweaty anthropology, marked by the anthropologist's own bodily responses to the clash of encountering a world. Shankar, *Brown Saviors*, xiii–xiv, 250.

2   Gong, "Between Tolerant Containment and Concerted Constraint," 664–89.

3   Milenko Martinovich, "States with Right-to-Carry Concealed Handgun Laws Experience Increases in Violent Crime, According to Stanford Scholar," *Stanford Report*, June 21, 2017, https://news.stanford.edu/2017 /06/21/violent-crime-increases-right-carry-states/.

4   Dave Collins and Lisa Marie Pane, "Police Loosen Standards for Accepting Recruits," Police1, November 14, 2016, https://www.police1 .com/police-jobs-and-careers/articles/police-loosen-standards-for -accepting-recruits-3uCEoz8NBnvmy1G1/.

CHAPTER 4. JON & THE GLITTERY CROW

1   When state and federal prisons and county jails are combined, the
     male population that has been diagnosed with mental health is-
     sues is nearly 35 percent, and the female population that has been
     diagnosed with mental health issues is nearly 66 percent. For a more
     detailed breakdown, see Manuel Villa, "The Mental Health Crisis
     Facing Women in Prison," Marshall Project, June 22, 2017, https://www
     .themarshallproject.org/2017/06/22/the-mental-health-crisis-facing
     -women-in-prison.

2   Don E. Woods, "Bridgeton Celebrates Its Secret Identity as Batman's
     Hometown: Gotham City," NJ.com, October 2, 2016, https://www.nj
     .com/cumberland/2016/10/bridgeton_celebrates_its_secret_identity
     _as_batman.html.

3   Avery Gordon, in *The Hawthorn Archive*, writes of community as
     that which is capable of healing both the individual and the culture
     of sociality. That is to say, community is not a passive descriptor for
     people who know one another and occasionally hang out. Com-
     munity is active, it is intentional, it is part of the process of becom-
     ing free—or, better, it is part of the process of allowing freedom to
     unmake and remake those people who participate in it. There are
     three reasons Gordon offers as to why community must be part of the
     healing process: a person cannot do it alone; the community is where
     the dream is already real and the unreality is "the failure to make it
     work"; the community is where a person spends time after healing.
     This is not about aiming at structural reform but at the cultivation
     of interdependent community whose members are unavailable for
     confinement, for servitude (44–49). And Gordon is not writing
     about formerly incarcerated people finding community and ulti-
     mately freedom in the spaces of what Herc calls interdependent life;
     she is writing this for and of everyone. Gordon writes: "The com-
     munity is not a panacea for all ills, but it is the place where [Toni
     Cade] Bambara locates the practice of freedom, the second sight that
     gives us the knowledge that we have the sovereignty, the authority, to
     free ourselves on our own terms." Gordon, *Hawthorn Archive*, 47. Jon
     seems also to believe in the necessity of community to the possibility
     of life, of free life, of flourishing life in the downtown. It is manifest in
     his actions of care around my safety.

CHAPTER 5. CARL & WAKING BAKERY

1   Pearson, "Work without Labor," 179.

1   April Hunt, "Gun Group's Church Violence Stats Can't Be Verified," Politifact, August 1, 2014, https://www.politifact.com/factchecks/2014 /aug/01/georgiacarryorg-georgiacarryorg/gun-groups-church-violence -stats-cant-be-verified/.

2   "National Trends," Mapping Police Violence, accessed December 7, 2021, https://mappingpoliceviolence.org/.

3   Seth G. Jones, Catrina Doxsee, and Nicholas Harrington, "The Escalat- ing Terrorism Problem in the United States," Center for Strategic and International Studies, June 17, 2020, https://www.csis.org/analysis /escalating-terrorism-problem-united-states.

4   Stephen Semler, "Congress Has a Chance to Roll Back the Flow of Military Weapons to Police Departments," *Jacobin*, September 23, 2021, https://jacobin.com/2021/09/congress-1033-program-military-weapons -police-departments; Nick Routley, "Charting the $1.7B Transfer of Military Equipment to Police Departments," *Visual Capitalist*, June 26, 2020, https://www.visualcapitalist.com/billion-dollar-transfer-of -military-equipment-to-police-departments/.

5   Achille Mbembe argues that "war . . . is as much a means of achieving sovereignty as a way of exercising the right to kill" (Mbembe, "Necrop- olitics," 12). There is one way to interpret the entire Sheepdog program as dedicated to the invitation for white men (who are already excited) to see themselves as people who are not simply allowed but required to—must, for the sake of the family, church, and state—develop and exercise their capacity to kill. This is bolstered by the feature of the age of "global mobility" and globalizing capital and hegemonic West- ern imperial developmentalism wherein "military operations and the exercise of the right to kill are no longer the sole monopoly of state, and the 'regular army' is no longer the unique modality of carrying out these functions" (31). This is not simply about encouraging white men who are already amped up; it is also about tending to a US race regime that is wearing thin. Cedric Robinson developed his concept of regime maintenance through his expansive study of representation in nineteenth- and twentieth-century US film production, interpret- ing the budding cinematic fabrications of black people and blackness as constructions of whitewashed history that created new terrains of memories and meaning while concealing the consistent fact of black resistance and fugitivity. Robinson tears apart this era of filmmaking alongside the widespread development projects to build theaters in local spaces, urban and rural alike, across the country as a two-headed "agenda in the process of seizing domestic and international labor, land, and capital" while installing "black inferiority" into the veins of a

"shared national culture" (Robinson, *Forgeries of Memory and Meaning*, 125–26). In short, the film industry was a ruling-class tool for helping to produce a national context in which, among other things, viewers repeatedly learned that white men were superior, white women were in need of protection, black people were inferior, and antiblack violence could or perhaps should take place without interruption. The Sheepdog event we have just worked our way through conjures a world that shares many ideological conceits with the representations in these early films. The typology of humanity reinforced racial hierarchies with white men as the superior group. The representations of women consistently depicted weakness, frailty, and the need for (white) men's protection. The selected historical recounting ignored any mention of the numerous midcentury Klan attacks against Christian churches and erased entirely the contemporary acts of antiblack white-man violence. Even the grainy, soundless surveillance footage recalled the minstrel-like depictions of the earliest silent films. But there is one notable difference: Sheepdog Seminars were and are not sponsored by the monied elite. This particular event in Bridgeton was funded by local church congregations, the Bridgeton Police Department, and the county prosecutor's offices. And this is consistent for Sheepdog events across the country. Regime maintenance is thus also happening in a more uneven, patchwork way. This is precisely the tangle in which the distribution of retired military weapons aids, bolsters, and stabilizes the work of racial regime maintenance.

6   For the most thorough study of prisons as sites of domestic warfare, and police and corrections officers as soldiers paid to carry out that war, see Orisanmi Burton's *Tip of the Spear*.

7   For example, Denver police officers in July 2022 after spraying their pistols into a crowd in the entertainment district; Ryan Donald in 2015 after shooting and paralyzing Bryson Chaplin; Solomon D. Simmons in 2021 after shooting and killing Donovon Lynch; Jeronimo Yanez in 2016 after shooting and killing Philando Castille; Ray Tensing in 2015 after shooting and killing Samuel DuBose; Darren Wilson in 2014 after shooting and killing Michael Brown; Timothy Loehmann in 2014 after shooting and killing Tamir Rice.

CHAPTER 7. MS. REID & HER BOY

1   Pearson, "After the Riot," 777.

2   Stefano Harney and Fred Moten write of needing to protect ourselves and one another from critique, from unending fighting with the state and its infinite modes of confinement, containment, and destruction

because the state and its politics are toxic, poisoning not only our sociality but our being with energies that kill us as we try to kill it. Harney and Moten, *Undercommons*, 19.

CHAPTER 8. TEN & TWO

1   For one ethnographic example, see Didier Fassin's *Enforcing Order*, which documents how police officers in the banlieues of Paris work to maintain order through violence and intimidation directed against poor black people.

CHAPTER 9. MR. CANTALE & THE COMMUNITY

1   Grace Hauck, "Cars Have Hit Demonstrators 104 Times since George Floyd Protests Began," *USA Today*, July 9, 2020, https://www.usatoday .com/story/news/nation/2020/07/08/vehicle-ramming-attacks-66-us -since-may-27/5397700002/.

2   Cameron Peters, "State-Level Republicans Are Making It Easier to Run Over Protesters," *Vox*, April 25, 2021, https://www.vox.com/2021/4/25 /22367019/gop-laws-oklahoma-iowa-florida-floyd-blm-protests-police.

CHAPTER 10. FRED, KEN & INTENSIVE SUPERVISION

1   Associated Press in Almocageme, "Black Panther Arrested in Portugal Decades on from Hijacking US Flight," *Guardian*, September 28, 2011, https://www.theguardian.com/world/2011/sep/28/black-panther -arrested-portugal-hijack.

2   Joseph Shapiro, "As Court Fees Rise, the Poor Are Paying the Price," NPR, May 19, 2014, https://www.npr.org/2014/05/19/312158516/increasing -court-fees-punish-the-poor.

3   Matthew R. Durose, Alexia D. Cooper, and Howard N. Snyder, "Recidivism of Prisoners Released in 30 States in 2005: Patterns from 2005 to 2010—Update," US Department of Justice, April 2014, https://bjs.ojp .gov/library/publications/recidivism-prisoners-released-30-states-2005 -patterns-2005-2010-update.

CONVEYANCE II

1   See Frantz Fanon's "On Violence" in *The Wretched of the Earth*, where he discusses how decolonial fighting is about establishing a new rhythm that helps to bring about a new humanity on the path toward liberation (2–3).

CHAPTER 14. HERC & PRISON ON THE OUTSIDE

1   See David Harvey's *Limits to Capital* (2006) or, more recently, *Redesigning AI* (2021), by Daron Acemoglu et al., for agreement with Herc's analysis that new technologies (rather than offshoring labor) are most responsible for the displacement of low-wage workers.

2   Mike Frassinelli, "N.J. Inmates Make More than a Million License Plates Each Year," NJ.com, February 27, 2012, https://www.nj.com/news /2012/02/nj_inmates_work_to_make_licens.html.

3   Nas, "The World Is Yours," track 4 on *Illmatic*, Columbia Records, 1994.

4   Matthew R. Durose and Leonardo Antenangeli, "Recidivism of Prisoners Released in 34 States in 2012: A 5-Year Follow-Up Period (2012–2017)," Bureau of Justice Statistics, July 2021, https://bjs.ojp.gov /library/publications/recidivism-prisoners-released-34-states-2012-5 -year-follow-period-2012-2017.

CHAPTER 15. THE LAWYERS & THE AMISH MARKET

1   Mike Cummings, "Do Body Cameras Affect Police Officers' Behavior? Not So Much," YaleNews, October 27, 2017, https://news.yale.edu/2017 /10/27/do-body-cameras-affect-police-officers-behavior-not-so-much.

CHAPTER 16. THE SPOT IS AN ALTERNATIVE SPACE

1   See Pearson, "The Prickly Skin of White Supremacy."

2   Avery Gordon's *Hawthorn Archive* (36–48, 281–87) outlines the practices of community that enable people to be unavailable for servitude.

CHAPTER 18. SHAKES & THE PACE OF CONNECTION

1   See Didier Fassin's *Enforcing Order* for a similar analysis about police officers who patrol the banlieues surrounding Paris.

APPENDIX I. LOCAL HISTORY OF CONFINEMENT WITH ARCHIVAL PICTURES

1   Dowd, *The Indians of New Jersey*, 42.

2   Cooley, *A Study of Slavery in New Jersey*, 9.

3   "Allegations of Racist Guards Are Plaguing the Corrections Industry," SPLC, December 6, 2000, https://www.splcenter.org/fighting -hate/intelligence-report/2000/allegations-racist-guards-are-plaguing -corrections-industry; William Finnegan, "Law Enforcement and the

Problem of White Supremacy," *New Yorker*, February 27, 2021, https://www.newyorker.com/news/daily-comment/law-enforcement-and-the-problem-of-white-supremacy.

4 Woods, *Development Arrested*, 90.

5 Chris Franklin, "Holy Cow: In This State Program, Prisoners Double as Dairy Farmers," NJ.com, July 24, 2017, https://www.nj.com/cumberland/2017/07/see_what_happens_in_dairy_that_is_run_by_state_inm.html.

6 Marx, *Capital*, 440–42.

7 Robinson, *Black Marxism*, xxx.

8 Robinson, *Forgeries of Memory and Meaning*, xii–xiii.

9 Wright, *Afro-Americans in New Jersey*.

10 Du Bois, *Black Reconstruction in America*, 46 (italics mine).

11 Karl Marx highlights a similar point in the first section of *The Communist Manifesto*, writing that the struggle against the ruling class "is *carried on by individual laborers, then by the workpeople . . . in one locality, against the individual bourgeoisie who directly exploits them. They direct their attacks* not against the bourgeois conditions of production, but *against the instruments of production themselves . . .* they smash to pieces machinery, they set factories ablaze" (480; italics mine). In other words, workers banding together do not (could not) attack the "conditions" of production; they break the machines and set ablaze the floors of their own factories, which, coincidentally, also happen to be the instruments of their bondage.

12 "Gas Balks Rioters on Jersey Farm," *New York Times*, July 10, 1934, https://timesmachine.nytimes.com/timesmachine/1934/07/10/94549184.html?pageNumber=1.

13 These insights and more were gleaned from letters written in the 1990s by Japanese Americans who were confined on Seabrook Farms during the war. They are held online by the New Jersey Digital Highway, "Invisible Restraints: Life and Labor at Seabrook Farms," in the subsection: "I Remember." See, especially, the letters written by Paul H. Noguchi, Rei R. Noguchi, Fusaye Kazaoka, and Robert Hasuike.

14 "Black Panther Arrested in Portugal Decades on from Hijacking US Flight," *Guardian*, September 28, 2011, https://www.theguardian.com/world/2011/sep/28/black-panther-arrested-portugal-hijack.

15 Robert Hanley, "Leesburg Prisoners Stage Brief Protest," *New York Times*, June 10, 1978, https://timesmachine.nytimes.com/timesmachine/1978/06/10/110861559.html?pageNumber=49.

BIBLIOGRAPHY

Acemoglu, Daron, Rediet Abebe, Aaron Benanav, Erik Brynjolfsson, Kate Crawford, Andrea Dehlendorf, Ryan Gerety, et al. *Redesigning AI: Work, Democracy, and Justice in the Age of Automation*. Cambridge, MA: Boston Review, 2021.

Burton, Orisanmi. "Captivity, Kinship, and Black Masculine Care Work under Domestic Warfare." *American Anthropologist* 23, no. 3 (2021): 621–32.

Burton, Orisanmi. *Tip of the Spear: Black Radicalism, Prison Repression, and the Long Attica Revolt*. Berkeley: University of California Press, 2023.

Cooley, Henry Scofield. *A Study of Slavery in New Jersey*. Baltimore, MD: Johns Hopkins University Press, 1896.

Dowd, Gregory Evans. *The Indians of New Jersey*. Trenton: New Jersey Historical Commission, 2001.

Du Bois, W. E. B. *Black Reconstruction in America*. Oxford: Oxford University Press, 2007. First published 1935.

Fanon, Frantz. *The Wretched of the Earth*. New York: Grove Press, 2004. First published 1961.

Fassin, Didier. *Enforcing Order: An Ethnography of Urban Policing*. Translated by Rachel Gomme. Cambridge: Polity, 2013.

Gong, Neil. "Between Tolerant Containment and Concerted Constraint: Managing Madness for the City and the Privileged Family." *American Sociological Review* 84, no. 4 (2019): 664–89.

Gordon, Avery. *The Hawthorn Archive*. New York: Fordham University Press, 2018.

Gordon, Avery. "Theory and Justice." In *Keeping Good Time: Reflections on Knowledge, Power, and People*, 99–105. New York: Routledge, 2004.

Greenhouse, Carol. *The Paradox of Relevance*. Philadelphia: University of Pennsylvania Press, 2011.

Harney, Stefano, and Fred Moten. *The Undercommons: Fugitive Planning and Black Study*. New York: Autonomedia/Minor Compositions, 2013.

Harvey, David. *The Limits to Capital*. London: Verso, 2006.

Kelley, Robin D. G. *Race Rebels: Culture, Politics, and the Black Working Class*. New York: Free Press, 1996.

Li, Tania Murray. *Land's End: Capitalist Relations on an Indigenous Frontier*. Durham, NC: Duke University Press, 2014.

Mahmood, Saba. *Politics of Piety: The Islamic Revival and the Feminist Subject.* Princeton, NJ: Princeton University Press, 2011.

Marx, Karl. *Capital.* Vol. 1. Mineola, NY: Dover Press, 2011.

Marx, Karl. *The Communist Manifesto.* In *The Marx-Engels Reader,* 2nd ed., edited by Robert C. Tucker. New York: W. W. Norton, 1978.

Marx, Karl. *The German Ideology.* In *The Marx-Engels Reader,* 2nd ed., edited by Robert C. Tucker. New York: W. W. Norton, 1978.

Marx, Karl. *The Grundrisse.* New York: Penguin, 1993.

Mau, Søren. *Mute Compulsion: A Marxist Theory of the Economic Power of Capital.* London: Verso, 2023.

Mbembe, Achille. "Necropolitics." *Public Culture* 15, no. 1 (2003): 11–40.

Moten, Fred. *In the Break: The Aesthetics of the Black Radical Tradition.* Minneapolis: University of Minnesota Press, 2003.

Moten, Fred. *Stolen Life.* Durham, NC: Duke University Press, 2018.

Pearson, Heath. "After the Riot: The Capitalization of Justice and the Refiguring of Racial Politics." *Anthropological Quarterly* 91, no. 2 (2018): 763–90.

Pearson, Heath. "The Prickly Skin of White Supremacy: Race in the 'Real America.'" *Transforming Anthropology* 23, no. 1 (2015): 43–58.

Pearson, Heath. "Work without Labor." *Cultural Anthropology* 36, no. 2 (2021): 167–92.

Robinson, Cedric. *An Anthropology of Marxism.* 2nd ed. Chapel Hill: University of North Carolina Press, 2019.

Robinson, Cedric. *Black Marxism: The Making of the Black Radical Tradition.* 2nd ed. Chapel Hill: University of North Carolina Press, 2000.

Robinson, Cedric. *Forgeries of Memory and Meaning: Blacks and the Regimes of Race in American Theater and Film before World War II.* Chapel Hill: University of North Carolina Press, 2007.

Shankar, Arjun. *Brown Saviors and Their Others: Race, Caste, Labor, and the Global Politics of Help in India.* Durham, NC: Duke University Press, 2023.

Turner, Frederick Jackson. "The Significance of the Frontier in American History." *Report of the American Historical Association* (1893): 197–227.

Woods, Clyde. *Development Arrested: Blues and Plantation Power in the Mississippi Delta.* New York: Verso, 2017.

Wright, Giles R. *Afro-Americans in New Jersey: A Short History.* Trenton: New Jersey Historical Commission, 1988.

INDEX

Abu-Lughod, Lila, 5–6
activism, 3, 24–29, 76–82, 86–90, 93–100, 111, 177–78. *See also* civil rights; resistance
An Anthropology of Marxism (Robinson), 11, 213–14n21

Bayside State Prison, 102
Black Liberation Army (BLA), 102–3
Black Panther Party for Self-Defense, 7, 32, 102–3, 201. *See also* Wright, George
black voters. *See* voting
Boumediene, Houari, 102
Brown, Michael, 29, 86

carceral logic, 10. *See also* policing
Christianity, 57–69
Christie, Chris, 84–85
civil rights, 83–86, 128, 176–77. *See also* activism
Cleaver, Eldridge, 102
commissary prices, 108–10
concentration camps. *See* internment camps
corrections officers, 5, 53–54, 78, 83–87, 92, 99, 102–3, 116–18, 128, 135, 147–49. *See also* policing
criminal justice system, 35, 177

Development Arrested (Woods), 9
drugs. *See* war on drugs

education system, 91–94, 97–99, 103–4, 107–8, 114, 117–18, 135–38. *See also* school boards

employment, 51–56, 101–3, 106–8, 143, 145. *See also* prison work

fees, 105–6, 110
foreclosures, 5
Forgeries of Memory and Meaning (Robinson), 216–17n5
formal economy, 55

The German Ideology (Marx), 1
Gilmore, Ruth Wilson, 92
Gordon, Avery, 9–10, 215n3
Greenhouse, Carol, 23, 211n14
gun laws, 58–59, 63–68
gun statistics, 33, 39, 64

Hall, Stuart, 9
Hearns, Radazz, 79
highlanders of Sulawesi, 4
homelessness, 51
housing, 41–48, 101, 106, 113–14
Hughes, William J., 140
Hurston, Zora Neale, 211n12

imagination, 1, 6, 85, 88, 111–12, 119, 138, 211n14
Indigenous people. *See* Native Americans
informal economy, 55
Intensive Supervision Program (ISP), 101, 104–11
interdependent community, 11, 141–42, 150–51, 157–72, 177, 179, 183–93. *See also* social life (discussion of)
internment camps, 7, 10, 16–17, 20–22, 28, 48, 70–71, 118. *See also* Seabrook Farms

Japanese Americans. *See* internment camps

Kant, Immanuel, 10–11
Kelley, Robin D. G., 5–6
"Knowledge of Freedom" (Moten), 10–11, 212n18

land ownership, 174–75
Lenni Lenape, 7, 17–20, 45, 71
Li, Tania Murray, 4

Mahmood, Saba, 11
Marx, Karl, 1
Marxism, 11
Mau, Søren, 15
Mbembe, Achille, 216–17n5
mental health, 34, 58–59
militias, 66–69
misogyny, 62
Moten, Fred, 10–11, 212n18
Mules and Men (Hurston), 211n12
Mute Compulsion (Mau), 15

Native Americans, 7, 17–20, 45, 71
"Necropolitics" (Mbembe), 216–17n5
New Jersey Department of Corrections, 140
nonprofit organizations, 5, 51, 71–72, 113, 180–81

Obama, Barack, 148

The Paradox of Relevance (Greenhouse), 23, 211n14
People's Organization for Progress, 77
plantations, 9. *See also* slavery
"The Prickly Skin of White Supremacy" (Pearson), 164–65
policing: and brutality, 78, 167–68; and corruption, 26–28, 37–38, 48, 80, 94, 122–23, 147, 149, 168, 177, 183; and domination, 29–30; and education, 137–38; and intimidation, 16, 31–32, 181–82, 186; militarization of, 4–5, 9, 37, 64, 68,

156; and nostalgia, 32–36, 39, 44, 48; perspectives on, 155–56, 158; and race, 8, 23–29, 37, 40, 67, 85–88, 94, 102; and religion, 57–64, 66–67; and resistance, 6; and salaries, 5; and shootings, 33–34, 36, 77–82, 86–87, 93, 130; standards, 35–36, 39, 66; tactics, 95–97, 99. *See also* corrections officers; racism; war on drugs
The Politics of Piety (Mahmood), 11
poverty, 113–14, 123
prison fix, 92
prison work, 146–48. *See also* employment
protesting. *See* activism
public funding, 55–56, 70, 110, 118
public schools, 17. *See also* education system

"Race, Articulation, and Societies Structured in Dominance" (Hall), 9
Race Rebels (Kelley), 5–6
racism: and capitalism, 11, 22, 48, 70, 148–49, 151; and prisons, 9; and profiling, 152–55; and resistance, 10. *See also* internment camps; policing; slavery; white supremacy
recidivism, 35, 51, 108, 150
regime maintenance. See *Forgeries of Memory and Meaning*
Reid, Jerame, 23–29, 72–73, 76–82, 86–87, 90, 93–95, 99, 111, 130
resistance, 5–11, 80–81, 129–31, 188–89. *See also* activism
Robinson, Cedric, 6, 11, 200, 213–14n21, 216–17n5

school boards, 5, 92, 97–99, 115–18, 128, 135. *See also* education system
Scott, James, 5–6
Seabrook, C. F., 10, 22, 66, 98, 118
Seabrook Farms, 7, 13–14, 20–22, 48, 70–71, 101. *See also* internment camps
Sheepdog Seminars, 57–69, 72, 82, 111
"The Significance of the Frontier in American History" (Turner), 15

slavery, 7, 9, 21, 70. *See also* plantations; racism

socialism, 11

the socialist impulse, 6, 213n21

social life (discussion of), 2–4, 6, 8–9, 11–12, 100, 139–50, 157–59. *See also* interdependent community

social services, 43

South New Jersey, 173–74

South Woods State Prison, 103

Sulawesi, 4

terrorism, 37, 40, 59, 62–65

Turner, Frederick Jackson, 14

unruly sociality, 11, 22, 98–100, 185. *See also* Moten, Fred

violence (statistics on), 61–62

voting, 124–28

war on drugs, 4–5, 11, 34–40, 84–85, 105. *See also* policing

white supremacy, 60–69, 72, 164. *See also* racism

Woods, Clyde, 9

World's Greatest Heroes, 46

Wright, George, 7, 102–3

LIFE BESIDE BARS

LIFE

BESIDE BARS

HEATH PEARSON

CONFINEMENT
AND CAPITAL IN AN
AMERICAN PRISON TOWN

Duke University Press *Durham and London* 2024

Printed in the United States of America on acid-free paper ∞
Project Editor: Ihsan Taylor
Designed by Matthew Tauch
Typeset in Merlo Tx and Anybody by Westchester Publishing Services

Library of Congress Cataloging-in-Publication Data
Names: Pearson, Heath, [date] author.
Title: Life beside bars : confinement and capital in an American prison
town / Heath Pearson.
Description: Durham : Duke University Press, 2024. | Includes
bibliographical references and index.
Identifiers: LCCN 2024008009 (print)
LCCN 2024008010 (ebook)
ISBN 9781478031147 (paperback)
ISBN 9781478026921 (hardcover)
ISBN 9781478060130 (ebook)
Subjects: LCSH: Prisons—Location—Economic aspects—New Jersey—Cumberland
County. | Prisons—Location—Social aspects—New Jersey—Cumberland County. |
Corrections—Location—Social aspects—New Jersey—Cumberland County. |
Corrections—Location—Economic aspects—New Jersey—Cumberland County. |
Community development—New Jersey—Cumberland County. | BISAC: SOCIAL
SCIENCE / Anthropology / Cultural & Social | SOCIAL SCIENCE / Ethnic Studies /
American / General
Classification: LCC HV9475.N5 P437 2024 (print) | LCC HV9475.N5 (ebook) |
DDC 365/.974994—dc23/eng/20240802
LC record available at https://lccn.loc.gov/2024008009
LC ebook record available at https://lccn.loc.gov/2024008010

Cover art: Sitting in front of the Spot. Photo by author.